The Long Silence

The Long Silence

Civilian Life under the German Occupation
of Northern France, 1914–1918

Helen McPhail

I.B. Tauris *Publishers*
LONDON • NEW YORK
in association with
New European Publications

Paperback edition published in 2001 by I.B.Tauris & Co Ltd
6 Salem Road, London W2 4BU
175 Fifth Avenue, New York NY 10010
www.ibtauris.com

In the United States of America and in Canada distributed by
St Martins Press, 175 Fifth Avenue, New York NY 10010

First published in 1999 by I.B.Tauris & Co Ltd

ISBN 1 86064 653 0

A full CIP record for this book is available from the British Library
A full CIP record for this book is available from the Library of Congress

Library of Congress catalog card: available

Typeset in Minion by moda design partnership
Printed and bound in Great Britain

Contents

Illustrations

A Brief Chronology Relating to the Western Front

1914

28 June: Assassination of Archduke Franz Ferdinand
1 August: General mobilisation in France and Germany
3 August: Germany declares war on France
4 August: Germany invades Belgium
    Great Britain declares war on Germany
7-16 August: The British Expeditionary Force lands in France
18-20 August: French offensive in Lorraine
20 August: French armies retreat
21-25 August: French defeat at Charleroi
5-10 Sept: Battle of the Marne
17 Sept-18 Oct: the 'Race to the Sea', extending the Western Front
    to the Channel coast
12 Oct-11 November: 1st Battle of Ypres
17-29 Dec: Battle of Artois
20 Dec-15 Jan.1915: 1st battle of Champagne

1915

10-13 March: Battle of Neuve Chapelle
22 April: 2nd Battle of Ypres
4 May-18 June: 2nd French offensive in Artois
9-10 May: British offensive, Aubers Ridge
15-25 May: British offensive, Festubert
25 Sept: French offensives in Artois and Champagne,
    British offensive at Loos

1916

21 Feb: German attack on Verdun
31 May: Battle of Jutland between British and German fleets
1 July: opening of the Battle of the Somme
August-Nov: Battles of Verdun and the Somme continue
19 Nov: Official end of Battle of the Somme
12 Dec: Germany offers conditional peace
18 Dec: Official end of Battle of Verdun
18-19 Dec: Italy, France and Great Britain reject the peace offer

1917

1 Feb: start of unrestricted submarine warfare
21 Feb: German withdrawal to the Hindenburg Line
6 April: U.S.A. enters the war
9 April: British offensive: the Battle of Arras, capture of Vimy Ridge
16-19 April: French attack: the Chemin des Dames
late May-early June: French troops mutiny
26 Sept: Third Battle of Ypres
23-26 Oct: French success on the Chemin des Dames
30 Oct-11 Nov: Battle of Passchendaele

1918

21 March: major German offensive towards Amiens
9 April: German offensive in Flanders
27 May: the Germans reach the River Marne
15 July: German offensive in Champagne
18-28 July: French counter-offensive
8 August: the German advance is halted, start of Allied advance
12-26 Sept: U.S. successes at St.Mihiel and the Argonne
27 Sept: Anglo-Canadian offensive at Cambrai
11 Oct: Germany accepts Wilson's peace conditions
9 Nov: Collapse of the Imperial régime in Germany
11 Nov: Armistice

Acknowledgements

As a francophile, translator and frequent visitor rather than a professional historian, I have learned about the land beyond the Western Front in France through personal enquiry, through friends and chance acquaintances. Perhaps the random selectivity of the material that I have encountered and used—often the result of lucky coincidence—reflects the nature of daily life for the people discussed here, both repetitive and incomplete, dealing with events as they occurred.

The Historial de la Grande Guerre, Péronne, and its historians is a constant source of ideas and information—I am grateful to Annette Becker of the Université de Lille-III for hospitality, for reading the ms and for her helpful suggestions, to Jay Winter of Cambridge University for his interest and encouragement and to Jean-Pierre Thierry at the Historial itself for his detailed knowledge of people, places and publications.

Also in France I would like to thank those who have been generous over several years with both time and practical help, including survivors of the First World War and their families, and the owners of records and diaries who very kindly allowed me to use material from their books or unpublished family diaries: M. Jules Delva, Ors; M. Robert Embry, Péronne; M. Bernard Fleury, representing the families of Elie Fleury and Paul Seret, St. Quentin; M. and Mme Michel Gauchet, Le Nouvion-en-Thiérache; M. Jacques Landouzy, St. Quentin.

The staff and libraries of the Imperial War Museum and Nanterre University, Paris, (the BDIC) provided invaluable material. Professor Hugh Clout of London University confirmed some elusive figures, and Philip Guest and Tom Miles of the Western Front Association found unexpected details in British military records. Stanford University Press kindly gave permission for me to quote from *Public Relations of The Commission for Relief in Belgium: Documents* (Gay and Fisher), and a short extract from Henry Williamson's *The Wet Flanders Plain* is reproduced with the permission of Gerald Gliddon.

I did not set out to write a full-length book: as indicated above, my original purpose was to discover a few facts for myself and perhaps accumulate enough material for a talk, possibly a short article or two. *The Long Silence* has grown out of this personal search—the reason for the sometimes rather limited notes—and I hope that this hidden personal and communal history will be fully recognised.

Introduction

What happened to ordinary French civilians who lived beyond the Western Front? What was the First World War like for those who lived through it as temporary German subjects? From my first visit to the area, I wanted to know about the Great War in the communities and farms that were cut off from the rest of France, on the far side of the battlefield.

Approaching the Western Front from Great Britain – whether literally or mentally—still seems to mean approaching a substantial barrier: we look at the front line and not beyond it—or at least not beyond the immediate trench and battle areas. For many British observers, the almost mythic nature of the Western Front seems to act as a mirror; it is too easy to gaze at our own reflection, to observe the long struggle of the British troops in their trenches, and fail to see beyond.

For the British in 1914-18, the war progressed from invasion and rapid movement to stalemate, and eventually once more to movement, advance and victory, a military and political episode of British history which occurred in a foreign land. In such a war, civilians may appear to military eyes as a complicating factor—people who do not understand how to behave, how to look after the troops (except to exploit them), or how to keep out of the way. Written by combatants, leaders or humble soldiers, military memoirs ignore those who are not in uniform, or refer to them with patronising impatience, even while the writer yearns for his own home and family.

In 1914-1918, this sense of the army as something distinct from ordinary life was different in France from the civilian view of military life in England. The French troops knew about the army from their military service as conscripts, a normal but separate element of early adult life, while the British army in 1914-18 was vastly expanded from its original professional core to take in men who in normal times would never have seen themselves as potential recruits. One nation had a fully trained potential force, familiar with military language, practice and expectations, while the other was forced to deal with hundreds of thousands of inexperienced civilians in uniform. For both nations, however, the realities of this particular war lay far outside the expectation or comprehension of families at home.

Accounts of personal encounters between officers or soldiers on leave and their civilian counterparts sometimes reflect this lack of mutual comprehension. The failure of imagination and lack of mutual comprehension affected both groups, prefiguring the postwar unease and the gap between those who fought and those without direct experience of combat and contributing to enduring myths about the war. While soldiers' comradeship in all the armies developed in the structured and enclosed condition of active service life, the civilians in the occupied north of France were forced to suffer the pressures and dangers of war in an alarming atmosphere of oppression, tedium and uncertainty. Everything in their daily life was undermined and altered, in both fact and perception. Morale and pride had to be sustained in ignorance of military or political events, in a much-diminished local community structure. Most people survived on a personal dogged resolve, concern for family and neighbours, and a scorn for the occupying forces which infuriated the more perceptive or sensitive among their German overlords.

For the French civilian population within the invaded territory, stalemate and stabilisation represented loss of autonomy and identity, a permanent foreign presence—a major personal and communal crisis without the support and comfort of the accustomed national framework. Not surprisingly, the result of this small-scale world was that each event and injustice was felt by the victims of the occupation to be unique: in fact, almost every episode quoted here for one location could be repeated for others, and whatever is shown in relation to one individual or community should be regarded as typical of many others. If episodes or attitudes seem confusing, it is often because the reality was complicated and uncertain, continually changing without warning or explanation. This explains the apparently repetitive nature of some sections—the recurrence of similar episodes underlines the static atmosphere of the war, when the natural rhythms of life had been eliminated. It is also characteristic of almost any occupation, with information and individual freedom of action withdrawn. Although those who found themselves the victims of the occupation felt that it was unprecedented, it was in fact an age-old situation—a reversion to mediaeval life, when only the privileged had freedom of movement or of decision over their daily life.

The fragmented recording and understanding of the war in the occupied territories has contributed to its later neglect, as has its comparatively undramatic nature. There was little here that could be seen as noble, few opportunities for publicly recognisable courage or the glamour of major military events: no equivalent of 'The Somme' or 'Verdun', not even a dramatic list of losses. After 1918, the knowledge that they had lived through a different war from that of either the troops or the civilians in free France was held within the families and communities themselves; they suffered as much as the veterans from a lack of comprehension in the national mentality yet had no claim to the respect, honour and consideration which were the right of the ex-combatant. Memoirs from outside the occupied territory make virtually no mention of the French people cut off from the rest of the nation, and this includes a number of otherwise admirable and valuable records. The majority of the population was not directly concerned with the occupation, and even books written several decades later, when a broader approach would seem appropriate, refer to civilians and their war-time experience only in terms of the free 'home front', without any indication that a small but significant part of the country had been occupied. Among historians, Richard Cobb (in his *French and German, German and French*, published in 1983) is almost alone in acknowledging and describing this aspect of the war, although modern social historians are now recognising its importance.

II

We should press on past this barrier of the imagination, and explore the French landscape beyond the fading line of the trenches, into the *départements* of the Aisne, the Nord, the Marne or the Meuse, to consider them now and as they were between August 1914 and November 1918.

For most of the war the frontier between France and Germany was a semi-permanent series of trenches. Visited today, this battle zone can be traced as a sequence of towns and modest villages with famous names and very few old buildings—but the traveller exploring further to the north and east across France will find few names that are familiar in British histories of 1914-18. From the Western Front to the modern international frontiers and beyond, that first war of the twentieth century has left a different memory—personal, diffuse, domestic, complex and anecdotal, it exists as the muted echo of an initial defeat that was intended to be permanent.

The war memoirs published in the 1920s, on which much of this account is based, reveal as much of their authors' social and educational background and expectations as they do of the war experiences that they describe. We learn little or nothing of the industrial working classes, people for whom the war often meant simply a different set of authoritarian voices giving orders. The records I have drawn on here were written in general by the better-educated, by professional or leisured people—independent, active, accustomed in normal times to managing their own lives and community affairs, often unfamiliar at a personal level with the living conditions of industrial workers or the unemployed poor even when surrounded by them in their city factories or small-town markets. Most of the industrial poor in the mining villages of the north and the big manufacturing centres or the landless rural workforce, who would be familiar with the tyrannies of poorly-paid, irregular or seasonal employment that might also be dangerous, are present in this wartime world only as groups or statistical elements. Another (purely coincidental) feature that tends to confuse the picture is the number of people with very similar names: the reader who considers that the name 'Louise' appears too often in Chapter 5, for instance, or that full names are spelled out too often, has my sympathy—but that should not detract from our sense of their individuality.

Any assessment of historical events is liable to be coloured by the date and nature of the records on which it is based. Part of the material used here comes from daily diaries, written up regularly while the war was in progress (contrary to all regulations) in ignorance of its eventual outcome. Much of it provides mundane but vital information on daily life; above all it shows the minutiae of subordination. Another strand comes from material published in the 10-15 years following the Armistice, usually when the reconstruction work was fairly well advanced but while memory was still fresh for those who had lived through the war. Here the tone may be triumphalist and self-justifying, presenting French citizens as noble, brave and selfless, but usually giving a broad view of a particular community. Both of these elements are very clearly the product of their own times.

The third strand comes from later records which help to give a broader background. American publications were particularly useful in investigating Herbert Hoover's war effort (see Chapter 3); this is little known in modern times, presumably because his later political career and reputation eclipsed his achievements in the First World War. Indeed, many features of the non-military American contribution to the war deserve greater attention from modern British commentators. The hard work undertaken by churches, aid and fund-raising committees, the Red Cross and big business in the U.S.A. was significant from the very beginning of the conflict.

This book should therefore come with a warning, not only that the records on which it is based are partial in two senses (both incomplete in terms of French society at the time, and almost entirely French in origin), but that there remains much to be discovered. Investigation of German records of the occupation, and of American contributions outside the food aid campaign, would contribute further valuable material but lie outside the scope of this book. I am particularly conscious of the missing German point of view in this account: a fully balanced narrative would illustrate the policies, practices and difficulties faced by the invading forces, at all levels, in their task of pacifying and administering this new and uncooperative territory.

I am also aware of having dealt inadequately with one part of France, Alsace-Lorraine. As a consequence of the 1870 Franco-Prussian war, these provinces spent the years between 1870 and 1914 as a region of Germany, a factor which affected attitudes to the First World War within both its population and the invading forces; regulations and control over civilians and language were different here, and the people of Alsace-Lorraine suffered acutely during the 1914-18 war from being neither fully German nor fully French. (Tactfully, their war memorials record the names of those who died as members of the armed forces without indicating which uniform these men wore.) What we have here is based on French accounts from a few specific places, the victims' own record of their lives for those 52 months.

There is no sympathy here for their 'masters', although for many of the occupying troops life was as dreary—and, in the end, almost as hungry—as it was for the French themselves.

These civilians were essential to the local management of the war when they worked the land, operated factories or brought coal and iron ore out of the ground, or serviced domestic life for the occupying forces, but in other respects they were a drain on German supplies and supervisory manpower, and on French political concern.

III

Once the invasion period and the appalling early battles were over, the nations who had expected that 'it would all be over by Christmas' were faced instead with a long-drawn-out struggle. In northern France the invaders were concerned to make the most of their economically wealthy new province, while the residents did their best to counter their efforts. The years of occupation became a continual battle of wills, strength and endurance, carried on in individual households, small communities, workplaces, farms, factories and shops.

It is not hard to see why this German occupation of France has been generally ignored. It affected only a limited area, military expediency was not directly concerned, the hard-pressed politicians of the day naturally focussed on military and international matters—and many of its elements, repeated on a much larger scale in the Second World War, have been thoroughly explored since then with specific reference to that more recent occupation. Meanwhile, of the innumerable English-language books that continue to appear on the First World War, the overwhelming majority deals with either military and political history or the remarkable body of English literature which arose out of the war years.

Life in an occupied community is not an obvious or particularly simple subject for investigation when it is no longer a matter of personal experience. When the occupying nation is eventually victorious, the occupied territory changes nationality and loses much of its independent voice, as in Alsace-Lorraine between 1871 and 1918; and when the original identity is regained the fact of the occupation is lost in more general and positive post-war recovery. A subjugated and disenfranchised body of people was increasingly prevented from making decisions about daily life, subject to total and frequently arbitrary control in matters of finance, housing, food, employment, movement, communication, leisure: it is hardly surprising that resentment as well as pride underlie the memoirs published in the 1920s and 1930s by people accustomed to such freedoms, and great pain, pride and anxiety were expressed both explicitly and implicitly in even the most matter-of-fact or positive accounts used here. The political events of the post-war decades, however, followed by the war and occupation of the 1940s, pushed much of their memories into the background, and although many families in the north recalled their lives in the First World War amongst themselves, for the rest of the country their bitter lessons had to be learned afresh and their patterns of resistance and endurance rediscovered.

There are difficulties in presenting the occupation in this particular war—no radio recording or record on film, few French photographs of the area taken between the invasion and the armistice, no correspondence. Damage to papers and archives during the final German evacuation in 1918, and again in the Second World War, meant the loss of many personal and official records of damage to be assessed after November 1918. More significant, perhaps, is the way in which the later war seems to have eliminated France's memories of that first twentieth-century occupation—it is not until much later, when both wars can be seen as part of a continuous thread running through the whole century, that historians can look closely at life in those closed-off communities. In this modest survey of a vast and multi-faceted subject, I hope that this account will show those whose territory has never been invaded or occupied what daily life can feel like under enemy occupation over a long period.

Of the two and a half million people in occupied northern France during the First World War, we see a few individuals, in a few places, whose story has survived. Some of them were extraordinary men and women who would have stood out in any age; the lives and activities of others, if the war had not overtaken them, would have passed peacefully, unnoticed and unknown. For a few individuals, names survive on plaques, or have been given to streets or schools; but their true character can be seen in their lives and their responses to experience, taking us into their families and illuminating a small but significant element of twentieth-century history. Mainly, this 'civilian' side of the war shows how a lengthy conflict makes victims of everyone concerned, and how no one can escape its effects, then or later.

Michel Corday, working in a government ministry in 1914, was aware of the pitfalls of recording contemporary events. In November of that year he wrote:

> It is difficult to secure truth in history. In the course of Poincaré's second journey to Paris [after the outbreak of war], some say that he was hissed, while others declare that he was cheered. Perhaps both were right. Perhaps it depended on the observer's particular viewing point, and the strength of the police.[1]

IV

All historical periods are routinely and casually characterised as either more innocent than our own, or more violent and depraved; some elements of the First World War have become a by-word for horror and outrage against human sensibilities, monstrous experiences that have set the standard against which later conflicts are still judged, while at other times we look back with comfortable nostalgia to an age of noble impulses and powerful comradeship. Both strands contribute to what has become a simplified mythic version of history.

However honest and dispassionate we wish to be, we cannot read about the Great War without applying its circumstances to ourselves, our own families and communities, or thinking of similar events awaiting the survivors and their children. As well as awareness of the terrible human losses of the First World War, an appreciation of the conditions and the atmosphere in occupied France during those years illuminates our understanding of French political and economic life in the years between the two World Wars, attitudes to the approach of war in the 1930s and the occupation of 1940-1944. Social patterns, thinking and practices have changed profoundly since 1918, making it particularly difficult to picture life in those years of the first occupation: to be without information of *any* events outside the immediate area and what your unwanted masters choose to tell you—how can we realistically imagine that? Television unknown, radio contact totally forbidden, newspapers, correspondence, travel—none of them available, no contact with the outside world.

In the late twentieth century we have become used to direct visual images of war—for most of those who were not actually involved, the Second World War, for example, lives in black and white news photographs and film and decades of war-story feature films. Since 1945 we have become used to watching war on television, as it occurs. Photographs of the First World War were taken in their thousands, but the true record of action, life in the front line, lies almost entirely in the written word. The British army has left innumerable vivid and moving documents—a myriad letters home and an immense body of literary record, created by men from every kind of background and education, about every aspect of war experience.

In contrast, there are very few photographs to illustrate life among the communities of north-eastern France—apart from propaganda pictures. There are plenty of shots of the ruin and devastation visible at the end of the war—but they show what was selected 'for the record' at the moment of victory, not what life was like when victory was not predictable or perhaps even imaginable. To build our own picture of lives in this occupation we must read the diaries and memoirs as well as the official documentation; we must try to enter the world of those who, forced to live in the most literal day-to-day manner imaginable, did not write down their daily experiences, who could not be certain that they would eventually be free. The pattern of their daily life was a persistent effort to sustain the fabric and pattern of the family, to retain some semblance of ordinariness whenever possible.

Tedium, restrictions and lack of news created the prevailing atmosphere between periods of fear and occasional hope; and anxiety, cold and insidious malnourishment intensified the misery of deteriorating living conditions. A permanent sense of uncertainty and lack of control over today or tomorrow was a challenge, even for the most steadfast. In many respects, descriptions of everyday life during this first occupation foreshadow later experiences, and also emphasise the depth of difference in national memory between countries which have experienced a foreign invasion and occupation and those which have not. A good deal of what appears from the first-hand reports and anecdotes seems trivial now; we have to remind ourselves that there was no advance understanding of what was likely to happen, and the war was almost universally expected to be short and sharp.

There were, of course, other and more positive features that occasionally emerged from the loss, humiliation and misery: as the twentieth century has continued to remind us, unwelcome domination by a hostile régime can stimulate pride, resistance and ingenuity as well as darker feelings of betrayal or despair. Local pride and dignity, and the industrial importance of the region, contributed to the civilians' powers of endurance and their subsequent recovery. Putting oneself into the shoes of these families, these individuals, these communities at war does not at first seem easy, after more than eighty years, but their letters, diaries and memoirs help to take us into their world.

No More Dancing

One of the broadest and most detailed accounts of life in the 1914-18 occupation can be found in a novel, *Invasion '14*, by Maxence Van der Meersch, published with tremendous success in both French and English in 1935. Although written as fiction, it is based consistently and directly on fact and many of the characters and incidents that I use in this book, taken from reliable official and first-hand records, appear in his novel. By choosing fiction for a record of the war published less than twenty years after its end, Van der Meersch was released from the need to honour real-life individual people with constant praise and enthusiasm, or damn them with images of unrelieved villainy. In his fictional presentation of real-life people and events, Van der Meersch shows a wide range of human character and society in adversity—a trend matched by the continuing popularity of fiction set in the First World War and similarly based on actual individuals and true events.

With the supporting evidence of Van der Meersch's 'faction', I have concentrated on factual records from the occupied territories themselves; but one personal history from unoccupied France impressed me with the strength of civilian feeling about the Great War and what it meant to the nation, as an illustration of a personal response to a universal experience—in this case with an unexpected result. In conversation with a French family more than eighty years after the outbreak of war I heard how Grandmother—born in 1900—faced the challenge to her country. With all the intensity of an idealistic adolescent, she was determined to express her profound patriotic commitment to her nation's crisis. Young and closely sheltered, far from immediate danger, she could see no effective way to help: she must dedicate an act of personal sacrifice to France's survival and victory.

After prayer and deliberation, she vowed to give up her greatest pleasure: until the great day of France's triumph and victory (never doubted, however long the war might last), despite her great love of the dance-floor—for her at least there would be no more dancing.

In the depleted farmlands, the desolate coalfields and the shabby crowded industrial cities of occupied northern France during the Great War, dancing was hardly an important issue—but perhaps this deliberate self-denial—deeply significant to her, utterly trivial to the outside world—can stand as a small symbol of the personal and domestic side of the war, and single-mindedness and disruption in everyday life between the invasion of 1914 and the Armistice in 1918.

(By the end of the war, Elisabeth was helping her country in a more mundane and practical way, working for the Red Cross as a trained nurse. But despite the pleadings and invitations of young friends home on leave, she kept her vow and did not dance until the war was over.)

Notes

1. Corday, Michel, *The Paris Front*

1

Invasion

'Everywhere in the world can be heard the sound of things breaking'
John Buchan, on August 1914

On August 26 1914, French national newspapers carried a statement by General Joffre: 'The position remains unchanged from the Somme to the Vosges'. It caused widespread consternation: for after the shock of mobilisation and being at war, most of France believed that the French armies were advancing northwards, pushing the invaders back across the frontier. How could the line be 'unchanged' as far into national territory as the River Somme?

Throughout August and September, the inhabitants of northern France knew better. They saw the invasion, the early fighting and the French retreat, recalling for many families the alarms and disasters of the Franco-Prussian war in 1870. These memories sent many thousands of people out onto the roads, and a disorganised and miserable mass of refugees, Belgian and French, poured down the roads with their children and most valued possessions.

Belgian civilians, women, old people, children, weeping with weariness, pushing carts and barrows and children's prams, revealing to all their scale of values concerning their most intimate possessions. Bedding might be put aside in favour of the old family clock piled up on top of the pots and pans; some loads were carefully thought-out and tidy, others piled up pell-mell.[1]

Some families had been forced to leave with barely ten minutes' warning. Michel Corday, a Paris civil servant, recorded a large group of refugees which reached the capital at the end of August 1914:

> A dreadful cavalcade of old men and little children, wearing slippers and weighed down with bundles. An antheap changing its quarters.[2]

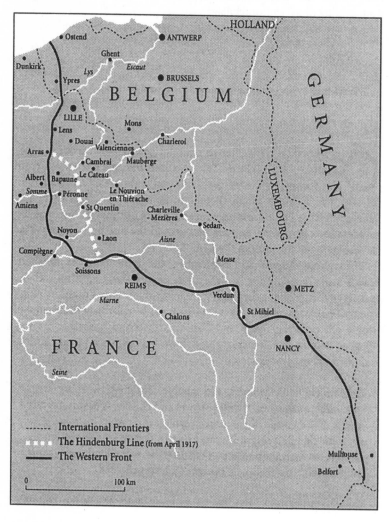

------- International Frontiers
■ ■ ■ ■ The Hindenburg Line (from April 1917)
——— The Western Front

Their flight was hastened by a cruel mixture of fact and rumour. The German invaders were determined to impress the Belgians and French that it was useless to resist: houses were fired, hostages taken, recalcitrance met with summary execution, and deliberate burning of ancient and much-loved buildings emphasised their determination. These refugees included many modest families from big industrial cities and from mining or agricultural village.

The war had immediate economic implications in the area, for the region they were leaving was a significant source of national wealth. Once the line of the Western Front became bogged down during the first winter of the war, it became clear that France had lost serious vital supplies for the duration of the war. The human and industrial losses were terrifying (see Appendix): ten *départements* were wholly or partially affected, and several million people were cut off from the rest of France.[3]

In 1913, France's total output of coal was 40 million tons and its consumption 63 million tons, the balance being imported from Belgium, Britain and Germany. On the outbreak of war, French coal production capacity fell to less than 20 million tons. In the front line area, the German army appears to have believed that French troops were likely to travel underground between one mine shaft and another, and would thus be able to emerge behind the German lines and attack them from the rear. First of all, therefore, they cut off ventilation to the pits near the front, cut the cables and let the cages fall down the shafts. After that the mines were left unpumped and gradually filled up with water, and later—in September 1915—explosives were lowered into the shafts and detonated. The same damage was also undertaken in the Liévin and Lens collieries, destroying in the case of Lens mines which before the war were producing more than four million tons each year. Surface installations were also deliberately destroyed, on top of the damage already achieved by shelling, and all records and plans were burned.[4]

The importance of Lille's textile industry is indicated in the scale of its equipment, for in 1913, the city had 2,700,000 spindles, in 76 establishments, producing 64,500 tonnes of thread of all calibres. The world record for fine thread was held here: 800,000 metres of thread from 1 kilo of raw material. The surrounding centres of Roubaix, Tourcoing, Croix, Wattrelos and Halluin employed 20,000 workers in 87 spinning factories, with another 23,000 employed in 93 weaving factories. In all, these works produced 90 per cent of the French total output, and 17 per cent of world production. Women, and children under 14, were also employed, often at home.

Lille, close to the Belgian borders, was one of the largest cities in France with a population of half a million in 1914. Together with its neighbours Roubaix and Tourcoing, it was the centre of a confident and successful industrial world with a thriving manufacturing and export trade, particularly in mining and textiles. As a major frontier city, Lille had a substantial fortress—but political moves and military lack of planning meant that on the eve of war the garrison forces and the fort itself were not fully armed or stocked. The first months of the war were confusing for all civilians in the north, but particularly in Lille, despite its size and status. Finally, in the first week in September, the city's male population was called on to leave Lille in a notice despatching all men between the ages of 20 and 48 to Dunkirk, and a great crowd set off towards the coast.

Buildings were damaged by shelling, and fires started. In October 1914, after several episodes of confusion, alarm, counter-order and failures of communication, reinforcement and combat, early in October the city was finally abandoned to the enemy as 'ville ouverte', with the loss of substantial supplies of food and ammunition. The Governor was accused, then and later, of dereliction of duty, and the inhabitants turned to the mayor of the city, Charles Delesalle, and their bishop, Monseigneur Charost, for guidance and support. Some met the onslaught with businesslike calm: after the Battle of Charleroi, one of the town's many *concierges* made good use of his usual notice ('le concierge est sur l'escalier', busy round the building) by crossing out and replacing the final word to indicate that 'the *concierge* is at the front'.

Diaries were started. Something extraordinary was happening, many of those who witnessed it wanted to record it, and although not all kept going until the armistice, some of their observations survived into publication after the war. In Guise, a young student hid his early war journal in an empty cellar in the cemetery, knowing that discovery would mean deportation. After seven months, worried about damp, he dug it up, to find that the string was rotten, the paper damp, and some pages lost. He buried it again, in a tin box inside a house, and recovered it after the war in good condition.

Another observer, and one of the most meticulous, was Madame

Delahaye-Théry, a widow in Lille who noted down her impressions every day. The war occupied eight large note-books covered in black cloth, and at the beginning of each one she expressed the hope that the war would be over before she came to the end of it.[5] She would have been surprised to find that she had anything in common with another very effective recorder of wartime experiences, who had greater problems to contend with in keeping up her diary unobserved; but Marie Polvent, in the village of Ors a few miles east of Le Cateau, wrote her notes in school exercise books and slipped them into the rafters of her farmhouse every day, despite the regular presence of German soldiers and officers, the cramped conditions and unremitting hard work of running the farm during constant uncertainty and shortages.

While battles raged and the civilian population was aware that their country was being overrun, elements of ordinary life continued or were attempted: late in September 1914, farmers came in to market (with carts drawn by mules, or by dogs, or with children's prams) and several butter-sellers were there to meet them: but when Germans also arrived and enquired about the market, everyone fled into their houses, vehicles were shut inside farmyards and there was a general scattering in all directions. Everyone suffered from uncertainty, and lack of information: early in October 1914 Marie Polvent records a trip to Le Cateau, about four miles away—an hour in a horse-drawn wagon—in search of provisions. Gunfire sounded very close, and there were attempts to stop the expedition, but they went none the less; there was no salt, paraffin or sugar to be had, but they managed to buy soap, chicory and candles. They saw crosses marking soldiers' graves, and heard brisk gunfire from the Cambrai direction. Trains full of wounded men passed frequently. A week later, German troops came seeking horses, or bicycles, or pigs. Looting and requisitions, which were to become the common experience of the war years, make their first appearance in her diary.

'Fasol', Henri Douchet of Péronne, a market-town on the Somme, was another diarist, and a remarkable man of many talents: a baker-confectioner and caterer by trade, he was also a musician, writer, composer, pamphleteer and local historian, and contributor to the local newspaper. He too kept daily notes and published them after the war, incorporating the observations of other fellow-citizens.

When mobilisation was ordered, Fasol saw—as observers all over France must have seen—the local men hurrying to assemble. After a sleepless night of farewells and preparation, they were kept waiting all day for orders, grew restive and noisy in the heat, and brought plenty of custom to the local bars. Fired with enthusiasm and drink, the bolder among them scared the listening families with tales of war, until late in the afternoon they were reassembled and despatched with a rousing patriotic speech from the Mayor. The night-time departure (in a regimental train with a section which appeared to be the refuge of all the captain's friends) had its wagons laden and overburdened with all kinds of baggage. As each wagon came into the station, escorted by men without rifles or bags, some of the cargo collapsed: the train had to stop, and packages reassembled, amidst loud shouting, swearing and jeering.

By the end of the month, more fears than hopes were confirmed by the enemy's arrival in Péronne. Henri Douchet's journal notes for 28 August 1914:

> 5a.m. Shells are whistling over the houses. A desperate silence hangs over the town. Shutters and windows are tightly closed—but inside, everyone is watching. First there was an indefinable murmur, which grew quickly, and was pierced by the sharp note of a trumpet sounding a few notes in a sad minor key. The noise grew, became overwhelming. The troops were in the northern suburb and shot three women crossing the street.
> 5.30 a.m. An enormous wave, a tide of grey men shouting and waving, rushed into the town square. A simple-minded man was shot. Looting began, and the first fires. General Von Arnim's 4th Army Corps had arrived. The Mairie cellar became the temporary refuge of 'the municipality'—the mayor and his councillors and the local judge, who refused the German demand to lower the French tricolour flying over the town hall, and then saw it torn down by furious enemy hands.[6]

Very early next morning the frightened town shook to the rumbling passage of carts and caissons as several German artillery units marched briskly through. As day broke Péronne was quiet, with no civilians visible. By 7.30 a.m. a young German officer was banging on one of the shop doors, until the owner opened it.

'Where is the Mayor?'—'Gone'—'His assistants, and the authori-

ties?'—'Gone'. The officer was irritated. 'Well! You are a locksmith,
I believe?'—'Yes'—'Good. The Commandant insists that the town
should carry on as usual. I order you to warn all shop traders that
they must open up at 9 a.m. German soldiers will buy from them,
and will pay. Any shops not open at that time, and willingly, will be
opened by force and looted, and I require you to force the locks.'[7]

Under this threat, shop doors flew open on time and life went on, though
scarcely as normal, for heavy gunfire was clearly audible towards Albert
and Bapaume and hundreds of wounded soldiers were brought into
Péronne hospital. Nine hundred one day, seven hundred the next, almost
all Germans. Evacuation of the wounded went on steadily; an attempt to
use barges to take them by canal to Saint Quentin proved impractical
and trains were used instead.

Madame Delahaye-Théry witnessed the departure of the men of military
age from Lille early in October, just before the Germans finally occupied
the city. The diary lists the names of half a dozen young relatives whom
she saw setting off early in the afternoon of 9 October 1914. By early
evening it was too late to leave:

> Since 25 August all the regular troops and officers, all the military
> staff, all have gone. We have been abandoned. The Germans are
> coming. It's the end. The end for us, because the French army is
> somewhere out there but we no longer know where.[8]

She would have sympathised with Elie Fleury, owner-editor of the
Journal de St-Quentin, who in late August hastily despatched his
daughter and her child to relatives in Provence. (His six-year-old grand-
daughter was reluctant to go: 'If I'm not here, who will look after you,
Grandpapa?') Neither of his sons was liable for military service. His
second son, who worked with him on the newspaper, spent much of
August 1914 transcribing official telegrams: seeing beyond the tri-
umphant tone to the disasters afflicting the French forces that month,
with their desperate defeats and losses, he finally declared to his father:

> A few more 'victories' like those, and we'll be fighting in the streets
> of Paris! I'm off to enlist.[9]

(He served throughout the war, surviving trench fever and two wounds.)

During August 1914, English troops arrived in the towns along the railways of northern France, to march away at once towards the approaching German army or remain billetted in reserve in French households. In Le Nouvion-en-Thiérache, a small market town in the wooded pasture lands of the Aisne near the Forest of Mormal, Aline Carpentier was another assiduous observer and diarist. She expressed a fervent hope that, in view of the well-known English custom of 'le picpoket', [sic] she would be allotted an officer as lodger; meanwhile, the kilts of a passing Scottish regiment caused great amusement and curiosity, and she noted the British commanding officer's insistence that the troops should not be given or sold 'any intoxicating drink'.

In the same town the headmaster of the boys' school, Monsieur Leduc, began to keep the carefully detailed diary in which he noted daily activities and incidents throughout the war. Between 15 and 23 August, he records the arrival of English troops on their way to face the invading enemy, with the last contingent leaving the town on Monday 24 August—and next day a British artillery convoy passed through the town in the opposite direction, overtaking the hundreds of refugees trailing down the road with their flocks and their possessions. He saw two riderless German horses led into the town; an English soldier appeared and without a word jumped onto one of them and disappeared at a rapid trot, leading the second horse by the reins. The German cavalry reached Le Nouvion the same day, ahead of their infantry, and overwhelmed the few remaining allied forces. Methodically they set fire to the town, claiming as elsewhere that they had been shot at by civilian snipers. The Mayor was taken hostage and spent the night under guard in a cellar with other local notables. Many Le Nouvionnais, forcibly prevented from fighting the fires, spent the night out in the fields and woods, and even in the cemetery. In one of the town cellars a Belgian refugee gave birth to a daughter.

These scenes were typical of events across the whole of northern France. Péronne, happily unaware of the total evacuation and almost complete destruction to come, was also partly burned by the invaders.

French civilians who remained at home in the north faced two threats during these early weeks of the war: there were the passing refugees, pleading for food and temporary shelter, and implying that their benefactors would suffer equally in the days ahead, and there was the invading enemy. Near Laon, Marguerite Yerta was on holiday at her husband's family farm when the war broke out. Left there when her husband rejoined his unit, she wrote a spirited account of how she and his widowed mother and four sisters coped with events. They handed out as much food as they could spare to a trainload of refugees escaping from heavy shelling and fighting in Belgium, and sheltered a few Belgian soldiers at the farm.

Warned that the Germans were gaining ground, the women hastily hid their valuables. Silver, clocks and the best china were buried in the garden, and until its mechanism ran down the largest clock could be heard, eerily striking the hours underground. The roof space was opened up to hide linen, clothing, carpets and bedding, while mirrors and pictures were tucked away behind curtains and cupboards. The family considered escape, but there were no more trains, and no horses to be had. A neighbour with oxen offered to take some possessions, but then withdrew the offer. Distressed and unable to sleep, the women watched through the night as exhausted French and British soldiers tramped past in a confused rout.

Like so many, Marguerite Yerta and her family finally set out laden with bundles and dragging their dogs on leads, adding to the congestion on the hot and dusty roads of late August, and sleeping in ditches and haylofts. As Prussian troops approached they reached a relative's farm and hastily helped this household in its turn to hide valuables beneath an outhouse floor, covering the trap-door with dirt and straw. (But when invading troops stabled their horses there, the hooves sounded hollow on the trap-door and the hiding-place was discovered.) Discouraged, and assured that they were in no danger, the women returned to their own house. They found rubbish, rotting food and human excrement everywhere.

Food was running out, and it was impossible to obtain further supplies from Laon, the nearest town. International confusion added to their needs—the local people had given much of their food to retreating French troops and were happy to do the same again for the British; on at least one occasion small boys ran ahead of approaching soldiers, shouting 'The English are coming!' Everyone crowded round, offering wine and coffee, fruit and biscuits, a bucketful of lemonade. One woman spoke to the tallest man in the band, enunciating loudly and encouragingly: 'Well, as a reward, you will bring us Willhelm's head!' The man grinned: 'We no English, we Germans…!'

Farmers and farm-workers had to feed themselves and the German troops billetted on them. No tea or coffee, and sugar very scarce: the ingenuity which would be needed so extensively throughout the next four years was put into practice, as walnut leaves with liquorice made a drink of sorts and boiled beetroot produced a form of sweetening. A good crop of fruit from the farm orchard was a blessing.

Except to those directly involved, none of these experiences was a matter of high drama or great significance, but they were typical. The difficulties created by these large movements of people in a time of national crisis were not limited to areas of direct enemy action; quite apart from their own grievous distress and losses, the refugees posed considerable problems along their route and in the communes where they settled indefinitely until they could return home. The comments of an American observer in Belgium could equally well be applied to northern France:

> °As the German armies swept across Belgium, devastation and panic filled the roads with refugees and threw the nation's highly organised economic life into tangled disorder. Communications between communes were broken, business activities were suspended … Isolated communities began to feel the lack of the most elementary necessities and larger towns were taxed to provide food and shelter for the homeless. … Volunteer committees were formed to house and feed refugees and give aid to the destitute. These … were necessarily temporary expedients maintained with increasing difficulty as local resources disappeared.

Some of the 'local resources' had odd destinations: a group of Belgian bank officials crossed the frontier ahead of the invasion and turned up in Le Cateau, laden with a vast amount of money in cash. It was to be given to the Governor of Namur, who had disappeared, and they could not give it to anyone else. In desperation, they burned eight million francs in paper money, and reluctantly handed over the final million francs, in gold, to the French army paymaster.

For most of the refugees, their relocation lasted for the whole war. One rural doctor described their reception and lodging in a small town, identified simply as 'somewhere in central France'. When a large group of refugees arrived in mid-September 1914, a very modest lodging allowance was available, but the newcomers soon outstayed their welcome. There were murmurs at general unruly behaviour and apparent reluctance to work, as well as their inability, sometimes taken for unwillingness, to return home. The schoolroom where they spent their days was soon needed for the expanding needs of the local hospital—with the school itself presumably relocated elsewhere—and problems of accommodation continued to rumble on throughout the war. The local postal service was swamped by the mass of correspondence generated by the new arrivals; letters to men in the forces went post-free, and some women were writing half-a-dozen letters a day to their sons and husbands.

Meanwhile, in the frontier regions civilians hesitated, panicked, fled to join the crowds of refugees from further north, or sat tight, and many did all of these at various times during August and the weeks of early autumn. In Cambrai a serious and conscientious schoolboy, Gaston Prache, who had accompanied his father on the solemn walk to the railway to join his unit, knew that he must take his father's place in helping his mother, tending the garden and caring for the rabbits in their hutches—for food was already scarce. By the end of August there was news of Germans advancing, and the Prache household saw neighbours leaving for Arras or Bapaume to escape the invasion. Gaston and his mother hesitated too long and were prevented from leaving by the arrival of the occupying forces; Gaston records the swift change of circumstances at the end of August, with Cambrai occupied, Péronne fallen, and the enemy south of the River Somme. He wrote too of the courage of their English allies who were so sturdy and cheerful as they passed through Cambrai only a week earlier.

Surrounded by the tide of rumours, the only way to be sure of anything at all was to see it. Those who lived in the threatened north knew well that there had been heavy fighting and that vast numbers of people were on the move, both refugees and armies, but the rest of France was in ignorance, for one of the earliest moves of the war, introduced at the same time as the general mobilisation, was the suppression of detailed reporting and the introduction of censorship. On 3 August all French newspapers were ordered to submit copy to the Press Office so that public opinion 'could be directed and chloroformed'. Even in Paris, the stringent official secrecy meant that President Poincaré was kept in ignorance of the early battles in Lorraine and at Charleroi, knew little of the terrible early losses, and was prevented from visiting the French front line or the border with Alsace.

Accounts of the war as a whole are concerned with large-scale events and historic currents, but the domestic scale should not be overlooked. Late in September, 'Fasol', Péronne's assiduous note-taker, recorded that

> What everyone feared yesterday has happened: this morning there is no bread ... for lack of flour ... how could the reapers operate in the fields in the middle of these endless battles which occupy the whole area for the last fortnight?[10]

Food on the table was not far removed from everyday labour in the surrounding countryside, and housewives were well aware of the close link between farmland strewn with the debris of battle and the lack of supplies in their local shops. The war created one particularly poignant visual effect: it was normal to see the cornfields splashed with the red of poppies, but this year there were different splashes of red which marked the fields of battle—the French army still wore its traditional scarlet trousers, chosen to represent the soldierly spirit and alarm the enemy. In the débâcle of August 1914, they were fatally easy to aim at and showed up clearly when the battle and the living had moved on

Other needs were catered for, in Péronne at least: on 21 December 1914, 'Fasol' in Péronne records that:

> The Germans think of everything! They have just organised prostitution ... a first list of 35 women ... who have been required to undergo medical inspection. Four of the girls available have already been sent to a special hospital in Saint Quentin.[11]

He also observed the misery of people evacuated from the front line, who had left their houses dressed in their summer clothing and were now shivering in front of hearths without fuel; no coal or coke was supplied to civilians. Every day someone could be seen going out with a bill-hook or saw to look for wood, bringing back green bundles which would give more smoke than heat. Others again were burning anything they could lay hands on—doing, as Fasol remarks, what they blamed the Germans for doing.

By the time that Lille was finally occupied in mid-October, after a repeated to-and-fro of French and German control, the significant battles of Mons, Le Cateau, Charleroi, Guise and the Marne had been fought, and many thousands of French and British soldiers were dead. Many communes in the north of France had been in German hands since mid-August and in Le Nouvion-en-Thiérache Aline Carpentier wrote in her diary of 'the long and weary occupation of two months' duration'. The constant movement of those early weeks, the unexpected and alarming events, threats and dangers without detailed news from the wider world, gave the impression of a sudden whirlwind, nothing to do with life elsewhere; each body of men and women, each city, hamlet or farm felt that it was fighting its own war, isolated from any great overall design. The rapidly shifting scenes of action and the losses and dramas of the Allied retreat could only be guessed at by the civilians who saw their armies plodding southward in the late summer heat, lacking food, water and, apparently, cohesion.

Those whose houses lay on or near the northern battles and skirmishes crept back home cautiously when the fighting ceased, and found monstrous sights, of slaughtered soldiers by the hundred blackening in the sun around battered and often looted farm buildings. Aline Carpentier in Le Nouvion—not far from Guise and the French army's battle there on 29 August—gathered such news assiduously for her diary and records the sickening smell of dead horses lying unburied in the fields.

Some may have guessed at the rate of losses during the first weeks of the war; others perhaps recalled the assurances of one newspaper, *Le Temps*, on 4 August:

Statistics taken from recent wars indicate that the greater the efficiency of the weapons used, the lower the number of casualties.

How many of its readers were aware of the total French losses during the first 45 days of the war? Of 3,700,000 men mobilised, 600,000 were dead, wounded, or captured, or had disappeared.

When the wearisome war of attrition set in, with the front line shifting little from the end of November 1914 to the spring of 1918, the frontier between Germany and France ran, in effect, from the Belgian coast to the Vosges, with trenches of increasing complexity marking the new boundary. To the east and north of this line, visible to the French and British armies along the Western Front, lay the conquered lands of Belgium and northern France.

As the opposing armies dug themselves into their trenches during the winter of 1914-15, their civilian counterparts in all the cities, villages and farms on the German side of this new frontier were learning a new way of life, imposed by their new masters. The mobile drama of invasion solidified into a state of occupation.

During those early months, instinct and human kindness prompted innumerable acts of practical help and concealment, or shared food and shelter. Men of combat age still behind the front line, who had lost their units in the turbulent weeks of the late summer, and others in the reserve or territorial units, were in danger: some were discovered and sent to Germany or held as hostages, but a considerable number managed to evade capture and go into hiding.

Lille was large enough to provide a degree of anonymity, a place where a number of sophisticated and successful men and women could work together and draw on many forms of expertise. Individual soldiers and civilians potentially liable for service as reservists remained in Lille and in the surrounding countryside, some wounded, others in hiding after losing their units, others simply trying to avoid the war: the number was never established. One young English clerk in a Roubaix textile firm, John Whitaker, was at home in Manchester on holiday when the war broke out. Hearing that all his employers' office staff of military age were being mobilised, he felt it would be easier to explain in person that—as a British subject—he was not liable to service in the French army despite his residence in France. By mid-September he was back in Roubaix, confident that the Germans, by now facing successful resistance along the Marne, would not take Lille or Roubaix. A month later, however, he saw the German army enter Roubaix, marching through massed and silent crowds. With the occupation of the twin cities, all business stopped and Whitaker felt that perhaps he would be better off after all on the English side of the channel. Setting off by a roundabout route, he was stopped and turned back, returning to Roubaix in time to see the effect of the new régime on his employers' mills.

Proclamations from the newly installed governor of Lille, General von Heinrich, made clear the risk to those who protected soldiers in hiding:

Any civilian, including the civilian staff of the French government, who helps troops who are enemies of Germany, or who acts in a way injurious to Germany and her allies, will be punished by death.

The pattern was the same across the whole of the occupied zone. Late in the autumn of 1914, posters appeared in prominent sites, stating that all French, Belgian and British soldiers hiding in the care of local inhabitants must give themselves up—they would be treated as prisoners of war. After 4 December they would be regarded as spies, and shot.

The speedy invasion and confusion surrounding the retreat to the Marne left a number of British soldiers behind the German lines. In the hamlet of Vertigneul, near Le Cateau, a young officer was hidden for four months by the mayor in his large farmhouse—clearly remembered ever afterwards by the mayor's son, then aged six. The German Commandant of the area suspected the man's presence, and there were constant demands and threats to all inhabitants to give up any such fugitives. The Commandant respected the Mayor and his household to some extent, which was fortunate—the young Englishman was extremely casual and on occasions had to be physically bundled out of the kitchen and into the cupboard which was his hiding place. Finally he was despatched in workman's overalls, carrying his uniform and revolver in a bag slung over his shoulder. While travelling towards safety he was challenged in German, but escaped successfully; in 1918 he passed near the farm and sent messages but was unable to return. His sword, which he was persuaded with some difficulty from taking with him when he set off in disguise, was buried somewhere in the farm and has never been found.

In Saint Quentin, three Irish soldiers missed the last train that took British army units out of the city at the end of August 1914. Thomas Hands, of the Kings Own Regiment, John Hughes, of the Royal Irish Rifles, and their companion (listed only as 'Mac Nell' in French records) managed to exchange their uniforms for civilian clothes. Two of them found safe lodging, but Hughes, 19, was found weeping in the street. Madame Preux, whose children found him, reluctantly took him in, and was impressed by his behaviour: as she remarked after the war, 'I treated him like one of my family, I had seventeen children, eight of them have survived.' Hughes, who was known to the family as 'Henri' never left the house. The city's central administration paid Mme Preux ten *sous* per week for his maintenance, the same amount as for everyone else in the household. It must have been a crowded household; Hughes slept each night on a mattress laid on the kitchen table.

Hands, however, was not so sensible; he went out frequently, enjoyed brawling with German soldiers, and began a romance with a French girl. It seems probable that she betrayed the three British soldiers for the sake of the reward it brought her. 'Mac Nell' was arrested on 20 October; his host, M. Contant, escaped and lived in hiding for the next three years, while the Germans did their best to find him. Madame Contant, meanwhile, was sent to prison and 'Mac Nell' himself sent to Germany. Together with their French host, M. Preux, Hands and Hughes appeared in court in February 1915 and impressed at least one observer by their dignity. When asked why they had not given themselves up, Hughes stated: 'Because our king sent us here to fight or die.' What about the poster, calling on foreign troops to surrender? 'Yes, I saw it, but anyone can put what they like on a poster, that doesn't give them any rights'.

Attempts to convince the court that as foreign soldiers caught behind enemy lines they should not be treated as spies were met with disdain. The two Britons were condemned to death and Preux to fifteen years in a German prison.

On 8 March the two soldiers learned of their approaching execution, later that day. From mid-morning until the mid-afternoon they were allowed to walk around in the prison, and spent the time singing Irish songs. In the absence of Irish shamrock they pinned violets on to their caps (smuggled in from Madame Preux) and were executed in the military barracks.[12] Six years later the girl who betrayed them was brought before a French court and sentenced to life imprisonment.

From the earliest days of the war and invasion, there were people who needed protection. In the immediate aftermath of those early battles, French soldiers who sought to hide from the victors were easily spotted by their scarlet uniforms. As the Germans took possession of Péronne, on the River Somme, a few French soldiers were hidden in sheds or outhouses. A local priest cared for them, and showed them how to steer a boat. When German observers noted continual visits to his garden shed and came to search, the priest opened the door to them and pretended not to understand while the fugitives took to their boat and sought refuge on an island in the lagoons of the river marshes.

It was known that men of various nationalities were in hiding around many towns and villages throughout the autumn, taking food and shelter where they could find it, or helped by local residents; communes were subject to substantial fines for shielding these strays from the new masters—if more soldiers were not brought in to surrender within four days, according to a proclamation in Le Nouvion on 25 October, a heavy fine would be payable, the mayor would remain a hostage liable to be shot, and his councillors sent as prisoners to Germany.

In Le Nouvion, Aline Carpentier wrote up her diary:

Friday 20 October 1914: Monsieur Lemaire [confusingly, the assistant to the Mayor, Monsieur Page] and two councillors prepared to leave for Guise with the 1,000-franc fine. First the Kommandant's message was proclaimed, that the local populace must urge the English soldiers known to be in the area to surrender, to lift the threat and achieve the release of the Mayor. This was distributed to all the surrounding communes. What would happen? Will the English surrender? In any case, they should not be betrayed. We can still hear the guns ...

Monday 2 November. Requiem Mass for the dead, and especially for the soldiers killed in battle. The church has never been so full— and yet, there were so many missing. The councillors have been to Guise three times, hoping to obtain the release of Monsieur Page, but their trouble was in vain.

Tuesday 3 November. Mlle Marchand called out to me, 'Hurry, Madame Carpentier, come and look, here's an Englishman who's surrendering!' I rushed out and saw a poor boy, he looked so young, walking down the street all on his own. Our hearts were touched to see him, after suffering these weeks of deprivation, trying to keep his freedom and now deliberately giving himself up—what wretches they are who must have denounced him! Another five men passed us on their way to surrender, looking miserable, and party dressed in civilian clothes, walking between German soldiers who held their rifles cocked at them. We wept to see them pass, and prayed for them, brave men, they have surrendered to save our mayor and commune.

Wednesday 4 November. The sacrifice of the British soldiers was not in vain, for Monsieur Page [the mayor] was released yesterday.

Men hid in woods and abandoned houses, torn between remaining concealed and trying to rejoin their units. Aline Carpentier's 11-year-old son and his friends, playing in the woods near Le Nouvion, discovered a group of twenty British soldiers, in uniform and armed, hiding in the undergrowth; in her diary, his mother describes how the boy recognised one of the men, who had bought postcards in the village before the

Borough of Ramsgate.

Town Clerk's Office.
Albion House.

TELEPHONE Nº 201 & 202.

A. BLASDALE CLARKE,
TOWN CLERK.

AVIS AUX ETRANGERS

La ville de Ramsgate, avec sa belle plage, située
à une heure de Douvres et une heure et demie de Folkestone,
(deux heures de Londres) est particulièrement adaptée aux
demandes des réfugiés étrangers.

Les Français et les Belges qui se rendent à Ramsgate,
y trouvent un accueil des plus sympathiques.   Les
Catholiques peuvent assister aux offices à l'abbaye béné-
dictine de Saint Augustin où se trouvent des prêtres
français et belges.   Il y a aussi plusieurs couvents
pour les jeunes filles ainsi que des pensions pour les
garçons.

Une dame interprète, portant un ruban tricolore, sera
heureuse d'aller chercher à la gare de Ramsgate Town les
voyageurs dui lui auront envoyé une dépêche lui annonçant
l'heure de leur arivée, et de leur fournir des adresses
de pensions, de familles, d'hotels, ou de maisons à louer
dont les prix sont modérés.

Il y a à Ramsgate un consulat belge.

S'adresser par lettre ou par telegramme au:

Town Clerk (Secrétaire de la ville)
Albion House,
Ramsgate,

A notice welcoming refugees to Ramsgate

retreat. In a real-life adventure tale, the boys guided the men across country, acting as scouts and look-out, and brought them bread and salt to eat with the eggs they had been given.

The dangers of remaining in hiding were all too obvious. Late in the autumn of 1914 a group of eleven men from the British Army took shelter in a village mill near Le Nouvion-en-Thiérache. In February 1915, the German Commandant of Le Nouvion, Waechter, announced that the eleven men had been denounced; they and their protectors were shot and their houses burned. This sad ending to what one woman, who had cared for the men, described in court as 'simply her duty as a good French citizen', contrasts strongly with the astonishing case of a British trooper who, cut off after the battle at Le Câteau late in August 1914, spent the rest of the war hidden in a wardrobe. He returned home safely, and his guardian eventually received recognition and financial support.

In Péronne an employee of the local *Gazette* was arrested as a spy because notes had been found in his house, recording the numbers of troops passing, and their regiments. Under interrogation he unwisely remarked that many others were in the habit of doing the same. It must have been typical of so many incidents across northern France, as local indignation and curiosity clashed with the invaders' wary determination. A local citizen, M. Quentin, was arrested, together with his wife, their maid, and a clerk. The whole house, in the main square, was searched, and two neighbours who called unawares while this was going on were also arrested and interrogated before being sent on their way.

M. and Mme Quentin were well known and thoroughly honest and admired citizens—but as a well-informed amateur historian who took a passionate and detailed interest in all local happenings, he naturally took notes on whatever occurred, in order to maintain a full record for posterity. If the fact of copying the text of posters and official announcements exposed the note-taker to prison, everyone who kept a diary—i.e. most of the town at this time—had reason to feel uneasy.

Friends and neighbours did their best to help him; his brother approached the Commandantur several times but was finally arrested too, while suspicion fell on everyone he had spoken to. For the week of his incarceration he was kept incommunicado, although it was possible, with care and discretion, to see him at his prison window and make signs to him.

By the end of 1914, northern France was coming to understand that

Germany intended to take full advantage of her newly-conquered territory. The burden of the occupation gradually became clearer as the invaders showed their disregard for the ordinary human needs of their new subjects while the French civilians did their best to sustain their morale and to show the occupying forces as little respect or interest as possible. All resources were to be used for the benefit of the German economy, not simply as hostile terrain to be kept under control. An administrative network was imposed, with a Governor at the head of each major regional division and a Commandant at each local headquarters. The local mayor and his assistant and clerks, relieved of all authority—except that of becoming a hostage when necessary, a useful role for the mayor—were required to transmit messages and impress on all citizens the importance of cooperating with the new regime. After the fears, dangers and uncertainties of the war's first weeks, the self-assurance and firmness of purpose shown by the invaders was impressive, but deeply disturbing. They clearly knew what they wanted, and intended to stay in possession of their newly-won lands.

Where the mayors remained at their post, or others stepped forward to replace those who were missing, they were tolerated—but removed for the slightest misdemeanour and replaced by a nominee of the German occupying forces. Whoever served as mayor, whether the original officeholder or German nominee, was used as the point of contact with the local population and if necessary as a hostage, held to ensure good behaviour or as punishment for infractions in the commune.

In an orderly fashion the administrative system of each Commandantur looked at the various French resources available, and by the end of October, a month after first entering Le Nouvion, the local citizens were learning what to expect from their new masters. A typical announcement was recorded in Le Nouvion, from the regional Governor based in Guise: all men between the ages of 18 and 48 must report to the German authorities on the first and third Monday of each month, otherwise carrying on with their normal work. They must parade twice a month to confirm their continued presence, and any who failed to appear would be sought out and sent to Germany. This affected the men who had not been mobilised as reservists, and also some who had been called up at the outbreak of war but sent home because their headquarters could not cope with the numbers. Sent home 'to await further definite instructions' and delighted to return to their families, particularly for the harvest if they were from rural homes, many were overtaken by the rapid German advance of late August and early September and were still at home when the Germans occupied the north. The 'appel' on 8 November in Le Nouvion brought in a total of 600 men, of whom 250 lived in the town itself and the remainder in outlying hamlets and farms. Aline Carpentier's diary describes the lines of men, and her distress at seeing so many strong young men under enemy control, liable to become prisoners of war in Germany instead of fighting for their country. Had she been fully aware of the scale of French losses she might perhaps have been more relieved than distressed at their preservation from active warfare.

After the human head-count came the farm produce and livestock: five-sixths of the 1914 harvest was immediately seized to feed German troops in France and civilians at home in Germany—an augury of shortages ahead. A detailed count of livestock in the commune of Le Nouvion was complete by the end of November, listing the age, sex and condition of all animals. On the basis of this census, the commune, like all others under occupation, had to hand over hundreds of cattle to the invaders, also a foretaste of future demands. Colonel Waechter, Commandant of Le Nouvion, issued a formal notice that no animal was to be sold without official permission. By mid-October all dairy farms round Le Nouvion were directed to deliver their butter to a specified dairy at a set price and by the end of the month the commune was instructed to deliver 800 kg of cheese, in 50 kg packages, to the Commandantur—the local German headquarters, more familiar to local residents as the Hotel de Ville, or town hall.

All such instructions were carefully noted by Monsieur Leduc, the schoolmaster. At the end of October he records the first use of what was to become a dreaded word throughout the region: Requisition. On this occasion the demand was for 100 pigs, together with hay, straw, corn, carts, harnesses, strong horses, young horses, and wine. The demand at the end of November was for 200 cows, each with a strong rope, and all horses not used for farm work.

In addition, all pigeons were to be killed: this was a regulation stringently imposed in all areas, urban and rural—not for culinary purposes, but to prevent their use as message-bearers. As in England, the industrial north of France was passionately enthusiastic about breeding and racing pigeons and for many fanciers it was heart-breaking to be forced to kill their favourite birds.

What the cities could not offer the invader, in the form of livestock and agricultural produce, was available in the form of machinery, manufactured goods and raw materials in the great warehouses supplied and exported by rail and canal. Lille, the proud textiles capital, saw its stocks of finished goods vanish in train-loads and lorry convoys, along with reserves of food. As well as these end-products—textiles ready for sale or making-up, food for immediate consumption—the city's mills and factories of all kinds came under close scrutiny.

In the first weeks of the occupation, factories were closed down, cleared of machinery, or kept in working order under German control. A typical report on a textile factory speaks of all its 315 looms broken up with heavy hammers and the essential leather straps removed. One particularly important piece of machinery was dismantled and sent to Germany, the others destroyed, at the rate of six looms a day. Most of their looms, among the most modern in Europe, were dismantled and sent to support the German textile industry, together with stocks of machine tools and heavy engineering equipment. Modern equipment was sent back to Germany, particularly from the most up-to-date textile works, some coal mines were kept working, and owners of establishments which were of no use to the invaders were told to lay off their workers. In Cambrai 150 workers were retained by another textile mill to maintain the machinery after the stocks were removed in 1916, but early in 1917 the machinery was destroyed—a task which occupied some British prisoners of war for about three months. In many cases the workforce refused to work for the enemy and some, in a new-born spirit of resistance, delayed and mishandled production through sabotage or obstruction to reduce stocks which might aid the German war-effort.

In Denain the great steelworks, employing 4,000 men and producing 350,000 tons of steel per year, were destroyed. (After the Armistice, Denain remained unproductive for ten years during reconstruction, while Germany was able to sell steel to France.) Where managers refused to work for the invaders, their works were closed down; civilians and prisoners of war were forced, at pistol point, to place explosives and the factories were blown up, with 50 or 60 large explosions each day.

Fabrics, raw materials, machine tools and sugar-refining equipment were loaded up and sent to German factories, while old or worn-out machinery was taken for scrap. As one observer recorded in Lille, 'Every form of production which made the name of the city famous throughout the world, the fruits of its labour and the mark of its skill, disappeared bit by bit'.

An example of an important and valuable product of the northern textile factories, easily overlooked in later times, was linen thread—an essential item in a pre-plastics age when leather, textiles and equipment of all kinds needed vast amounts of linen thread for manufacture, maintenance and repair. The war created an insatiable demand for sandbags, made up from coarse jute sacking and stitched with hemp or linen: fine thread normally produced for lace-making had to be diverted to their manufacture. (Another large-scale local product, of great significance in a horse-drawn world, was the harvest of oats for the thousands of horses which were an essential part of everyday life.)

French gold coinage was taken in various ways, as fines for infringements, or as 'war contributions', and municipal treasuries were cleared of money. These forced contributions were often described as fines, for alleged misdemeanours or instead of hostages; or they were simply taken as a contribution to the new administration's war effort.

The presence of enemy troops and of incoming refugees felt overwhelming in some places, and houses became desperately crowded. By December 1914 the French population of Péronne—2,750 inhabitants—was host to 1,320 refugees, quite apart from the presence of German officers and soldiers billetted amongst them. Conditions were exacerbated by initial damage to houses which made some of them wholly or partially uninhabitable.

Throughout the war, there was no possibility of contact with the rest of France, or indeed with other occupied areas: no news, no newspapers, above all no radio and no letters. There were accusations that French inhabitants were corresponding with their free families through the Red Cross; this would be regarded as espionage. It is of course universally acknowledged that true facts are impossible to discover in war-time. All civilians had to interpret the news released to them with an eye on the need for propaganda favouring the dispenser of the information, but the French residents in the occupied area had to contend with a doubly distorted image: what little news reached them about free France and the progress of the war was the German propaganda version of French news, itself already presented to suit official propaganda requirements without any counter-balance of neutral interpretation or comment.

By the end of 1914, the occupation had become a fact of life, reflecting the static conditions prevailing in much of the active combat areas. Amidst the uncomfortable adjustment to this new status, the feeling of isolation was intense.

Notes

1. Corday, Michel, *The Paris Front*
2. Corday, *The Paris Front*
3. The number of French people affected by the occupation varies according to the criteria used, but there are three main scales. The whole population of the ten *départements* affected (i.e. including areas on the Allied side of the front line) was just over 6.5 million, or 4.7 million in the 'war zone', in 1911; the core of the civilian population in the occupied zone during the war, as calculated by the Committee for Relief (see Chapter 3), was around 2.25 million.
4. Extensive and detailed documentation surviving from this period, covering other mine-shafts in this coal-field, are held at the Mining Museum at Lewarde, near Douai.
5. Mme Delahaye-Théry's main reason for keeping the diary was that she was cut off from her children and grandchildren and feared that she would never see them again. When the family was reunited after the war she did not mention the notebooks, but they were discovered after her death and published in 1933.
6. Douchet ('FASOL'), *Péronne sous l'occupation*
7. Douchet, *Péronne*
8. Delahaye-Théry, Mme Eugéne, *Les Cahiers Noirs*, Éditions de la Province, 1934
9. Fleury, Elie, *Sous la Botte, Histoire de la Ville de Saint™Quentin pendant l'Occupation Allemande, Août-Février 1917*, Elie Fleury, 1925-6, Les Éditions de la Tour Gile, 1996
10. Douchet, *Péronne*
11. Douchet, *Péronne*
12. Their graves, with Commonwealth War Graves Commission headstones, are in Saint Quentin communal cemetery.

2

Occupation

'A wearisome thrusting against a pressure of evils'
H. G. Wells, *Mr Britling Sees it Through*

Once the mobile war had passed on, the developing stalemate of trench warfare was reflected in the northern regions. In the unoccupied bulk of the country, the French and their allies struggled with their heavy losses and then the stalemate conditions of trench warfare, while the inhabitants of the northern occupied regions assessed the aftermath of the invasion. With the despatch of all natural and manufactured products to Germany, all activities of the conquered population must be henceforward be directed towards the exclusive benefit of the invaders. In Péronne, 'Fasol' recorded in early November 1914 the invaders' attentive visits to wine-cellars: bottles were inspected, counted, and taken—sometimes on the pretext that it was for the wounded, from both armies. Occasionally it was possible for servants of the house to smuggle bottles back again during the loading-up. The visits were apparently at random—never a sequence down one street and up the next, but unannounced, to catch residents off-guard. It was not only wine that was taken—one of the town's patissiers had thousands of eggs preserved, ready for his kitchens, but saw the German inspecting officer designate them for the Casino, the Officers' Mess. To save time, the eggs were scooped up in metal buckets from their preserving tanks—with the result that almost as many were broken as were removed whole.

He also records the indignation of the populace on hearing that, although the French bakeries had almost no flour to make their bread, German cavalry billetted in neighbouring villages were using local unthreshed corn to feed their horses. On 23 September, Aline Carpentier noted in her diary that the housewives of Le Nouvion crowded in to the market, for many of the regular suppliers had been missing for several weeks. A sudden blast on a car hooter announced the arrival of German officers, and everyone fled—except for a few of the market traders, who sold goods to the Germans.

Instead of continuing with the existing local government structure (as happened in Luxembourg), the German forces removed all powers and took over all administration. Six German areas were established, based in Valenciennes, Charleville, Stenay (or Laon), Cambrai, Vervin and Vouziers. The scale of operations was considerable, with the Charleroi general headquarters consisting of some 600 officers.

The movement of refugees during the first weeks of the war soon ceased as the German troops settled in and took control, but a different kind of involuntary civilian movement developed. Hostages were taken, frequently community leaders such as the mayors; many were sent to Germany where they were lodged in rough barracks, initially without any form of heating. One group of sixty hostages was kept in Lille as assurance against damage caused. This policy developed in places into a rota of citizens held hostage locally, and imprisoned or fined in case of fire or damage occurring during their 'tour of duty'.

Further east, the two provinces of Alsace-Lorraine, which had been German since 1870, made up a special category in 1914-18. Soldiers from these provinces were considered 'an enemy within' and sent to the Eastern front, while German propaganda promoted the concept that both soldiers and civilians from these areas should be regarded as potential traitors. Responses to German success were certainly more complex here than elsewhere, and there was considerable evasion of military service, with men escaping across the Vosges mountains into free France. The modern French *département* of Moselle represents the part of Lorraine which had been part of Germany since the 1870 Franco-Prussian war, and the remainder (the modern *départements* of Meurthe-et-Moselle, Meuse, and the Vosges), which had remained French, was now invaded and considered totally German by the invaders. The drive towards Germanisation which had marked local teaching and administration since 1870 was intensified.

The region's recent history meant that the Germans regarded it as particularly suspect and about a hundred of the more important citizens of Metz—elected representatives, mayors and priests—were deported to Germany. The French army's brief incursion into the part of Lorraine which had been German since 1870 was greeted with delirious delight at the 'liberation'; but when the Germans returned they punished the local population severely for their 'treachery' and sent many people to camps in Germany. Some remained until the Armistice, together with other civilians deported from front-line villages in the partial clearance of front-line zones. Altogether several thousand individuals spent the war as civilian prisoners. Escapes and evasions of military service were greater in Alsace than elsewhere, and although Lorraine men in general accepted their requirement to serve in the German army, some 200-300 men from the Seille region reached the French army and enlisted there. In Alsace, the Vosges mountains providing valuable hiding places.

Back in Picardy, 'Fasol' recorded in Péronne that a group of civilian prisoners was brought back to the town in the following spring, not to be released but to undertake local labouring work. Thin and bearded, they described the conditions in their camp near Frankfurt. It contained ten thousand prisoners, soldiers and civilians, and including some British and Russians, although most were French. They lived in vast barrack huts, each housing some 200 men, counted and numbered like convicts, and closely guarded. Within the barbed-wire fences the ground was a mass of insanitary mud; their food was rotten, and inadequate. Large numbers of men died. Their duties were to carry out labouring duties, stone-breaking and road-mending.

Only one northern *préfet* remained, in the department of the Nord, and he was left with no real authority; he was a minor cog in the administrative system, superfluous. Occasionally the invaders deigned to humour him with some reply to his protestations. The mayors were the only official representatives of the local community allowed to remain in post. The mayors were the conduit through which all instructions were passed on to the inhabitants and through which information must be passed back up the chain to the Commandant. 'Rumours and gossip' among the French themselves were strictly discouraged. It was also the mayors' task to encourage proper behaviour—to see that the French saluted or greeted German politely: hats must be removed, and the penalty for incorrect behaviour would be 20 marks' fine and three days' arrest. It was not considered polite to put one's hands in one's pocket in the presence of a German officer. One determined citizen of Péronne took to carrying empty bags or suitcases around so that his hands were legitimately occupied and he was not required to salute. The commune survived as the lowest level of the German administrative system, and all other sections of local government were suppressed. The new hierarchy consisted of the Army, the *Étappen* (districts), the Commandantur (local German headquarters under a German officer) and the French mayors.

As movement became more restricted and the means of transport vanished in the hands of the requisition teams, community cohesion and morale depended increasingly on local leaders. Official pre-war status had little importance, but those who could retain their personal integrity and dignity were increasingly valuable. Very often this would be the mayor, who was treated as the representative of his commune even when he retained virtually no powers, and religious leaders were also important in many communities. Lille provided good examples of both; the Bishop, M. Charost, spoke out boldly in his pulpit and resisted blandishments and orders, and Charles Delesalle, the Mayor, matched him. In a typical gesture in October 1917, M. Delesalle refused to accompany the German military governor of Lille to the inauguration of a new memorial to German soldiers killed in the war unless the governor agreed to salute the French dead in return.

'*The earliest form of transport...*'

Local civic offices were manned by German soldiers at first but later, as the need for fresh troops grew greater, many were sent off to fight and were replaced in the Commandantur offices by German civilians transferred into France for the purpose. A few French were employed—the mayors became the conduit for communication between the occupying forces and the subservient population, and a few of the more educated French men found work as clerks, protecting themselves in this way from deportation to Germany or, later, desperate physical exhaustion in forced labour gangs.

The scale of administrative organisation naturally depended on the area to be managed: Lille had a general as its governor, while Valenciennes had a colonel. Avesnes, a medium-sized town, had a colonel and a lieutenant, with 21 junior officers, large towns had their own Commandantur, with a separate establishment for the surrounding district and a few important features such as the Forest of Mormal—a substantial stretch of woodland which needed thorough patrolling and which was also a significant source of timber—had their own Commandantur. At the lowest village level, the establishment consisted of a single officer with a few soldiers. Meanwhile, two industrial centres in Lorraine marked out for annexation into Germany proper were subject to a different system of special civilian administration.

La Capelle, with nine communes and just over 7,000 inhabitants, was typical of smaller centres; here the Commandant was a major, assisted by a lieutenant. There were two chaplains—one Catholic and one Protestant—a chief administrative clerk, a judge, two cashiers, a sergeant and four non-commissioned officers, two women secretaries, two doctors and one veterinary officer, and an agricultural manager. In addition, an industrial labour section consisted of 62 French workmen with an overseer; there was also a laundry and a sawmill with 14 men, a group of Russian prisoners with 37 horses, a civilian group with 47 horses; sections for road and general maintenance, fuel and food distribution, forestry work, a stores manager, and requisition services. Any further labour required was recruited from the local French population. This administrative system was responsible for the smooth running of La Capelle's railways, shops, police patrols, postal service, anti-aircraft guns, two dairies, three pig-fattening units, the telegraphic service, and military dogs.

Local government clerks and treasurers were officially still operative, but the French courts were relieved of all jurisdiction except for the most minor infractions and an imported German judge administered justice in all other matters. Police were in charge of traffic, passing on orders, enforcing requisitions and keeping an eye on men of military age, as well as detecting subterfuge designed to evade food or other regulations. The military police force generally consisted of soldiers who were unfit for front-line service. Some were uniformed, with a special armband, while others formed a secret police force whose job was to detect espionage, resistance or escape plans.

The mayor became the link between the new masters and the new subjects. He and his clerks—often women who took the place of men who were absent in the French army—would have to deal with demands of all kinds. Frequently this would mean finding billets at very short notice, for soldiers and horses needing overnight lodging and food. One of the most disagreeable tasks for the mayor was to supply manpower for local maintenance work. Fasol describes the work and how it was regarded in Péronne:

> Forty men were needed every day. This application to our citizens of German laws which forced all the inhabitants to work for the invader was extremely badly received. We had become used to inactivity in Péronne. Perhaps if everyone had stayed shut up indoors, the Germans would have left us alone, but the sight of so many men and lads wandering around and ferreting about here and there made them uneasy. But instead of organising this unpopular and unrewarding work themselves, they made the town do it... so the *mairie* drew up a list of names more or less at random, and informed those concerned; but next day hardly anyone turned up. The next day, they were asked for again—and were met with certificates of incapacity or illness. In the end the mayor and his assistants had to give the names to the Commandant, who had the men rounded up the night before and held with the civilian prisoners, to make sure of attendance the next day. So the mayor found himself accused of being a German supporter.[1]

Services of this kind, and tasks such as shoe-repairs, laundering and cleaning, were paid for at the town hall with 'bons', or vouchers. There were some advantages in the early days of the war, for the German army dentist put his skills at the service of the town, and for several days the first question between French people meeting in the street was, 'Have you been to the dentist yet?' The French, who had thought themselves supreme in the art of bureaucracy, found themselves outdone in their own domain of pedantry, as lists were made out in triplicate or, in the case of wages, in quintuplicate, as sheaves of paper sped or dallied between the town hall and the Commandantur. Confusion was added to mistrust and resentment, and the French officials needed superhuman qualities of flexibility and tact.

'*The St Quentin city treasurer...*'

Money management was worrying and complicated, and Fasol describes how it was dealt with in Péronne—the same system was applied throughout the occupied area. In the summer of 1915 the town was told that it must issue its own paper money: a polite refusal, because it was completely illegal under French law to print bank-notes, raised smiles from the German authorities. The sum to be printed, they said, must represent 1,860,000 francs, in notes bearing the same face values as the ordinary French currency. The next objection was the shortage of suitable paper and printing presses. 'No problem!' came the answer, 'We will supply it, and some of you can go to Lille to discuss the printing.' Paper was available within a few days and three people were given unprecedented permission to leave the area and travel to Lille to arrange the printing. A German officer accompanied the fortunate three; after a good lunch with liberal wine he decided to enjoy himself further, and went off to Brussels, leaving the Péronne trio to complete their investigations and return home.

The system of local paper currency operated for the rest of the war, and helped to control the local population since they could not use this 'money' outside the area. Civilians were in any case not allowed to move around freely. Their chief role was to serve the occupying forces, not to get in their way, and to do as they were told. The great majority of the French in this occupied area naturally wanted to help their own forces, but this was extremely difficult; in the occupied zone of 1914-1918—far more restricted than in the Second World War—the high ratio of occupying Germans to resident civilians meant that opportunities for active resistance were limited, with plenty of ways to enforce at least outward compliance with regulations. Freedom vanished as a flood of prohibitions and instructions rained down, with new posters appearing almost daily.

The need for food brought degradation to everyone, no matter what their peace-time status: former land-owners could be seen doing the washing-up for the German officers lodged in the Casino, farmers' wives washed and ironed clothing for the soldiers, and others who could no longer work or could not find employment were grateful for hand-outs of old clothes which in peace-time they would not even have put down for their dogs to sleep on.

As Fasol remarks, everyone's moral values were undermined: it was recognised that all the civilians employed at the flour-mills filled their pockets with flour, used what they needed and sold the rest; but others made use of their enemy by betraying their fellow-countrymen, pointing out their hiding places. Girls were forced into prostitution by their wretched conditions, and then lacked nothing—their lovers brought them fine white bread, coal, dresses and furs. A different question of conscience exercised the people of Péronne, and their senior priest; one of the town's most respected citizens sought guidance—was it permissible, given the opportunity, to consume food taken from the enemy, such as a slice of ham or a piece of Dutch cheese? The priest dealt with the question wittily: 'To assess whether this is sinful or not, let me consider the quality of the food - bring me a slice of this ham and a piece of this cheese and we shall see!' From this remark to advice to his flock that stealing from the Germans was permissible was only a small step.

The German authorities were aware of the need to maintain good relations: a poster was pasted up entitled 'The Soldier's Orders', specifying that he must respect the households in which he was billeted, show that he was not a barbarian, not be untidy ... and avoid all relationships with the inhabitants.

Manpower needs affected many households. Men considered of 'mobilisable' age - between 17 and 50, or in some cases 60—were ordered to present themselves regularly to be counted and inspected. Some were kept in France at the service of the Commandants, while others were sent to work in Germany. In Douai a weeding out procedure resulted in one-third of the men being sent to Germany, and early in the war men in Le Cateau were seized off the streets and despatched to Germany, recalling the British press-gang system of earlier centuries.

In Chaulnes the male population of three hundred was reduced to 17, young adolescents or old men. Of the men considered useful, the young were sent to Germany, and the older men to Péronne where they joined a 1,500-strong group from 20 communes. (They stayed in Péronne for nearly two years, undertaking various kinds of work, until in the general evacuation as the Germans fell back to the Hindenburg Line in the spring of 1917 they were taken further north, and only returned home after the Armistice.) As part of this macabre dance of shifting civilian populations, Péronne acquired incomers from many far-flung communes during the early months of the war, and also a group of 90 Russians who were billetted in the château in a state of virtual starvation and destitution. In Sissonne an announcement in November 1914 made it clear that 'All men not working in the fields and without other occupation will sent in a labour gang and required to work there'.

In Germany it was announced that the men arriving from France were criminals or snipers, and they were treated accordingly. At the French end of the chain, the departure of so many men to Germany was a highly effective guarantee of good behaviour among those who remained. For those who were left at home—everyone else in the occupied region—life was strictly regulated. All clocks were set to German time - which caused considerable resentment - and each house was required to post a list of residents by its street door, showing the full names, ages and professions of all who lived there. In villages, the household's livestock must also be listed. Doors were to remain unlocked by day, and also at night when shelling might force German soldiers to take shelter. German street names appeared on the walls. Identity cards must be carried at all times, and no more than three people could gather together on the streets. Travel between communes was forbidden, except with a special pass, available only in exceptional circumstances—which did not include visits to sick relatives. The issue of these passes was later restricted to a fixed number per commune, and excluded private movement. Their cost was gradually increased, from 0.08 pfennigs (10 centimes) to one mark. Eventually they became obligatory for going to fields or hamlets within the same commune. The oppressive burden of these controls were quickly felt. In the autumn of 1914 Elie Fleury, in Saint Quentin, wished to travel with a young friend to seek news of her husband's family in their village some seven kilometres away, which had been shelled during the invasion. Fleury knew that it was hopeless to ask for permission if the reason was given as 'seeking family news' and in his negotiations with the authorities stated instead 'looking for potatoes'. As one of the German troops remarked to him, such petty restrictions which had come to cause such irritation and distress over the past three months had been part of daily life in Alsace for more than forty years.

Travel to Belgium was forbidden, as was any correspondence except with prisoners of war in Germany, to whom one postcard per month could be sent. This correspondence occasionally brought news of free France, heavily disguised, since prisoners in Germany were allowed to receive letters from both sides of the Western Front. News was always wanted, both personal and public, and no one knew what or who to believe; as a Paris civil servant observed in the autumn of 1914, from the privileged viewpoint of his central government post,

> When one compares the first despatches announcing the destruction of the cathedral of Rheims with the photographs of this edifice, its majestic outlines almost unchanged, one realises that tendency towards exaggeration against which one must steel

oneself if one is to be fair.

One may not mention that the Germans, according to the first rumours which are reaching us, have cleverly organised the invaded territories, stimulating industrial production (of which they commandeer half).[2]

The same observer recalled a novel about Germany which he had read before the war, which included a word coined by the author for people who make their living out of war: 'the belliculturists'. He would probably have applied the expression to those whom he wrote about in the spring of 1915:

> Paris is remote from the war. The restaurants are crammed. What a contrast with those tortured towns of eastern France, that endless stream of wounded down from Les Éparges into Verdun ... That is one of the great tragedies of the time—the enormous gulf between Paris and the front.[3]

News management, as it would later be called, was a vital feature on both sides of the front line; in the occupied area there was only German-approved news, while in the free part of France all papers were required to submit copy to the Press bureau 'in order that opinion should be directed and chloroformed'. Although civilians may have accepted what the were told, the troops adopted the universal approach—then as later—that anything might be true, except what appeared in print. Certainly no news about the conditions and destruction in the occupied area could reach the rest of France, not only because the territory was out of reach of reporters but also because everywhere war damage was reported as 'insignificant', and filtered by official censorship.

Commerce too was strictly controlled: after 3 November 1914, all wholesale trade outside the area was forbidden in Roubaix, and a month later Lille was forbidden to trade with foreigners. In the same month, Roubaix manufacturers were instructed that they must not continue any industrial manufacturing without permission. A year later, the sale or transport of wholesale goods outside the area of the Commandantur was forbidden, no import or export was allowed, and trade and manufacturing both largely ceased in what had been a thriving and substantial industrial city.

Domestically, the same effect was achieved through the sequence of requisitions which gradually stripped houses of their contents and fittings. Every record of the 1914-1918 occupation includes long lists of items requisitioned; as early as November 1914, the following example from Avesnes is typical in its domestic range:

Inkwells, a broom, two lavatory buckets, bells; 2 coffee pots, 8 coffee spoons, 8 sets of table silver and crockery, 3 forks, a coffee mill, 2 lamps.

Such lists might be issued at random, simply specifying items that the local German contingent wanted, or it might be based on a list drawn up after inspection. In Le Nouvion, the schoolmaster M. Leduc recorded a list of livestock in the commune; it was as detailed as a potential agricultural sales bill—horses, cattle, pigs and sheep were each listed in four categories (stallions, mares, colts, workhorses; breeding bulls, milk cows, heifers and bullocks—further subdivided into those under and those over 12 months old—and draught cattle, etc.). It was strictly forbidden to dispose of any of the animals, and soldiers would collect them as required. Other diarists—such as Marie Polvent in Ors, near Le Cateau - record the 'census' of livestock, including hens, geese, ducks, turkeys and rabbits. Orders came in, in due course, to take all horses to Le Cateau; Marie Polvent records which mare was taken by her brother, and how a number of horses were sent back again; next day, hens were demanded and, at the end of the week, wheat. Ors had none left, was threatened with searches, and finally satisfied the Commandantur with promises of hay.

As well as livestock and farm produce, each commune was required to supply ten lamps for the trenches, two communes had to find 600 kg of hay and 2,500 kg of straw, while another had to supply 110 litres of wine and 12 wreaths for monuments to German soldiers. Later in the month came demands for four dressing-gowns, a stove, a quilt, a pair of slippers, garters, smart gloves, three vehicles, and a thousand bottles of wine. Vouchers were handed over in lieu of cash payment. In November 1914 many mayors were called together to be told that these receipts, valid for all kinds of goods and services, 'would be repayable in cash in the fourth month after peace was achieved'.

Food control was naturally one of the most important matters: by the end of November 1914, inhabitants of Le Nouvion were instructed that no hens or eggs were to be taken out of the district without official authorisation. A demand for 200 cows was, however, satisfied by provision of half that number.

'How many chickens Madame?'

New bodies were created. The German Management of the Mines in the Nord, in Valenciennes, and the 'German Mine Management', were established to control and direct the French and Belgian coal mines. The aims of industrial management was, first, to make factories work for the profit of the invaders, and second, to expel owners from management. They were replaced by German managers, who thus acted as agents in the mines, and gas and electricity production.

Each army had an Economic Committee for each *Étape*, or region, with a 'general evacuation agent'. He was concerned with merchandise, consisting of prime war materials, agricultural materials and war seizures. The natural consequence was that all prime materials were hidden, and a secret police system, denunciations and requisition units developed. The French population was required to supply food for the troops stationed locally, and requisitions of this kind affected all local resources.

The condition of being outlawed, or prisoners, in their own country was brought home to Madame Delahaye-Théry in Lille when she went to church as usual one Sunday morning on 22 November 1914; her local church was closed to the French for the 8 a.m. Mass because it was reserved for the Germans to hold a Protestant service in honour of Saint Cecilia. Earlier in the same week, she wrote of the pain of not knowing what was happening to her family, and recognised that no one was likely to receive news from unoccupied France until they were liberated.

She describes an uncomfortable winter season. By the end of 1914 bread and coal were in very short supply, and everyone went home very early every day. January 1915 was the month when the realities of continuing war began to be felt, and on 3 January a series of names was read out at Mass, listing military prisoners and evacuees encamped in Wesphalia. Next day a new paper was published, the *Gazette des Ardennes*, similar to the *Gazette de Lorraine* which had first appeared in Alsace-Lorraine in September 1914; written in French and beautifully illustrated, it was edited by 'a German and by traitors', in Madame Delahaye-Théry's words; 'absolutely openly, it is intended to turn us again our allies'. She was honest in her diary writing, about herself as well as about what she saw. On the Emperor's birthday, special lights were lit and the German troops celebrated the occasion. Madame observed of the day:

> I don't feel strong enough to describe the illuminations even in private houses which are occupied by German officers. German flags are everywhere. But there is no one in the streets, no one goes out except for absolute essentials. Those who have never suffered an enemy invasion in their own land can never understand what war truly is.[4]

She records with bewilderment that the inhabitants of Lille were not allowed to visit the cemetery on the edge of the city, as they were accustomed to do: a pass was needed. When a funeral procession needed to go there, the priest walked between two armed German soldiers. None the less, on one occasion a British soldier, on the run after his escape route through Belgium was interrupted, managed to put a funeral procession to personal advantage: as a large group of people left Lille for a burial in the cemetery outside the walls, he managed to slip past the guards and return to the secure household which was part of the well-used escape system.

On 23 January 1915, all men in Lille aged between 17 and 50 were required to register, under pain of imprisonment if discovered. This was an improvement on the original threat of being shot—the fate recorded for two French officers discovered near Lille earlier in the month. The next day, a woman was shot for harbouring and hiding two French soldiers. This was the month when a Frenchwoman was overheard in a tram, remarking to her companion, 'When shall we be rid of these pigs?' She was fined 3,000 francs. Further to the east, the local residents were finding their recent years of German nationality being emphasised. In Sarreguemines, instructions were posted in February 1915 that use of the French language was forbidden in the street or in public places.

Just occasionally, a public notice caused amusement instead of alarm. During the first winter, Lille was informed that 'Maurice is lost': Maurice was the Commandant's dog, and was inclined to go missing. Commandant Hoffmann offered a reward of 5 francs for his safe return—the equivalent of more than half a day's pay for a skilled working man. Once the war was over, Lille's first carnival featured figures of Hoffman and Maurice.

The prohibitions against keeping pigeons caused problems beyond the reluctance of proud owners to kill their favourite birds. In 1914, research was in progress in Alsace on vaccination against tuberculosis. The professor in charge, M. Calmette, knew that resistance to the order meant arrest and possible execution, but insisted on retaining his research 'team' of pigeons. A German doctor passing through the area wished to get in touch with M. Calmette, whose work he knew, and was horrified to find him under arrest and awaiting trial. He became very active on the scientist's behalf and achieved his release; Calmette subsequently went on to create the successful vaccine.[5]

Other pigeons were kept in secret and against common sense. Aline Carpentier records the disaster that overtook acquaintances in Le Cateau who handed over their carrier-pigeons, as instructed, but then kept two or three which had found their way back home. The unfortunate pigeon-fanciers were executed by firing squad in the main square in Le Cateau, for harbouring pigeons contrary to orders, despite offers to pay large sums as a voluntary fine and despite the lack of any charge such as spying.

The people of Le Nouvion wondered whether their fellow French citizens, free on the far side of the front line, had any idea of the hardships being suffered under the occupation. Lists of requisitioned goods appear almost daily in Madame Carpentier's diary—the commune was required to supply coal, farm livestock, butter, cheese, 140 lbs of beef per day, four sheep, etc.—the land faced ruin. The fears of the French population were not relieved by the knowledge that there still remained a few English soldiers in hiding near Le Nouvion in mid-December. Some were desperate for alcohol, some would appear in French houses at night, particularly where there was only one person, demanding money, food or coffee.

Christmas brought a more cheerful mood, despite the German requisitions of turkeys, geese, duck and chickens, together with wine to accompany their feast. There were efforts to entertain the children; one child who still believed in Father Christmas was overjoyed to find what appeared to be a special Christmas card apparently dropped by a bird carrying out a delivery from Father Christmas. The young Madeleine was completely convinced by his message that this year he could not visit her as in previous years because just as he was setting out for distant lands he was seen by moonlight by soldiers who took him for an airman and fired at him—he was wounded in the foot and must rest for some weeks, and so had to limit himself to sending letters this year.

There was no Midnight Mass for the congregation of Le Nouvion for Christmas 1914, for no one was allowed out of their house after 6 p.m; bell-ringing was forbidden, and public clocks and carillons must be silenced.

In the spring of 1915 Péronne received the first indication that some of the civilian population would be allowed to leave the occupied area: the categories included Red Cross nurses and priests, and also indigent families, the sick or old, people who were a drain on the local economy and who could not make any practical contribution. Those who were to remain frantically wrote letters, or addresses for messages, to pass information to their families and friends in free France. The most likely messengers were the needy families who would welcome a financial contribution to their expenses - surely the German police would not search seven hundred people very closely! Some people wrote their messages on fabric and stitched them into hems, others hid letters in their umbrella covers, or inside their knitting wool; and some wrote several copies in the hope that one at least would get through. One letter was written out 17 times - in the event, many of the departing 'messengers' were frightened of compromising their departure and destroyed the letters, but three copies did arrive safely.

Occasionally the French population behind the front line would see some of the direct effects of war. In January 1916 two German military telegrams were displayed—in French—outside the local administrative headquarters in Saint Quentin (better known in peacetime as the local head office of the Crédit du Nord bank). They announced a successful attack south of the River Somme (which had been audible in the city) and the capture of over 1,250 French soldiers and officers, and a few English troops.[6] The next day, it became known that the prisoners would be brought into Saint Quentin, and people in the streets were pushed into shops and told not to look out of the windows. Elie Fleury describes the poignant scene:

> The French, in their bluish uniforms and helmets, at first looked little different from the Germans, but as they came close we could see their stony expressions. Dirty and passive, they did not look impressive. When you read a communiqué about 'We took X prisoners' you don't think anything of it, but when you see them, how painful it is! There are grey-beards there, and very young men. They don't all have helmets, there were balaclavas and old képis.[7]

A few days later they were marched out again and by now they looked better—rested, cleaned up a little, they responded proudly to the acclaim of the inhabitants. It turned out that the 'few English prisoners' was a single individual who, unfortunately for him, was visiting the French lines on the day of the attack.

Eight British prisoners were brought in a month later, in driving February rain. They were well equipped and their magnificent boots were soon removed and handed over to German officers. The town hall was instructed to find more shoes or boots for them—no simple operation—and in the meantime the prisoners were forced to go around in their socks. Each time that British prisoners arrived with good footwear, the same 'exchange' took place.

The French population was naturally inclined to look favourably on

British prisoners, but Fleury also records approvingly the German doctors' impressions of their British patients - commenting that they evidently considered it a sign of weakness to complain of pain during their treatment, however arduous.

Notes

1. Douchet ('FASOL'), *Péronne sous l'occupation*, Péronne, 1928
2. Corday, Michel, *The Paris Front*
3. Corday, *The Paris Front*
4. Delahaye-Théry, Mme Eugène, *Les Cahiers Noirs*, Rennes, Éditions de la Province, 1934
5. The implementation of mass BCG vaccination, made possible by Calmette's work on his pigeons in war-time Alsace, was interrupted for several years by a muddle in which babies in Lübeck were vaccinated by mistake with a very virulent strain of the bacillus; full use of the BCG vaccine was finally achieved in the 1950s.
6. Fleury also quotes the French announcement of the same engagement, showing without any need to spell it out how each side proclaimed its own success in halting an attack.
7. Fleury, Elie, *Sous la Botte. Histoire de la Ville de Saint-Quentin pendant l'Occupation Allemande, Août-Février 1917*, Saint-Quentin, 1925-6, Noyon, Les Éditions de la Tour Gile, 1996

3

Food

'In every respect the land is like a vast concentration camp'

Herbert Hoover

After the terrors of the attack and invasion, the first concern was food. In the first days of August 1914, even before the outbreak of war was officially confirmed, housewives checked their larders and stocked up. In Le Nouvion-en-Thiérache, Aline Carpentier kept a record of prices. On 2 August, she describes:

A steady procession since yesterday to the *familistère* [the workers' communal housing and store] and other grocers and the bakery next door to us. Everyone is afraid of running short, already the grocers have run out of paraffin, pasta, rice and haricot beans. The great fear is of running out of bread. I have bought in some stores: candles, matches, biscuits, noodles, lentils, chocolate, sugar, salt, and four kilos of flour.

She began her diary in August 1914, and recorded butter at 1 franc per pound, and eggs at 1.80 francs for 25. [In 1915, £1 = 26.5 French francs. Prices should be set alongside average wages in the autumn of 1914, when unskilled labourers might earn less than 1 franc per hour, and a metalworker was paid between 6 and 11 francs per day.]

In rural areas there were vegetable gardens and suppliers bringing their goods into market from small-holdings and farmers' poultry yards, but in larger cities and heavily developed mining regions there was no local source of fresh food available to housewives. Fresh foods shot up in price. The newly-installed German Commandants requisitioned supplies and livestock, and most of the year's harvest was taken to feed the troops or to send back to Germany.

The problem was not one of simply bringing in supplies as after a natural disaster, considerable though that might be; a whole nation—Belgium—and part of another, northern France, both highly industrialized and densely populated, were cut off abruptly from all their markets to which exports were sold and from which raw materials and much of their cereals (in the case of Belgium) were imported. All levels of society were affected, immediately. The invasion came at harvest time; crops were destroyed, food was confiscated, and grain left standing in the fields in the panic of the first weeks of war. In the areas near the front line roads and railways were taken over by the armies. Consignments of foodstuffs were requisitioned for military use, held up by congested roads and railways or delayed by lack of wagon space.

Total food supplies dwindled as local resources were used up, with the major urban centres suffering most severely. Farming was controlled by Germans who might not have any experience of agriculture—and who in any case were ignorant of local soil and conditions. Labour was lacking, and although women, children and grandparents did what they could, many draught horses and oxen had been requisitioned and there was a natural reluctance to cooperate with foreign supervision. The livestock suffered, with foot-and-mouth disease prevalent in the cattle in January 1915; this may explain the regulation that month that meat supplies in Lille must come only from the municipal abattoir, with no animals to be killed anywhere else. The 1914 harvest was brought in under very difficult conditions, for most of the men were away in the army and those who remained were too old, too young, or unfit. Farm horses were already being requisitioned by the invaders, the movement of people and goods was heavily impeded by disruption of the railways, with bridges and communications destroyed in areas directly affected by the war; it was difficult or impossible to move supplies of corn from farm to city.

Local committees sprang up everywhere to make the best use of what could be found, and Belgian refugees reaching other countries told the outside world of the shortages and difficulties.

Dried goods soon became scarce: by late September Roubaix reported that sugar, salt, rice, pasta and flour, dried vegetables and cheese were in short supply or unobtainable. In the same week, the mayors in the *département* of the Nord were requested to submit reports on the amount of threshed and unthreshed wheat, oats and barley in their commune.

Fresh food was highly appreciated, and everyone was concerned to keep it away from enemy eyes: in Péronne, young women came in from the countryside with contraband eggs tucked into the bottom of their babies' prams, or smuggled cheese or jam inside their heavy shawls. One of the greatest triumphs came when a number of fat pigs were herded through the town from the station to the German headquarters; when one beast wandered into a side alley, a swiftly-closed door kept it safely out of sight and reach, and plenty of families appreciated a better meal than they would enjoy for a long time to come.

This particular animal was butchered and distributed without the charade employed near Le Nouvion, where a newly-killed carcass was hurriedly disguised as a dying grandparent. German searchers saw the 'invalid' shrouded with shawls and blankets in a dim light and surrounded by weeping relatives, and departed apologetically. At the farm of La Désolation outside Guise (aptly named, for it was at the centre of the battle there in August 1914, when its returning owners found devastation and bodies piled in and around their buildings) the family managed to falsify their records: a hidden pig was fattened and slaughtered without the knowledge of the troops billetted on them. The time-consuming tasks of butchering had to await a suitable moment; meanwhile, the criminal carcass was hidden in the stables—under the straw where German horses were stabled.

Following the invasion, all trade had ceased in occupied France as each German administrative area—known as an *étape*—became a distinct administrative unit treated separately from its neighbours. Some towns were allowed to seek flour supplies from other areas, but by January 1915 permits were refused into the cereal-growing regions around towns such as Guise, Marle and Cambrai. Prohibitions proliferated: food and livestock must not be taken outside the *étape*, livestock must not be killed without authorisation—which was almost always refused. Food supplies were seized for the army.

Rations were established for what remained: 150 grammes of rye and 250 grammes of potatoes per day, 150 grammes of fresh meat per week. Rye came from Germany, in very small and irregular quantities, bread other than rye was forbidden and flour mills could only operate with official permission. The French did their best to conceal any supplies of grain and ground it up in cattle-fodder machines or coffee-mills. In Cambrai the rye ration was reduced to 108 g for adults and 70 g for children. Mézières had no bread at all for twelve days. Luckily the markets could still provide a few vegetables, potatoes and eggs, which were less strictly regulated, but the supply would not last long.

The great city of Lille was strictly regimented under its newly-installed German Commandantur, and Madame Delahaye-Théry made careful notes in the first of her black journals, the *Cahiers Noirs*. As one of the few diarists whose surviving records cover the whole war she gives a particularly valuable record; and the following extracts below give an idea of the prevailing atmosphere in the city. These extracts are typical of her experiences, and of the daily struggles in all the occupied cities.

- (30 January 1915) Bread very poor in quality. People try to make it at home. Meat going up in price.
- (6 February 1915) Lighting is a problem: no paraffin or candles. Gas and electricity working, but costly for the poor.
- (14 February 1915) No Lenten fast this year, since every day is necessarily a fast day.
- (16 February 1915) Bread is scarce: the ration is to be 160 g per adult, 40 g per child, per day. No flour. Bread is the prime anxiety for everyone.
  [Local records show that the average daily consumption of each inhabitant of Lille, a few years before the war, was 600 g of bread and almost the same quantity of potatoes.]
- (18 February) Two women fined (2,000 and 500 francs) for outstaying the curfew by ten minutes.
- (19 February 1915) Terrible shortage of bread
- (25 February 1915) Starving!
- (26 February) A newspaper (*Le Gaulois*) dropped by plane, enclosing a letter to be delivered - which it was.
- (4 March) French prisoners marched through town. Women with small tricolor cocarde in buttonhole arrested, together with those who shout 'Vive la France!'. The author's brother-in-law and nephew arrested for taking off their hats to the prisoners, held overnight in prison. [They were finally released on 15 April.]

- Result of Lille's expressions of support for French prisoners:
  - the city fined 500,000 francs;
  - ten hostages to spend a night, by rota, in the Citadel until 20 March;
  - curfew extended, lasting from 6 p.m. to 7 a.m;
  - no wearing or showing of French national colours;
  - no one to speak to prisoners, or make contact of any kind (i.e. giving food) to prisoners;
  - no gathering of more than ten people;
  - no public demonstrations;
  - no derogatory remarks about German announcements;
- (7 March) Gloomy atmosphere, gas lit at 3 p.m, shops closing at 4.30, everything quiet by 5 p.m.
- (8 March) Two nuns, daughters of a civilian prisoner, talked their way into the fort to see him and his son. Conditions fair, one bed between two people. They play cards, and are hungry.
- (11 March) British bombing. Telephone lines cut. Fresh meat ration reduced to 150 g per person per week while waiting for fresh supplies from neutral territory; this equals $10^1/2$ g per head per meal. Joke notice pinned to the town hall beside this announcement: please supply a magnifying glass to find the ration.
- (13 March) Continual firing, ambulances full of wounded. Roubaix citizens required to stay indoors after 3 p.m. after mocking German troops recovering from Ypres.
- (17 March) Declaration of death penalty for those harbouring or aiding two English airmen brought down in Lille on 11 March.[1]
- (23 March) Letter received from daughter in free France, via England, the Netherlands and Belgium. Hope for deliverance. Enthusiastic church attendance, as always.
- (26 March) Terrible gritty bread.
- (1 April) Bread inedible. News that the United States will supply flour which should arrive in one month's time.
- (3 April) Easter. No bells ringing. Crowds in church, local cannon firing, no substitute for the bells.
- (4 April) No bicycling without a special permit. Penalty, prison and fine. Some residents may be sent to free France; candidates such as those unable to work, women, children, old people and those maintained by the city are invited to put forward their names. This offer is

not open to men between 17 and 50. The Germans claim that the bread is bad because of the way it is made: 'It is kneaded incorrectly in order to inflame the populace'.

In fact the grain used to make bread in Lille consisted of no more than one-third wheat flour; the rest was made up of one-third rye, one-sixth rice and one-sixth maize. The news on 1 April that flour was on its way from the United States brought fresh heart to the depressed and hungry residents. The unoccupied regions of France were reasonably well-fed, and while they struggled to replace the supplies of coal and steel now cut off beyond the western front by expanding operations in other parts of the country or through imports, their allies' command of the sea meant that food shortages could be replaced fairly easily from allies or neutral states.

In the north, however, the removal of food stocks and the 1914 harvest affected everyone quickly, in the cities naturally more than in the countryside. Official propaganda reached a high point in 1916 when a German newspaper proposed that hunger was, after all, no more than a habit or a purely psychological phenomenon!

Prices were a form of rationing, with many items available only to those who could afford to pay more. In theory, it was of course the occupying nation's responsibility to ensure that everyone was adequately nourished, but their deliberate removal of the harvest made it clear that they did not see this as their concern. In Lille Madame Delahaye-Théry noted shortages of bread from January 1915 onwards, with a proposed ration of 160 g per adult per day and 40 g per child. Confectioners had no more flour, and the bread problem was distressing everyone; by the end of February half the bakeries were closed, with bread very hard to find and very poor in quality.

The daily ration that this provided for each person was not great—indeed, as Herbert Hoover[2] remarked in the memorandum which included this list,

I submit that the above ration is not as good as that of a prisoner in the English goals, and that if it were submitted to any dietary expert he would state that it is hopeless to withdraw any part of the ration. By 18 January 1915 the bread ration was reduced from 250 g to 200 g per adult per day, and from 125 g to 100 g for each child, with the prospect of a further reduction to 140 g per adult. Bread was made out of stray amounts of corn, or out of the bran normally discarded or fed to livestock after the corn was threshed.[3]

Complaints about lack of food were met with suggestions that it should be bought from neutral territories. Finally, approaches were made to the American aid system that was already heavily engaged in keeping the Belgians from starvation.

In 1870, Switzerland had provided aid for starving communities: in Laon the mayor was now given permission to visit Switzerland to seek help once more. The question was being considered all over the occupied territories, and recognised among the allies on the Franco-British side of the new frontier: two million French citizens, and six million Belgians, were effectively condemned to death by starvation if international aid was not forthcoming.

'A piratical state organized for benevolence'[4]

The way in which northern France was fed during the occupation is an extraordinary one, involving complicated international politics.

Although food supply conditions in France were more severe than in Belgium, the system that evolved after the initial crisis began in Belgium, and the numbers involved were far greater there. In the autumn of 1914 more than seven million Belgian civilians under German rule were threatened with failing food supplies. Their crops were damaged by battle or left ungathered as families fled, industry closed down, and trade and communications ceased. The solution lay not inside the country, but across the North Sea in London.

Into the desperate confusion, alarm and approaching despair of the winter of 1914-15 stepped an unexpected figure from a neutral nation, the American mining engineer Herbert Hoover. A classic 'poor boy made good', Hoover applied his determination and Quaker principles to the rapidly expanding world of mineral mining and processing. His considerable commercial success may be judged by his remark (in 1913) that if a man 'has not made a million dollars by the time he is forty he is not worth much'.

At the outbreak of war Hoover was working in London, and helped the 100,000 U.S. travellers stranded in Europe to return home. Both

Hoover and his wife were active in organising loans, arranging transport and reassuring anxious fellow-Americans, businessmen and leisure travellers followed by long-term residents whose livelihood had vanished, and German-Americans visiting relatives in central Europe and now unable to return to the U.S.

As Belgium was overwhelmed and thrown into chaos in the first weeks of the war, food stocks in Brussels fell dangerously low and costs soared. Industry ceased, food was not coming in from the surrounding farmland, and the poorer citizens could not afford to buy what remained on sale. Business leaders set up a private charitable body to buy and distribute food to the needy and unemployed. This 'Comité Central de Secours et d'Alimentation' (Central Committee for Aid and Food) secured the formal patronage of Brand Whitlock, American minister in Belgium, and his Spanish counterpart, the Marquis of Villalobar. Two American businessmen helped to set up the committee.

A system was worked out which would use American funds to locate and buy food and deliver it to Belgium. The Comité National would operate inside Belgium, dealing with the local population and centralising control over all locally-formed relief committees. Guarantees must be obtained: from the Germans, that supplies would not be seized, and from the British government, that goods could be exported from Britain to neutral ports on the continent. Working capital would be needed, and approval from all the combatant nations. Subsidies from the Allies were also necessary. Public sentiment must be encouraged to favour the scheme.

The British government was at first keen to support Belgium, and the Foreign Office was willing to let food supplies travel in neutral ships from neutral sources to Belgium via Rotterdam, provided that the Germans agreed not to interfere.

Almost immediately, however, Asquith's Cabinet divided and on 21 October a substantial section expressed their strong disapproval. It was the Germans who were under an obligation to feed the subservient civilian population, how could supplies be kept secure from German interference?—and of course such imports would enable them to requisition more food locally for their own use. Many senior politicians objected, including Lord Kitchener, Lloyd George and Winston Churchill. Their protests were overcome, and Hoover was confirmed as the chairman of the new organisation, which would be known as the

Commission for Relief in Belgium—or, most often, most widely and most enduringly, the C.R.B.

The C.R.B. was founded officially on 22 October, 1914, with a nature and status unlike any other official body. It had no obvious legal basis, although it resembled an independent state rather more than a private institution: established to engage in worldwide commercial activity under its own flag, spending large amounts of money and dealing with both sides of an extensive war, it formed treaties with the combatant nations, its ships were granted unique privileges, and in the occupied region its representatives enjoyed prerogatives normally enjoyed by independent nations. It was neutral, frequently involved in controversy with both sides of the conflict, and received aid and essential co-operation from North and South America, southern Africa, India and Australasia. It was an international public body operating under the patronage of diplomatic officers of the United States, Spain and the Netherlands.

In return, it was accountable to all the nations concerned in the war in helping the civilian populations, collecting and distributing money, goods or services. In terms of money or goods, its resources amounted to nearly a billion dollars in pre-1920s terms (roughly equivalent to the United States' net national debt just before the outbreak of war).

By the end of October 1914 the C.R.B. had already bought wheat, rice, beans and peas in much greater quantities than authorised under the Belgian Comité's original proposals. Hoover appealed to the United States, invoking local and national pride and proposing to state governors that food, or money to buy food, should be collected locally: 'This is not a question of charity or relief to the chronic poor, it is a question of feeding an entire population.' The press was drawn in, and reported widely and supportively.

Meanwhile, a network of shipping, dockside and barge capacity was taking shape. Food was to be shipped to Rotterdam, then taken on by canal into Belgium for distribution by the Comité National and businessmen-volunteers, who built up an interlocking system of local committees.

How was all this food to be paid for? About half of the four or five million dollars' worth of food imported each month would be paid for by individual recipients, but German regulations prevented the export of Belgian currency to countries with which Germany was at war, while increasing numbers of civilians could not afford to buy food from any source.

Hoover's business experience, political instincts and stubborn personality, and his determination to work without pay, attracted great good-will and practical support and the plight of refugees from Belgium drew enormous sympathy on all sides. American railway companies and docks managers offered free use of their facilities and shipping firms transported C.R.B. supplies without charge.

A large loan was guaranteed in Brussels and the Belgian government in exile in France (in Le Havre) provided £1,000,000 to back up charitable contributions to the Comité National. Once the food imports were inside Belgium itself, however, distribution was difficult. Towns were completely isolated from each other, continual negotiation with the German authorities was necessary for documentation and permission to move the cargoes, and young French-speaking Americans were recruited to protect the imports and ensure that the system operated as agreed.

Late in November 1914 Herbert Hoover visited his newly-acquired operation. His cross-Channel journey involved stripping off all his clothes twice for searches, and as he passed through the barbed-wire border fence he felt that he was entering a prison. He visited C.R.B. workers and stores—but, more importantly, he saw the end result of their work. The sombre gloom of the prevailing atmosphere was very striking, and he observed the faces of the many people thrown out of work by the war and the mothers waiting with their babies for food rations. By early December 1914, more than one-third of the people of Brussels—over 200,000 adults—were receiving their food, free, in canteens. They lined up with ration cards for bread, soup and coffee, waiting in the rain with their bowls and the municipal ration cards that entitled them to a meal. Hoover, a brusque and practical man, was much moved.

The political background to the C.R.B. was uneasy. It was the British blockade which made the German government dependent on locally-produced food, and the British government was not particularly sympathetic to efforts at overcoming the effects of the blockade. Hoover argued that the C.R.B. relief was beneficial to England, since it encouraged passive resistance and sustained the Belgians as a nation, it was a practical expression of humanitarian aid which Britain owed to Belgium to prevent mass starvation, and, if known, official British reluctance to support the C.R.B. would have a bad effect on popular attitudes to the war, in America as well as in Great Britain.

He won his point and grain waiting in the ports was released. The C.R.B. was given full control over the imported food until its final distribution in the communes, as the best way of protecting it from outside claims or from falling into military hands. Through diplomatic channels, German assurances were gained that British vessels - suitably identified and documented - could bring in relief supplies without challenge, and the necessary complicated system of paper-work was established. Insurance, a severe obstacle, was finally agreed, with a policy of Belgian indemnification for any damage caused to British ships while transporting relief supplies.

With figures growing greater day by day, the key to the whole scheme was finance. Inside Belgium, the Comité National was building up funds from the sale of food to those who could still afford to pay—but the money could not be transferred to the outside world, where the food must be bought. Over a period of several weeks late in 1914, Hoover and his staff worked out an ingenious system for covering their costs: the Belgian government-in-exile would give the C.R.B. a monthly subsidy in London, and the Comité National inside Belgium would distribute an equal amount from its food sale money, as salaries and pensions to people who normally received funds from the state—government employees, retired civil servants, etc. This, however, supposed a steady supply of money to the exiled Belgian government, which was receiving no tax income and was dependent on loans from its allies.

Staff too posed a problem: an eager group of Rhodes scholars sent to Brussels to help distribute the food aid proved too idealistic and immature, and had to be recalled. One enthusiastic but ineffectual volunteer told the C.R.B. that God had called him to go to Belgium: Hoover managed to persuade him that God had called him back home again.

By January 1915, 20 per cent of the Belgian population could not afford to buy enough bread for their daily needs. Across the frontier in France, Aline Carpentier recorded restrictions in Le Nouvion, and of complaints at not having sufficient wheat flour or white bread. In January 1915 she noted:

The bread that we buy now is dark, half wheat and half rye. In the newspaper of 18 January the Germans say that they are requisitioning wheat flour and giving us rye in exchange; but since they sell it dear the price is very high, a 1 kg loaf costs 60 centimes. The poor will be wretched and I feel that it is only now that our distress is really beginning.

When white bread became available briefly, Aline and her neighbours ate it very sparingly, not caring if it was a week or ten days old - but after that it was back to black bread once more. It was better baked, but with an extraordinarily hard crust which was almost impossible to cut—one neighbour had attacked it with a bill-hook and a hammer to break through. Inside, the loaf was heavy and glutinous and stuck to the knife, and despite their limited rations the bread was generally considered almost inedible. The allowance at this time was set at 140 g per head per day.

Other supplies of fresh food were erratic, although gardens and the surrounding areas continued to produce a certain amount of eggs, rabbits and vegetables. The last remains of the 1914 harvest were being used up, there was no surplus in store, and no fresh supplies were appearing. The Allied blockade kept the ports closed, industry could not bring in its necessary raw materials, and many people refused to work for German managers.

In London, the government was determined not to provide direct financial support to a scheme which effectively helped the enemy; but eventually Lloyd George accepted that Britain must support the C.R.B. as an essential element in their declared war aims of supporting the Belgian nation. The British government also recognised that American backing was crucial to the Allies in wider aspects of the war, and that it was wise to keep on good terms with this source of equipment, shipping, food and moral support.

The scale of the operation created tensions, both public and private, and constant disagreements between the main C.R.B., driven and managed by Americans under Hoover, and the Belgians' own Relief Committee; but by the end of February 1915 the C.R.B. was a clearly-defined organisation. It involved many thousands of people throughout most of the world: fund-raisers, farmers, engineers, bankers, merchants, shippers, accountants, diplomats, dockers, cargo crews, gathering supplies and bringing them to Belgium; and inside the country, further thousands, volunteers, who managed the central warehousing and distribution through the communes. The whole elaborate international organisation, the equivalent of a complete small nation, had been created within four months, effectively by one man, and was led by him and a small group of fellow-Americans based in London. Supplies being imported into Belgium in March 1915 included 60,000 tons of wheat and flour per month (as a strict minimum), 1,000 tons of lard and bacon, and large quantities of rice, peas and beans, maize and potatoes. Salt and dried fish would be tried out, and salt meat was being sought.

In the spring of 1915 Hoover sent a telegram to the C.R.B. representative in Paris stating the monthly food requirements of the population under occupation in northern France:

> Studies of our people indicate we could handle two million French people on supply of thirteen thousand tons wheat, twelve hundred tons beans, five hundred tons bacon, twelve hundred tons rice per month. This implies smaller ration than Belgium and could be managed on subsidy of three hundred thousand pounds per month. ... what we want is this money, and in view of critical condition cereal market we should have the money placed at our disposal at once so as to be able to procure and pay for three months' supply and thereafter three hundred thousand pounds per month ... March, April, May, June, July, five months, making total one and half million pounds ...[5]

It included such items as condensed milk, coffee, salt, soap, cooking oil and 'Cerealine', a cereal preparation suitable for children, the sick and the old. Vegetables were available, and a little meat.

As starvation threatened the great cities of northern France in the first winter of the war, the C.R.B. crossed the frontier to help two French districts which were now administered by the German government in Belgium. Other districts appealed to Hoover when he visited Belgium in December 1914, but without political and financial support from the French government he could not stretch his aid further. He angrily threw out a former American consular official who offered to share a deal with him, in which C.R.B. grain would be sold to local merchants in Lille, with the profits going to himself, Hoover and their colleagues; but Hoover (who throughout the years of the C.R.B. operation took no personal salary or expenses) could not operate alone.

First, Berlin must confirm that aid going into France would not be impeded. Following the Belgian precedent, this was not difficult, but in Paris, Poincaré's government was intransigent. Hoover set out the challenge and sought support: the C.R.B. was already helping 400,000 French citizens - and it could not afford to continue:

> It is no use dividing the food between the Belgians and the French in order that all may die. We have no right to take money provided to feed the Belgians and give it to the French.[6]

The French government resisted the idea as a matter of principle: they had been deprived by force of vital industrial and agricultural supplies, and more than two million French citizens were held prisoner against their will under foreign domination—it was the moral responsibility of the invaders to feed them. In February 1915, Hoover was prepared to state publicly that the C.R.B. had been feeding people close to the frontier but could not afford to continue, and that responsibility for French starvation rested with the French nation:

> If the French government are not prepared to give us positive reply, I propose make statement to press of world that we have up to now fed the people along the border, that our resources do not permit us to continue, that we have applied to French government for aid, that we do not believe this is a proper appeal to the world's charity, that the responsibility for the death of these people rests on the French nation itself, and I propose to do this simply to free this Commission from responsibility as to what will follow our withdrawal of our present supplies.[7]

The French did not want to admit the C.R.B; the Allied blockade was very stringent, permission to bring supplies into northern France could justify a German claim to import food into Germany and, in addition, official recognition of the C.R.B. would represent official acquiescence in German behaviour.

Poincaré was aware of growing pressure at home to feed the north, and did not want to be seen to refuse, but he was considering alternative plans. Relief money could be raised in France; instead of crossing the North Sea to Rotterdam, food could be shipped in to Marseilles, on to Switzerland by rail, then across Germany to northern France; two Swiss officers offered to take charge, with French agreement. Then the French government suggested that they might evacuate the entire population from the invaded territory to free France.

Hoover responded firmly. French public subscription could not possibly meet the need, but would 'merely relax the pressure on the French Government to deal with it in a broad and efficient manner'. Evacuation of two million people was impossible, and aid sent in via Marseille was 'wholly impracticable, too expensive and too slow.' The C.R.B. was the only solution.

The French government finally agreed to pass money to the Belgian government-in-exile, to be used as needed and 'no inconvenient questions' would be asked. By early March the Belgian government in Le Havre agreed to this indirect subsidy plan, provided that Germany agreed not to requisition the imported food and that at least five American C.R.B. representatives could be on hand to inspect the distribution.

Late in March 1915 the Belgian Minister of Finance sent an official note from Le Havre to Herbert Hoover in London:

> The Belgian Government, in conformity with the view of the French Government, advances to the C.R.B. a sum of 25 million francs, for which the French Government will reimburse it later. This sum is destined for the immediate purchase of a stock of provisions for provisioning the invaded part of France. The capital of Frs. 25,000,000 must be renewed by the sale of provisions at cost price to the population of the French invaded departments ...[8]

Supplies began to reach northern France immediately: the first consignment was distributed in the Valenciennes district on 6 April 1915, with Lille following four days later. As in Belgium, the C.R.B. was responsible for raising funds, buying, shipping and importing the food, while a local body, the Comité d'Alimentation du Nord de la France (the C.F.) handled the local distribution.

Two thousand local committees had been set up in neutral countries, notably in the United States, to raise money and track down supplies. Matters were more complicated in France than in Belgium, where, except in the actual front-line area, the occupied territories were regarded as civilian and administered by their own government. In France the whole of the occupied area was under the control either of the armies, in and near the active military zone, or of the *étapes* and their Commandants. The fact that each German Commandant had his own system and was free to make his own rules—or change them—and to cooperate (or not) with his neighbouring colleagues, did not ease matters.

The German administration divided its French territory into eight districts based round major centres. The total population of 2,110,467—which excludes the virtually abandoned communes along the front line—lived in an area of about 20,000 square kilometres. Another 126 communes along the front line were added early in 1916; and the population dropped by about 17,000 through repatriation and as deaths outnumbered births. Deportation took 24,000 people from Lille and the Ardennes; and three frontier regions (Givet, Fumay and Maubeuge) were supplied direct by the Belgian committee.

On 24 April 1915 Madame Delahaye-Théry observed that flour from America would be available from 3 May; when the resulting bread was put on sale, on 5 May, she proclaimed that it was excellent. But the difficulties of finding food, and the anxieties of the occupation, meant that by early June, she had lost two stone in weight. 18 June: 'our bread is rationed. Meat is rare, very poor in quality and very dear.' A few days later hopes were expressed locally, as she records, that the French would advance past Douai and Seclin, and that the Germans would abandon Lille; her son, editing the notes after her death, comments that another forty months would pass before their liberation. In Péronne, 'Fasol' noted that in the week of 8-14 May each inhabitant received one loaf of bread weighing one pound to last for four days. It was made without yeast, and was sticky, solid, and musty-smelling. All forms of food were running out at the same time.

Early in 1916, monthly imports into northern France are listed at 16,000 tons of flour, 1,600 tons bacon and lard, 1,000 tons of hard soap, 2,200 tons of rice, 1,650 tons of condensed milk, 1,650 tons of beans and lentils, 1,320 tons of sugar, 1,100 tons of coffee, 1,320 tons of salt and 2,200 tons of Cerealine. Supplies varied slightly according to the time of year and as population numbers changed—for example after the German withdrawal to the Hindenburg Line, or after 'useless mouths' were transported back to free France.

More and more food items were requisitioned. By the end of 1916, butchers' meat, eggs, butter and milk were unobtainable, and at this time the bread ration was slightly increased, to 400 g per day (500 g in Lille), with C.R.B. rations:

> 240 g American flour (to add to 100 g German flour)
> 14 g maize derivatives (cerealine)
> 66 g rice and dried vegetables
> 58 g bacon or salt meat
> 15 sugar
> 19 g coffee
> 19 g milk

The items available also varied considerably from one distribution session to the next, and from one centre to the next. Some items would appear in abundance for a while, then disappear completely. Precautions were taken against fraud, using someone else's card or selling C.R.B. rations. Anyone convicted for fraud was given a blue card, as a warning to the C.R.B. staff at subsequent distributions.

'*C.R.B. supply depot*'

Children, old people and the sick—which by late 1916 meant nearly half the population in the occupied area—received several foods which were particularly digestible, variations on a mixture of wheat and rice flour, sugar and cocoa powder. Dried milk was reserved for these categories. All children between 5 and 15 received biscuits (50-100 g per day) at school. The old and ill also received this amount of biscuits. The white American flour was kept for the frail or sick.

Distribution of bread and groceries, which required a large number of reliable and dedicated people, took place on set days, in schools and other suitable buildings. As the bread arrived from the bakeries it was weighed out in individual ration portions, while other items, such as bacon and rice, arrived in sacks and had to be cut or weighed. The amateur volunteer staff soon became used to their work, and in Lille each location distributed between 2,000 and 8,000 kilos of food in less than two hours.

42 per cent of the food came from the United States, 25 per cent from the British empire, 24 per cent from Great Britain and 9 per cent from other countries, particularly the Netherlands. Negotiations between the C.R.B. and the German government secured freedom for food shops from the *étape* authorities, and German staff officers were attached to the C.R.B. administration, as aids and supervisors. Food was brought into Rotterdam and distributed by canal to central depots, then to the communes.

Constant disputes arose between Hoover, as chairman of the C.R.B. and the Marquis de Villalobar, head of the Belgian Comité National. With claims that his home-grown organisation was the truly independent body and reports that the American-based C.R.B. men in Belgium were a 'group of high-living college boys having a good time', Villalobar drove a wedge between the Belgian government, based in France, and the C.R.B: but when Hoover threatened to withdraw the C.R.B., the banker Emile Francqui, who was also essential to negotiations, begged him to stay and in mid 1916, Asquith quoted Curzon on the C.R.B.: 'A miracle of scientific organisation'.[9]

The cost of these supplies to the inhabitants was kept as low as possible. The standard bread ration was distributed to all, and anyone who was destitute received rations free. German transport was provided, and American delegates were allowed to visit the distribution centres. The system suited the occupying powers very well; they laid down strict conditions and were inclined to take credit for their magnanimity - but they were relieved of the need to support their new citizens and at the same time took whatever they wanted from them. The manpower that they needed was fed and supported by others.

By late 1915, nearly a year after it began its work in Belgium, the C.R.B. had shipped nearly one million tons of supplies into Rotterdam, valued at nearly $69m. The C.R.B. was 'the biggest commissioning undertaking the world has ever seen', with 240 regional warehouses serving 4,700 separate communes, each with its own food store and local committee. In France and Belgium alike, children received special attention, with the 'soupe scolaire' for school-agers and separate canteens for the under-3s.

Everyone needed the bread, however, and many needed more than this; by the autumn of 1916, six million people in the two countries (double the number a year earlier) were dependent on relief supplies beyond a daily bread ration. Potatoes and other local supplies were becoming scarcer, and 1.5 million school-age children were showing signs of malnutrition. The cities of Lille, Roubaix and Tourcoing suffered particularly heavily, since their inhabitants lacked gardens. Seed potatoes and other seeds were needed, and more special supplies for children, as well as some pharmaceutical items. The correspondence between Hoover and the British Foreign Office illustrates other problems of domestic supply that had to be dealt with, in addition to simple shortage of food. For example:

Carbide: In the country outside the larger cities which are lighted by electricity, there is absolutely no illuminant, and people are going to bed at five o'clock in the afternoon. There are in circulation all over the country small miners' acetylene lamps, and it seems to us there could be no objection to importing carbide, as there is an ample supply of this material for all German purposes ...[10]

Despite the continuing scale and urgency of the need, internal squabbles arose again with the Comité National in Belgium, represented by Villalobar and Francqui. Internal and external politics complicated the balancing act between the need for funds and aid and personalities, internal stresses and efficiency, against publicly-stated claims and continuing need.

Final agreement was not reached until late December 1916: that the C.R.B. was to be 'entirely independent of control or participation of any of the belligerent governments and of any organisation of belligerent subjects' and it should have 'the sole administration of all relief activities exterior' to Belgium. Hoover did not like the British Admiralty, which had tried to destroy the C.R.B., and was appalled by the British habit of 'muddling through' crises.[11]

As to home-produced crops, some potatoes were left with the growers in France, although Belgian farmers kept their entire crop. Where possible, the goods were paid for, using the paper money, or '*bons*', which circulated in each area. The destitute, who had no money of their own or who could not work, and who therefore had no '*bons*', were supplied without payment, and they also received clothing, shoes and coal.

Matters became worse as time went on, as local resources were exhausted and as possessions of all kinds were increasingly requisitioned by the Germans.

By January 1916, when the rations imported by the C.R.B. were keeping the French civilians from starving, Lille had no potatoes, butter or eggs, virtually no vegetables, no milk. Not surprisingly, Madame Delahaye-Théry's notebooks recorded early in March that, with no meat, eggs, milk, butter or vegetables in Lille, and insufficient bread to satisfy hunger, food was the only topic of conversation. One day that month fresh cod was available from the C.R.B. distribution point; after waiting for eight hours, she was allowed to buy 200 g of fish for one franc. When supplies were available outside the imported ration, maximum prices were set, in February 1916, after a number of cases of outrageous prices being charged for cheese, sugar, jam and herrings. Such demands were liable to heavy fines. None the less, smuggled meat was offered late in March at 22 francs per kilo—but no one could afford to buy it, and next day meat arrived at a manageable price, from the 'American Committee'. It cost between 7 francs per pound—for the best steak - and 2 francs per pound for the cheapest stewing cuts.

Two weeks later, the week's ration was set at 3 kilos of bread per person, 125 g of rice, dried vegetables and Cerealine, 45 g of bacon, 10 g of sugar and 15 g of coffee. The condensed milk allowance would be increased. By early May, Madame Delahaye-Théry records prices of 140 and 85 francs for two hams, and beef, obtained unofficially, at 30 francs per kilo. Young rabbits, available before the war at 30 centimes each, now cost 2.50 francs each, crystallised sugar was 5.50 francs a kilo, potatoes at 185 francs for 100 kilos, olive oil 30 francs per litre, flour 8 francs a kilo, ordinary sugar 9 francs a kilo, steak 29 francs; a calf's head (without the brains, which were considered a great delicacy), 60 francs, Dutch cheese 16 francs per kilo and coffee 9 francs a kilo.

Other sources of food were not easy to find, and in August 1915 the residents of Péronne—located on the well-stocked River Somme—were told that henceforward fishing in the river was forbidden without written authority in advance. Food was a serious business: a Lille resident, condemned to several months in the city's central prison for having sold illicit spirits, was sent a suitcase full of underwear, clothes, ham, wine and chocolate by his wife, but when, on a brief visit, she enquired about the delivery, he responded that he had indeed received the suitcase—but with nothing inside it.

There were other matters to worry about, such as the great freeze of the winter 1916-17, and in such fierce weather and under wartime conditions Lille must have been a dreary place: the population had dropped from 216,000 inhabitants in July 1914 to 147,895 in January 1917. Eggs now cost 1.25 francs each (more than an hour's wage for an ordinary labourer), and turnips, the only vegetables available, were very welcome. In February vegetables were on sale at 3 francs a kilo, 2.80 francs for onions and 40 centimes for a single leek. A lamb chop cost 3.50 francs, while early in March carrots cost 2 francs per kilo and haricot beans 7 francs a kilo. There was no flour to be had; even the C.R.B. could not supply it, and were anxious about their future supplies. The difference between the C.R.B. supplies and food available direct was increasing, with butter at 6 francs from the Committee or at 28 francs from the open market. By the summer of 1917 the uncontrolled price of butter had reached 30 francs a kilo.

In October 1917, Madame Delahaye-Théry records several items: sugar 28 francs per kilo, peas and beans 15 francs, potatoes 4.75 francs, carrots 1.50 francs; eggs had risen to 1.40 francs each; salad oil 28 francs per litre. The price of a small bread roll, of the type which cost 5 centimes before the war, had increased to 25 times that amount. A month later eggs cost 1.70 francs, then 1.90 francs another week later, with meat at 30 francs a kilo. Three months later, in the spring of 1918, coffee had reached 100 francs a kilo and butter 42 francs; and in May 1918 eggs could be bought at 2.50 francs each.

Christmas brought a little free extra food each year, to the extent of another 100 g of flour per person for Christmas 1915, 100 g of plain biscuits for Christmas 1916, and a year later, surprisingly, 100 g of chocolate per head. Perhaps this was the inspiration for a wartime recipe for chocolate pralines, the invention of a housewife who wanted to offer her family a treat: it involved using 500 g of floury potatoes, which after cooking and sieving were mixed with sugar, butter, cocoa powder, breadcrumbs and almond essence. Formed into small shapes and rolled in chocolate powder, they must at least have looked impressive!

Lille perhaps suffered more than any other city; it became very rare indeed for any food to be available in addition to the American supplies, and frequently no amount of money could procure more that the meagre rations available through the C.R.B. Throughout the world, the Committee became known and recognised as the channel of relief in the occupied territory, with donations being collected in every country and administrative agencies based in the principal ports of north and south America, India, and Australasia. It was a wearisome task. Brand Whitlock, U.S. ambassador in Brussels and closely concerned with the negotiations, remarked in July 1915 that

> I am ninety-five years older than I was, and I wish I were on an unhabited island![12]

and in the spring of 1916 the energetic chairman wrote:

> ... I feel my entire inability to draw for you an adequate picture of the unutterable depression and despair of these people. We are the only link to their kindred and their allies, and we are thus the only mouthpiece by which they may express to you their prayer for more help. ... we, who for over a year have been ceaselessly endeavouring to alleviate this misery, are now forced to appear as an instrument of torture, since daily we must refuse the pleadings of a people whose sufferings will yet be told in terms reflecting neglect for which we are now daily blamed. Hoover.[13]

As a French report made clear after the war,

> The Germans took everything, leaving only just enough to keep from starving to death those whom they forced to work for them. The American supplies saved them from this catastrophe—a catastrophe caused not by the war itself but by the pattern of depradation practised by the Germans.[14]

Problems arose continually, complicated by negotiations as to what was available locally, what was taken by the Germans (so that C.R.B. imports might be subsidising the German invaders' needs) and how to ensure that the civilians were kept alive and clothed. An example of this type of difficulty arose in October 1916: the C.R.B. wanted to import boots into Belgium and northern France which were unsuitable for military use by Allied troops but which would be gratefully welcomed by farm workers in both countries; but the British government reluctantly forbade their import because they were in better condition than German army boots and would therefore be seized by the German forces. Two months later, however, the British Foreign Office relented and agreed to the import of 56,000 pairs of men's boots into northern France together with 100,000 woollen blankets. Both items

should if possible be stamped or branded or otherwise labelled in some indelible way and every precaution should be taken and every possible guarantee exacted from the Germans so as to ensure that none of these articles are used for any other purposes than for the destitute civilian population for whom they are intended.[15]

Hoover continued to face struggles with governments and accountants. Constant activity and persistence kept the subsidies flowing, but the money received was rarely adequate: almost all the income came from the French and British governments and they were themselves under increasing financial as well as military and political pressure. As the war dragged on into its third year and the world-wide cost of food soared, the C.R.B. operating deficit was not far short of £1,000,000 each month.

Once the C.R.B. system was operative, it was possible to be sure of staying alive, but it could not be claimed that this brought rich fare: only dried, salted or other preserved foods were supplied, with local sources providing whatever fresh meat, dairy foods, green vegetables or fresh fruit might be available. Because of large scale requisitioning raids and severe regulation of livestock, such essentials were scarce from the beginning, and grew scarcer.

The 'American' ration, as it was generally known, was very carefully defined, with everything set out in grammes per person per day. Portions were issued every two or three days, sometimes weekly, and payment was required except from those who were genuinely destitute. Payment was complicated because of the war conditions which made the food provision necessary: food was bought in a variety of countries around the world and had to be transported - so shipping had to be bought or hired, crews engaged and paid - and distributed through Rotterdam.

Prices were set at a modest level, taking note of the local economy so that this source of provisions was neither so costly as to be out of reach nor so cheap as to arouse hostility among the occupying German forces. This was an essential factor and grew in significance as the German soldiers and families suffered increasingly from the Allied blockade; although the C.R.B. staff were generally allowed to operate unimpeded, their neutrality and rigorous application of rules were closely supervised and any infringement or apparent leniency would mean instant withdrawal of cooperation. For this reason too the C.R.B. insisted on remaining the only source of imported food supplies, so that no arguments could arise over management, duplication of supplies or division of labour.

The goods available, the quantities allowed, and the prices, were indicated on notices displayed at each distribution centre and in the town's official newssheet. In the cities, the local committees managed their stocks with great care, never quite certain that they would receive more supplies for the next distribution; but in the countryside, with more local autonomy and greater local sources of food, the atmosphere was more relaxed.

'Soup distribution'

Apart from the destitute poor, the recipients paid for their meagre allowances with '*bons*'. These represented local currency, printed in a total of 66 cities or communities, with various face values and valid only within their own area, and issued in return for the French currency which had been taken as a contribution to the cost of the war. No profit was sought from the sale of the food, and those without any source of income or 'bons' were supported through charitable supervision; this was no light burden, for the number of indigent poor in the region was assessed at the end of 1915 as 212,000 men, 300,000 women and 323,000 children. This group also received clothing, shoes and fuel.

Despite the vast international exercise of charitable support, a degree of malnutrition was almost universal; and living conditions became desperate for many families as possessions were requisitioned. By the middle of 1916 the C.R.B. reported to the French government that mortality in Lille had risen from 17 per thousand to 40 per thousand.

Prices rose to unprecedented levels for any food available on open sale, not surprisingly. Bread cost 20 francs per kilo, flour 20 francs, condensed milk 8 francs. The lack of meat was particularly strongly felt, and for citizens of a nation which prided itself on the standards of its meals, some ingredients were extraordinarily bizarre. The episode in 1916 in Lambersart (near Lille), when thirteen horses vanished from a stable and only two were recovered, may have been unusual but was understandable. Horse-meat was already a normal part of French diet, and butchers and customers quickly ensured that no traces of the missing beasts could be traced. It was sold at 25 francs per kilo, but otherwise, by June 1916, horsemeat was not to be found anywhere and pork was also unobtainable. There were reports of seeing dog-meat pâté on sale, and of scuffles in the street over a bare knuckle of horsemeat bone that could be used to make soup.

The whole C.R.B. system was threatened by the German declaration of unrestricted submarine warfare at the beginning of February, 1917, with only a long narrow sea corridor remaining available to the relief ships; they would now have to travel round the north of Scotland. The problem was emphasised by the loss of the C.R.B. ship *Euphrates* on 3 February 1917, despite its German safe conduct pass, and of another ship two days later near the Belgian coast, with the loss of most of the crew in both cases. Hoover suspended all shipping operations immediately, while on land movement of food was halted by the exceptionally severe winter which froze all the canals, the main means of transport. Permission was obtained to move food by train, but the problem of sea transport remained unsolved. Neutral shipping became increasingly difficult to arrange, the new sea route was a thousand miles longer, and ships laden with food were waiting uselessly in British harbours.

Diplomatic relations were broken off between the United States and Germany on 3 February, and American relief workers in Belgium and northern France were immediately in great danger. Plans were in progress to operate relief without American nationals in Belgium and northern France when news came in that the American C.R.B. staff in Belgium and northern France could no longer serve in those areas; they must give up their cars, and be replaced by other, neutral, staff. Half a dozen Americans would be allowed to remain and work in Brussels. Brand Whitlock, the U.S. ambassador to Belgium who had worked hard to facilitate affairs, could also remain: but he would have no diplomatic status, transport or means of communication with the outside world.

It was an alarming moment. The future financial security of the C.R.B. was extremely uncertain, for a proposed U.S. loan scheme, as yet unsupported by the British Treasury, was making no progress, C.R.B. ships were unable to transport food satisfactorily and if America joined the war the prospects for relief and loans would be very uncertain. Hoover warned that the C.R.B. and the United States were willing to continue the relief programme, but only if their staff retained their privileges. Otherwise, they would depart, leaving the Germans solely responsible for the consequences. The Netherlands offered a Dutch committee to operate in Belgium in place of the Americans, and the Spanish announced that they would carry on with the C.R.B. with a Spanish successor to Hoover.

During this particularly severe winter, when German civilians were also suffering from shortages of food and coal, the notion of responsibility for feeding the civilians in Belgium and France passing to the occupying forces was not acceptable to either side: the announcement quickly came through that the Americans could remain and continue their work as before.

The Zimmermann note[16] meant the virtual inevitability of American entry into the war; the C.R.B. chairman stated that 'duty' required him to carry on as its head, and that its activities would continue as before. He may also have been influenced by a recent request from the exiled Belgian government, that the C.R.B. should help with Belgium's economic reconstruction after the war.

February 1917 was a month of crisis and Hoover was fiercely concerned to protect the C.R.B., to prevent a Spanish takeover, and to make himself available for direct war service if the Americans were drawn into the war. By early March he had arranged for the relief work to continue even if America entered the war. The only change would be inside Belgium, where a Dutch-Spanish committee would supervise distribution.

Supervision of the relief system in northern France was threatened by severe restrictions on C.R.B. delegates and conflicting demands from all the nations involved in giving and administering aid: but despite all the uncertainties Hoover launched his appeal for direct financial support from the American public, including a joint session of the New York State legislature followed by lunch consisting of a typical daily Belgian ration: a slice of bread, a small piece of bacon and a plate of soup.

Behind the scenes at the C.R.B. the struggle continued between Hoover and his old sparring partner the Marquis de Villalobar over future staffing in northern France (the two men had crossed swords long before the war, over commercial mining activities in China), while the German government was refusing permission for Dutch volunteers to take over the operation inside Belgium. In mid-March 1917 three C.R.B. vessels were attacked, despite clear markings and authorisation, and several crew members killed.

While the Dutch and Spanish governments each strove to gain control of the relief work in Belgium, Hoover travelled from Paris to part of France recently evacuated by the Germans as they withdrew to the Hindenburg Line. In Noyon, heavily damaged by the war, he met members of the French General Staff and mayors of thirty liberated communes who described how the C.R.B. bread had saved their own lives and those of their children.

On 6 April 1917, the U.S.A. declared war on Germany. Most of the American C.R.B. staff in Brussels had already left; the ten who remained, to settle the books and train their successors or because they had recently been in militarily sensitive areas, all left in early May. Before they left, the Comité National expressed the nation's feelings in a letter to Brand Whitlock; Emile Francqui, the banker who had also had many disputes

with Hoover years ago in China and again within the C.R.B., read it
aloud to the departing Americans:

> As you leave us you and your fellow-workers may take with you the
> assurance that Belgians will never forget the great work that has
> been realised through you. Each day the bread they eat, the food
> they enjoy, will recall them to the colossal work still carried beyond
> our frontiers by our American friends, a work on which the
> feeding and existence of the country absolutely depend. In the
> history of mankind there is no example of a generosity so noble,
> and the sorrowful history of Belgium will show that your action
> has resulted in helping us, not only to live, but also to preserve our
> faith in the greatness of humanity and in the possible beauty of the
> future.[17]

As the U.S.A. entered the war,
Hoover was invited to return to
America and take charge of food
supplies and management for the
American nation. He accepted—
but did not contemplate giving up
chairmanship of the C.R.B. Food
supplies in Belgium were critical;
supply ships had been sunk, deliveries in March were only a fraction
of their 1916 equivalents, rations
were reduced and the wretched
civilians shivering in the prolonged
severe winter suffered ever greater
privation. In mid-April 1917 the
British government seized a large
quantity of supplies and held up
cargoes arriving from America,
until the German responsibility for
sinkings was clarified. This was not

'Prices go up: ...'

until the end of May, after several weeks of intensifying near-starvation.

Potatoes were sorely missed. Farmers who grew them tended to hide
supplies, to push up prices—a practice punished by confiscation if dis-

covered. One report indicates that on 1 January 1917—in the hardest winter for many years—there was no meat, eggs, butter or potatoes to be found. By 1918, 99 people out of 100 were hungry; there was no rice, dried beans or meat. A little bread was available and a little jam, and the market offered a few lettuces and peas. Coal was running out, wood was scarce. One diary records a day's menu (15 March 1918): at mid-day, soup, carrots, cabbage, lettuce, a small slice of cake; in the evening, carrots and pickled cabbage. In the most heavily populated districts of Lille, Valenciennes and Saint Quentin, soup kitchens provided a half-litre of soup per person per day, based on dried peas and beans, with a small amount of fats, and local potatoes and other vegetables, but by June 1918 this fairly thin mixture was further reduced.

Garden produce was requisitioned. In the country, rabbits were raised, but in the towns there was nothing to feed them on—grass along

COMPTES DE LA MÉNAGÈRE EN 1916		COMPTES DE LA MÉNAGÈRE EN 1918	
Lait condensé (boîte) ..	4.75	Lait condensé (boîte)..	9.00
Un œuf	1.20	Un œuf	2.25
Un kilo de beurre. ...	25.00	Un kilo de beurre. ...	46.00
» de fromage...	32.00	» de fromage...	60.00
» de sucre	16.00	» de sucre	36.00
» de chocolat...	38.00	» de chocolat..	98.00
» de café	12.00	» de café	80.00
» de pain ...	6.00	» de pain	10.00
» de farine...	8.00	» de farine....	16.00
» de pommes de terre	1.20	» de pommes de terre	4.25
» de riz	12.00	» de riz....	18.00
» de haricots ..	6.00	» de haricots...	44.00
» de bœuf	12.00	» de bœuf....	28.00
» de jambon ...	18.00	» de jambon ...	60.00
» de poivre...	25.00	» de poivre....	125.00
» de sel.....	0.25	» de sel....	0.75
» de carottes ...	1.10	» de carottes ...	2.45
Une bobine de fil ...	0.75	Une bobine de fil ...	3.00
Total...	219.25	Total...	596.70

'... the housewife & her dog get thinner'

the outer roadsides or old city ramparts was reserved for the German army's horses. In Laon, a city set high up on a rocky ridge with little space for gardens, the inhabitants had no eggs or meat for three years: the best dish available was a mixture of rice, carrots, potatoes and turnips. Valenciennes saw all its potatoes requisitioned, and no meat was available for the final three years of the war. Occasional black-market supplies could be procured from the German abattoir, and once two horses were stolen from the commanding General. All wine supplies had been drunk or requisitioned—to the fury of the many wealthy merchants who prided themselves on their large and impressively well-stocked cellars— and although black-market barley or hops from the chemist could be used to make secret beer supplies, water was the norm.

Meat might be available by chance. A German soldier in Cambrai was sent to collect a requisitioned cow: a passing butcher saw him with it, negotiated a deal, and the beast was promptly slaughtered, cut up and distributed. It was milked first, however—a few lucky citizens gained a few litres of fresh milk for their babies and invalids. Gardens were cultivated, but the produce was often looted by night; when a night watch was officially instituted, it was found that German soldiers were among the thieves, and the watch was suspended. When the C.R.B. supplies were safely inside the house, they might still be inspected by *gendarmes* who looked into pots on the stove to see if any prohibited food was being prepared.

Markets existed in the main city centres, with set maximum prices. The German occupying forces made their selection first, followed by the civilians who gratefully bought up the left-overs, if they had enough money. This was where unrequisitioned vegetables could be found, but the quantities were insignificant and whenever possible it was better to go out into the suburbs where gardens were cultivated. Here too the Germans were feared and took first choice.

Fuel and lighting became difficult, then virtually unobtainable, and tightly-enforced curfew regulations meant that the French were unable to leave their houses from the early evening until the morning. Windows had to be shuttered or curtained, and it was forbidden to look out at night. Coal was supplied by the occupying forces, against payment in gold or French currency. As with most items of household consumption, supplies varied: near Lille in 1916 the allowance was 50 kilos of coal per household once a fortnight (an ordinary stove used 10 kg each day). These overall figures included the quantity put aside to produce gas, electric current and communal bakeries, so that households received rather less than the theoretical individual allowance. When the coal supply dwindled, people were told to 'go out into the woods'—but were forbidden to cut anything beyond a specified thickness, which might be as little as 7 centimetres. When gas and electric lighting failed or could not be afforded, light came from a wick set in fat or oil in a sardine tin. Such limitations reinforced the curfew, the shortage of fuel and lack of warm clothing, and people went early to bed—though as time went by their beds, blankets and mattresses were requisitioned and many slept with little covering on bare floors.

It is unlikely that the French inhabitants were much concerned with anyone's problems apart from their own, but the German troops billetted in their households also had plenty to worry about at home. The winter of 1917 was known as 'the turnip winter', and the civilian population suffered terribly from malnutrition and sickness, and lack of clothing and fuel as well as shortages of essential foods. Local administration took little notice of civilian problems, housing and medical matters were disregarded, and daily life in German cities had much in common with northern France.

At the same time, when the United States joined the war, the transition from American control of the C.R.B. to the joint Dutch-Spanish operation did not prove straightforward. Hoover wanted two new co-chairmen to take responsibility for one area each—a Dutchman for northern France, a Spaniard for Belgium—but the Marquis de Villalobar wanted both chairmen to supervise the whole area together, and the governments concerned were divided. Hoover finally won the day, after some trenchantly expressed despatches, and the Dutch and Spanish finally agreed to appoint their co-chairmen. By 1 May the new body was in action, under the name of the Comité Hispano-Hollandais pour la Protection du Ravitaillement de la Belgique et du Nord de France.

Money was still a serious worry. By the end of March 1917 the C.R.B.'s subsidy from the Allies was nearly $2,500,000 short of expenditure, and while the British War Cabinet agreed to increase its contribution, the French refused: they were already funding half of the Belgian part of the subsidy as well as the entire cost of feeding their own people, a total of 70 per cent of the overall cost of the operation. As the American entry into the war approached, Hoover proposed that the U.S. government should absorb all C.R.B. expenditure, covering the past, present and future duration of the war, and repay through the commission all sums lent to date by the Allies. It would make the U.S. the sole benefactor of the whole relief operation. Not surprisingly, this was not greeted with great enthusiasm in Washington, where Congress was extremely reluctant to take on Allied debts.

In mid-April, however, a loan was proposed, provided Hoover could satisfy the U.S. that it was wanted. This was no problem. The American credit would be in the form of a loan to the French and the Belgians for the C.R.B.'s provision of supplies to their occupied citizens, and would release the British from further outlay in this direction. It would also mean releasing the French from their subsidies to the Belgian requirements. Only the Belgians resisted the proposal, not wanting to be entirely dependent on the Americans: they preferred to be indebted only to the British and the French, seeing this as a preferable position in which to be placed when the war ended and the difficult peace began.

Finally, in May 1917 the U.S. government agreed to set aside $7,500,000 per month for Belgium and $5,000,000 for northern France, to be credited to the respective governments but to be used by the C.R.B. From then until the end of the war, the U.S. government was the C.R.B.'s only source of funds.

Hoover was, as he had wished, placed in an extraordinarily powerful position: as chairman of the C.R.B. he was responsible for feeding the occupied territories in Belgium and France, while at home, as chairman of the Council of National Defense's food committee, he became responsible for food management in the United States. It was a desperate moment: Allied shipping was being sunk in the Atlantic and food reserves in France, Italy and England were down to about two months' supply. He spoke to his fellow-Americans, urging them to reduce their food consumption:

> If we do not do it, we stand a grave chance of losing the war, because our allies cannot fight without food ... I feel it my duty to emphasize that the food situation is one of the utmost gravity, which, unless it is solved, may possibly result in the collapse of everything we hold dear in civilisation.[18]

By 1917, the C.R.B. had been in operation for nearly two and a half years and had handled over two hundred million dollars of charitable gifts and governmental subsidies. There had been no scandal or maladministration, and overheads for administration had taken well under one per cent of its funds. More than two and a half million tons of food had been bought and transported, across hostile seas, to Rotterdam and thence by rail and canal to 4,700 communes in Belgium and northern France. More than nine million people had been rescued from starvation. The body of volunteers involved numbered over 130,000, including 15,000 people in occupied France, while the C.R.B. itself in Europe was directed by a mere 55 people, only six of them in northern France; all the rest of the work was undertaken by French and Belgian citizens. As one of the main C.R.B. delegates wrote, it was a complicated undertaking:

> Take the one item of bread, for example. First the [C.R.B.] Provincial Representative has to figure out periodically the exact population of his Province, and the exact quantities of native wheat and rye and of imported wheat and maize on hand. From this he calculates the quantity of imported grain necessary to cover a certain period. This he reports to Brussels, and Brussels to London. London supplies the ships. New York purchases and sees to the loading. Rotterdam transships into canal barges. In the meantime Brussels has decided upon the exact quantities to be shipped to each mill in the country, and Rotterdam ships accordingly. The provincial man must see to the unloading and the milling. The milling involves questions of bran and flour, of mixtures of native and foreign grains, of the disposal of by-products, and so on.
>
> When the flour is finally milled, the real work of distribution begins. Sacks must be provided and kept in rotation. The exact quantity of flour required by a given Commune for a given period must be ascertained. Shipments by canal or train or tram or wagon must be made to every Commune dependent upon the mill. Boats and cars and horses must be obtained and oil must be supplied for engines and fodder for horses. When the flour has reached the Local Committee it must be carefully distributed among the bakers in accordance with the needs of each. Baking involves yeast, and the maintenance of yeast factories, and the disposal of by-products, and questions of hygiene and a dozen other minor matters. When the bread is baked it must be distributed to the population by any one of a dozen methods which guarantee an absolutely equitable distribution, each man, woman and child

getting the varying ration to which he is entitled, paying for it if he can afford it, and getting it free if he can't. All this involves financial problems, and bookkeeping, and checking and inspection, all along the line; and the whole process to the tune of endless bickering with German authorities high and low, and endless discussions with a thousand Belgian committees.

Now, if you have digested this, you have some idea of what it means to supply a nation with bread. But that is only one item among many. Lard, rice, milk, clothing, etc., etc.: each involves its own special series of problems.[19]

In addition to all this, by mid April 1917 nearly five million people in Belgium and northern France were not simply short of food but completely destitute. The C.R.B. supported a colossal network, including more than 2,700 local charitable committees and other more specialised institutions. Hoover calculated that by the spring of 1917 more than half the entire occupied population was receiving some kind of assistance. Three-quarters of Belgian children were receiving hot lunches at special canteens every day.[20]

An army of 55,000 volunteers was responsible for the C.R.B. on a day-to-day basis, and the full range of its work continued until the end of the war: women workers of all kinds in Belgium and northern France ran canteens for pregnant women, babies, orphans and sick children, organised workrooms and distributed clothing, while the men operated the vast and complicated food distribution service, the soup kitchens and canteens, the milling and breadmaking, and protected the imported supplies from fraud or theft.

The Commission brought its ships across the blockades for more than four years and delivered more than five million tons of provisions to the people of Belgium and France. Because of the different sizes of the two populations concerned—and because the aid projects began there—more has been recorded about the C.R.B.'s work in Belgium than in France; but it is clear that conditions were more difficult in northern France, and the proportion of people dependent on foreign aid greater.

Notes

1. A reference to the pilot Mapplebeck, whose exploits had serious consequences - see Chapter 5.
2. As part of his work for the Committee for Relief in Belgium.
3. Gay, George I., and Fisher, H. H., *Public Relations of the Commissions for Relief in Belgium: Documents*, (2 vols.), Stanford, Stanford University Press, 1929.
4. Description of the Committee for Relief in Belgium by a British Foreign Office official.
5. Gay and Fisher, *Public Relations*
6. Gay and Fisher, *Public Relations*
7. Gay and Fisher, *Public Relations*
8. Gay and Fisher, *Public Relations*
9. The possibility of helping other occupied nations, such as Poland and Serbia, was mooted. Hoover responded that if a neutral relief agency were found, he and his agents should administer it, despite the severe blockade. It was 'no use having the usual charity cranks'; there must be 'commonsense, solid business people, used to dealing with large affairs'. A competing operation was instigated, with a Swiss committee to help Serbia and then a Serbian request to the Rockefeller Foundation, but this, and another operation to help Poland, came to nothing.
10. Gay and Fisher, *Public Relations*
11. Hoover visited the front line in the summer of 1916, when he saw part of the Battle of the Somme while on a visit to the German GHQ. This was virtually his only direct observation of the military world, and unfortunately his reactions to it are not known.
12. Burner, David, *Herbert Hoover, a Public Life*, New York, Alfred A. Knopf, 1984
13. Gay and Fisher, *Public Relations*
14. Gromaire, Georges, *L'Occupation allemande en France (1914-1918), Collection de Mémoires, Études et Documents pour servir à l'histoire de la Guerre Mondiale*, Paris, Payot, 1925
15. Gay and Fisher, *Public Relations*
16. The British intercepted a telegram apparently from Zimmerman, the German foreign minister, to Mexico, proposing a German-Mexican alliance and promising German support in a Mexican reconquest of Texas, New Mexico and Arizona. Mexico was also to persuade Japan to shift its allegiance from the Allies to the German and Austro-Hungarian alliance.
17. Nash, George, *The Life of Herbert Hoover: The Humanitarian, 1914-1918*, London & New York, W.W.Norton, 1988
18. Nash, *Hoover: The Humanitarian*
19. Joseph C. R. Green, quoted in Nash, *Hoover: The Humanitarian*
20. It was not only the children who received special help. Belgium was famous for its lacework, and the absence of raw material because of the invasion and blockade meant that 40,000 women were out of work and losing their highly trained skills in idle frustration. The C.R.B. was able to import the thread

that they needed, and to sell some of their products abroad to keep the industry alive, while the sale of this fine Belgian lace in Britain and the United States helped to raise goodwill and awareness of their problems.

4

Requisitions and Regulations

'Occupied France can be seen from all aspects as a vast concentration
camp in which all forms of economic life are entirely suspended'
Herbert Hoover

Some aspects of the occupation must have reassured the anxious
inhabitants, after the uncertainties and turmoil of the invasion. In
Lille the ramparts and defences were repaired, streets were cleaned
and the tram service restored, to be used for transporting wounded
German troops. Dairies and greengrocers were allowed to circulate,
although meat was rare. By the end of 1914, however, the city had no oil
or candles, and gas and electricity supplies were reduced. Food supplies
were meagre and, until the C.R.B. system was introduced, no one could
see how they could continue to survive.

One of the most dreaded words throughout the war in the north was
'requisition', the removal of any and every form of household goods, livestock or food. Soldiers would appear, with or without official lists, and
demand specific items, or an individual German would give notice that
all households in a town, a district or even a street must hand over
anything made of a particular material, or a specific quantities of particular items of clothing or household equipment. Some of the demands
were for militarily significant materials—metals, or sacking (for sandbags), for example - but many were for officers' domestic use. At the end
of 1914, just before Christmas, there was a demand for apples (to be
handed over to the quartermaster-sergeant of the Third Company
Landsturm troops from Magdeburg); also 300 hand-towels and, to be
delivered on 23 December, three geese. The same week saw demands for

six barrows for charcoal-burners to use, six paraffin lamps for the guards and two light carriages with harness. Further requisitions during these few days before Christmas included two saucepans, 12 plates and knives, 2,000 nails (6 cm) and 200 nails (10 cm), and, for the officers' Christmas dinner, two chickens and 3 kilos of onions. As a variation, the final entry for 1914 concerned security and counter-espionage:

> Anyone in possession of wireless equipment or has knowledge of any such apparatus in anyone else's possession is hereby summoned, on pain of a heavy fine, to deliver it to the Commandantur in their commune or to indicate the premises where it is held. Delivery or information of amateur experimental equipment, or for use in schools, is also required.[1]

In Le Nouvion, January 1915 opened with a demand for 40 beds, followed a week later by a requisition for 100 blankets. By the end of January all communes in this *Étape* were to indicate how many animals could be pastured on their land and how many more animals could be fed than they currently possessed. From 25 January 1915 all graziers or dairy farmers must deliver their milk to the town dairy; butter-making at home was absolutely forbidden. A delivery service would be set up and each Saturday a list of suppliers and the amount of milk delivered would be handed to the Commandant. This week brought the requisition of another 25 beds for the officers, plus 14 ducks, 60 pounds of apples and 4 litres of sweetened cream. It would be impossible, and tedious, to give a full account of all the requisitions demanded from a single town, even a single street, but the following list represents a random selection of demands in various places at various times:

> anything made of rubber; stocks of woollens and cottons in the shops; brush-making materials; animal skins of all kinds; copper or brass weights and doorbells; writing tables, bedside tables, dressing tables, armchairs, dining chairs, carpets, linoleum, curtains, buckets, basins, crocks, jugs; washstand bowls and jugs; domestic crockery and cutlery; all household goods made of copper, nickel or tin; a piano; paint and decorators' supplies; 15 table settings, 100m of curtains, a declaration of all household furniture, linen, kitchen and household equipment; fabrics and silk

ribbons, blinds; 5 towels, ten rugs; glue made from animal bones; ducks and geese; mattresses; bicycles; 1,000 bottles of wine; unused stoves and piping; civilian clothes and shoes belonging to men absent in the French army; wallpaper; dressing-gowns; mercury from barometers; copper or nickel saucepan lids, copper pots and clocks; writing paper and envelopes [followed, two weeks later in the same town, by: ink]; the fruit harvest; smart gloves; anvils; arsenic; one pair of slippers and a pair of galoshes; sewing machines and thread; bronze or copper *objets d'art*; old iron; a quilt; gas water heaters; suits and personal linen, leaving a minimal supply for each person on the official register; and so on, indefinitely.

By the end of 1916 Lille had no leather, little fabric or personal linen, very little domestic hardware, virtually no paper. In August 1917 residents were told to hand over all lighting equipment and central heating and plumbing fixtures. Two months later, a second round-up of mattresses specified that people of 65 or over were exempt from the otherwise universal requisition; everyone else slept on a bare bedstead, if any remained, or on the floor.

Elie Fleury gives a detailed description of a requisition raid in Saint Quentin, in October 1916. His friends' house and its outbuildings had been searched, probed and pillaged three times already, but one of the workshops was regularly used by a group of German motorcyclists. (To borrow Fleury's phrase, 'none of them was worth an old burst tyre'.) The owner had refused to let them keep a stolen pig in the premises, and they took revenge with a denunciation

'Requisitioned mattresses awaiting collection, Lille'

leading to a further raid. Two officers, two soldiers with pick and spade, and a policeman were there, with the motor-cyclists standing by. The whole of the premises were searched, from attic to cellar, but the most careful probes found nothing. The policeman was launching furious blows with his pick at a block of masonry which concealed two hundred bottles of wine. The pick found its way through. And in an attic, essential leather straps from the textile factory were discovered. The Germans were delighted, but refused to issue a requisition receipt: 'These items were hidden, therefore they belong to us now'.

Immediately next to the motor-cyclists' sleeping quarters, a hundred sacks of dextrine sweetener were also discovered—but in this case, furious that the French household had retained something which the German troops were lacking, the officer issued a receipt. The final trophies of the day-long search were four cases of factory samples and more bottles of wine, taken from the family dining room. M. Fleury remarks drily that his friend felt ill at the end of the investigation.

The men who inspected houses and factories and preparing inventories were naturally among the most hated of the occupying forces. The entry in M. Leduc's journal in Le Nouvion for 8 December 1915 records a change of German commandant, and the departure of the soldier in charge of requisitions; the only comment that M. Leduc allows himself is to refer to him as 'the well-known corporal' and give his nickname, 'Caporal Voleur'—'Corporal Thief'. Other nicknames recorded were 'Monsieur Il Faut', or 'Monsieur Fouine' ('Monsieur You Must', 'Monsieur Ferret'/'Mr Nosy').

Farms were particularly carefully supervised, and one of the first requisitions in Le Nouvion, as in many agricultural centres, was for cattle (for consumption) and horses (for agricultural and military use). Nothing could be killed for meat without permission, all calvings, farrowings and litters must be reported and the young accounted for; this included chickens and rabbits kept in hutches. The numbers were checked and animals missing meant a fine for the householder. If permission was given to slaughter an animal, the head or hooves must be shown. At one moment there was a suggestion that wild rabbits should be counted and their capture for meat or skins accounted for, but it was reluctantly recognised that this might not be practical.

M. Leduc noted everything in his clear black writing. In March 1915, he records that:

the military authorities will supervise all reserves of hay and straw, in stacks or in barns, where it is not needed to feed horses. Where fodder is lacking, the livestock will be put out to graze.

All residents are required for farm work, as directed. Where the owners are absent the communes will undertake the harvesting of wheat, the digging of beet and storage in barns, etc.

The hours of work are set as follows: from 7.00 a.m. to mid-day; and from 2.00 to 6.00 p.m., German time.

All fit men are required to work during the hours indicated. Women and children will be given lighter work. Any breach of these regulations will be punished with a fine of up to 15 francs or imprisonment.[2]

Although many of the regulations imposed on the civilians were part of the planned use of their labour, possessions and produce, and recognised as straightforward exploitation, some demands were seen as pure irritants. These included some of the orders to residents to appear 'on parade'. In Bucquoy near Bapaume, the local doctor wrote:

General parades were frequent; everyone over the age of 16 had to appear, and absence on account of illness or old age was not allowed. These generally took place at 5.00 a.m. One night, however, the whole commune was called out at 1.00 in the morning; an old man of 92 asked to be allowed to stay in bed, but the troops made fun of him, pushed him out of the house and said that 'fresh air was good for the dying'. These parades had no serious purpose, they took place simply to annoy the inhabitants. People put up with them because, in the end, they were the least of our problems; but how we hated and revolted against, for example, the departure of young girls to work in the fields.[3]

In warmer weather there were instructions on protection against flies and mosquitoes, preventing contagious illness and maintaining clean streets, lavatories and stables. All milk must be kept in cellars or other cool places. Whether these instructions were really necessary, to keep careless farmers or resentful citizens in their place, or whether the occupying forces felt that they had to demonstrate their authority and concern, cannot now be known; but in June a proclamation called attention to the recent disappearance of a number of chickens, for reasons unknown. Each missing hen cost its erstwhile owner a fine of ten marks.

Increasing petty theft came as no surprise. In Ors, Marie Polvent records in September 1916 that farm produce was disappearing from the fields - apples, carrots, turnips are being stolen. In the terrible early months of 1917, when thick ice covered water tanks even indoors, the thieves became bolder; in February they took advantage of bright moonlight on snow-covered fields to steal two pigs from the Polvent farm (and an iron pot) while 30 hens disappeared from their neighbours' farm. Next night two turkeys, two cockerels and a guinea-fowl were taken from another neighbour, and elsewhere in the village chickens and rabbits vanished. Six weeks later, a calf was taken from a nearby farm, and someone managed to get into the Polvent farmhouse through the cellar grating - a basket of apples, quantities of beer, cider and cheese were missing next morning. (Despite the stringent regulations, food supplies were naturally more plentiful on farms than in cities.) Marie Polvent had rigged up an alarm system of a broom propped against the window, to fall against metal pots and make a noise if disturbed—but the nocturnal invader had been careful and silent. The next night she brought up all their dairy produce stored or maturing in the cellar; and arranged a broad cream skimmer so that it would fall with a crash if anyone entered. There were three further attempts to get in.

Elsewhere too, the balance between residents and occupying forces became no easier as time passed and the weariness of war accumulated. Three small industrial towns on the outskirts of Lille were each fined 50,000 marks because residents were considered to have shown too much sympathy for two hundred French prisoners passing through. In addition, all travel passes were withdrawn and residents ordered to remain indoors between 5 p.m. and 5 a.m. They were afflicted by constant fines and occasional bombs, dropped by French aircraft.

Bureaucracy was a burden everywhere, and took many forms. Typical was the close inspection of Le Nouvion's educational standards early in 1918, with all school buildings to be listed, the teachers' names and the style of their teaching: the number of pupils, the number of lessons each day and the use of time during the school day. Other orders continued to reach the little town's inhabitants: all molehills were to be flattened in the surrounding pastureland, all cow-pats to be broken up and spread out, all hedges to be trimmed and the thorns and debris to be cleared away immediately. Perhaps these instructions conflicted with educational demands, for the next day all boys and girls between the ages of 6 and 13 were instructed to attend school. Despite the enquiry into school premises, educational life was complicated and classes were held in the town abattoir for a while, then in a small artist's studio which had escaped the fire at the outbreak of war. Classroom equipment consisted of eleven tables large enough for two children, and a blackboard. Communities continued to take an interest in the future of their young people, with conditions of employment, training and apprenticeship very uncertain. In some cases clothing was distributed to apprentices, and classes gave advice to young girls on household management. As well as learning how to make the best possible use of the meagre materials available, the girls and their families found this good for their morale. It also provided a good opportunity to discuss wider topics and how they would feel and behave in the longed-for post-war world.

Classes in towns well behind the lines, however cold or disrupted their routine by military demands, were incomparably better than in the unfortunate communities close to the front line. In the mining town of Lens, school life continued underground and children were sometimes at risk from shell-fire as they made their way to their classes. In later years the deputy mayor of Lens during the war years recalled that occasionally, when everyone could be sure that there were no enemy ears close at hand, children were encouraged to shout '*Vive la France*' together, as loud as they could manage.

Until the evacuations of 1917, Saint Quentin suffered little from bombardment, although French aircraft were occasionally seen overhead and dropped bombs. Other cities suffered the double distress of enemy occupation and Allied bombardment. One example among many (Nancy, Reims, Amiens, etc.) was Soissons, which suffered intensive shelling from September 1914 until February 1915. Many people left the city, but many more remained, to see the fine and ancient city suffer severe damage, to be buried beneath their collapsing houses, to suffer death or wounding. Houses, apparently in ruins, might have a notice stuck on the door: *House still occupied*, with the names of its stubborn inhabitants. Cellars provided sturdy shelters from attack and explosives, and in between attacks shops and public services continued as normally as possible. Life was almost as dangerous for the brave or foolhardy civilian who insisted on remaining as for the front-line soldier. Occupied twice over and largely reduced to ruins, Soissons was at the heart of conflict until the last weeks of the war.

Public assistance, care for the destitute or abandoned, was a problem, with a distressing problem outlined by the inspector for the Nord *département* to the *Préfet*:

> 27 March 1915: Because of the nearness of the front line, those in charge of children in care in Aubers who did not follow the British army in its retreat were evacuated by the Germans to Tourcoing in October 1914.
>
> Recently the Commandant of Roubaix has decided to send these citizens of Aubers to non-occupied France. One of the guardians did not wish to be evacuated with his charges, but brought them to me [in Lille] so as to remove them from the German authorities - who, however, asserted that they would despatch them by force if necessary with the indigent poor who were being evacuated. Some of the children, aged between 7 and 15, had been taken by the *gendarmerie* and put on to the special train for evacuation.[4]

Money was a source of anxiety for almost everyone, and many households broke with every principle and sold possessions. Loan offices were set up where those with recognised assets could borrow cash, repayable after the war, and rent went unpaid. In Le Quesnoy, the municipality was paying out 25,000 francs each month for the unemployed by October 1916 and Valenciennes was paying out financial support for around 80 per cent of its population. Those who volunteered to work for the Germans received no money. In Fourmies, the mayor's office deliberately combined allowances for unemployment, indigence and the families of mobilised men, to avoid passing military information to the Germans. Some families managed their domestic finances effectively despite the rigours of war. When the Suel family in Roubaix realised that the invading troops were almost upon them in the summer of 1914, they divided their forces: Madame Suel remained with her younger children to look after the family home, while her husband and eldest son escaped southwards to avoid German military demands. Once the war had settled down into its interminable stalemate, money became a problem—and Monsieur Suel, safe in free France, was able to arrange for funds to be sent regularly via the embassies of Spain and Berlin, with sums of 100 or

500 francs being deposited in Madame Suel's name in Tourcoing. Each deposit came with a letter of authority signed by the King of Spain's authorised servants, the Spanish Embassy in Berlin, and its representative in Tourcoing: and each sum, once safely received, was acknowledged by a paper which passed in the reverse direction. The transactions took about three months to complete on each occasion, but none of them went astray.

Children were a particular problem in war-time and ran particular risks. Education suffered as institutions closed during the invasion and as the occupation settled in, but gradually school doors opened again. In many cases school buildings were taken over for use as billets, offices or stores, and classes were set up in private houses or outbuildings. Other schools, however, were in operation, and Lille records the reopening late in 1915 of the *École Industrielle*, or technical school.

In 1915, the teaching authorities in St-Quentin discussed their arrangements for *baccalauréat* candidates. This school-leaving examination was taken in the final year of secondary education, and only by pupils of recognised academic ability. Then—as now—it was the essential starting-point for any further professional education or profession. Seen also as an important element of French culture in a broader sense, it represented a key feature of survival under foreign occupation, and an indication of confidence in an independent French future.

Examination conditions were a problem; candidates would not be granted the necessary permission to travel to Lille, but after discussion three external examiners were allowed to travel to St Quentin to assess candidates from the surrounding area. Even with permission it was a difficult journey for the trio; railway travel was not normally available, just as letters, telephone calls and cars were forbidden for the French. Life felt like a return to the cave-man era, and they met no other civilians on the way. The city provided lodging for those who could not afford it. At the end of the session, the examiners discussed their assessment, and the German observer claimed the need to put an official stamp on the list of successful candidates.

'But we do not draw up a list. The names are notified by public verbal announcement'

'But the stamp must appear on the official record'

'But there is no official document of record'.

The examination was concluded to the full satisfaction of all concerned, except for the few French candidates who failed the rigorous examination—all others would be the proud possessor of a valid certificate to pursue their further education or profession after the war.

The winter of 1916-17 was exceptionally severe—this was when soldiers in the trenches were freezing to death—and schools were closed for several weeks. By mid-March they reopened, but as the year progressed it was clear that there might be further closures during the next winter, and the school holiday period was reduced in the summer to make up for lost teaching time in the winter.

The early start to the autumn term was turn reduced, however, so that teaching began two rather than four weeks early in the late summer of 1917: many of the teachers were of retirement age and were suffering from poor diet and living conditions—they needed the holiday period as much as their adolescent pupils. The debate in July 1917 about school opening in September concluded that '... the great majority of school premises are in a disturbing state of physical dilapidation and in urgent need of repair'.

The most senior among primary school children (in their early teens) were sent off on forced labour gangs, some to look after horses near Laon, others to look after cattle. In Charleville, a schoolmaster was 'called up' in October 1917, and despatched early next morning, together with eight more men, in charge of 200 children aged 11, 12 and 13. Divided into groups of 50, they were lodged in empty houses left by other deportees, and provided with straw palliasses to sleep on. In three teams, they worked from 7 am until dusk, with two hours off at mid-day, picking apples and pears, climbing the trees and slaving to complete the allotted task. Endless further examples are given by authorities—depressingly repetitive in their detail, dispiritingly inhuman in their effects.

Education continued to present difficulties. In November 1917 three teachers were not receiving payment because they refused to undertake work forbidden by the Hague Convention, while in the summer of 1918 an examiner was unable to undertake his official visit and assessment because his travel pass was refused, for 'disobedience'. Anxieties surfaced throughout the occupation: in May 1918, German soldiers were discovered measuring up rooms in Lille university, which was perceived as a threat to the studies which had continued under great difficulty for the past three years. One such problem had been recorded in December 1917 when pupils at an academic secondary school, housed since the outbreak of war in the university's Arts faculty, found their borrowed classrooms closed because of lack of coal to heat them. This was seen as a serious interruption of their education, and they were moved to buildings in a hospital where they shared the heating provided for the patients.

Children's health was a growing cause for anxiety and despite the C.R.B. food supplies, by 1916 the slow effects of undernourishment were appearing; in February 1916 Dr. Calmette reported the appearance in Lille of scurvy and beri-beri among old people in crowded areas, with pale and puffy skin, kidneys and heart beginning to fail, excessive skin dryness and hair falling out. Inadequate diet was blamed, with too much starch and no fresh meat or fruit.

Typhoid fever broke out in Lille in December 1915. One report suggested that it might be spread through holy water in the churches, and that a 'powerful disinfectant' should be added since 'it was unlikely that the Church would give up the use of holy water'. The (unnamed) public health official commented that '...I naturally do not wish to cast a slur on the sanctity of the holy water.' But in May of that year Lille recorded 245 deaths from typhoid; regulations to prevent its spread included banning the sale of fruit from itinerant vendors, and of fruit ices and confectionery. The same month saw major outbreaks of diphtheria, scarlet fever and measles.

The case of children in the care of the public authorities was causing concern, for the hospitals were overcrowded and cases of typhoid had to be nursed at home. The generally poor food was undermining everyone's health, but adolescents were particularly badly affected, and a request was made for 100 children in delicate health to be sent to the South of France, with four nurses. Permission was refused for a doctor to travel with them as far as the Swiss border; the children in the greatest need because of their fragile health were therefore taken off the list as too weak to travel without medical supervision, and other suitable candidates were found.

Although Lille's capacity to look after children in public care was for a maximum of only 120, the number had reached 205 by 26 February 1916 to 205, and a second evacuation was undertaken. This was followed by groups totalling nearly 200 children who were despatched in the first three months of 1917. At the end of March 1917 a group of 30 children with highly contagious ringworm were sent to unoccupied France, in specially isolated railway compartments with the seats covered with special sheeting. In separate compartments the same train carried two handicapped and mentally backward adolescent boys and a group with tuberculosis, a disease which was causing increasing alarm. Further groups of children were sent throughout 1917.

Other groups were sent out of occupied northern France but not always to the free regions of their own country. In April 1917, a thousand inhabitants of Wambrechies (on the edge of Lille) were sent to Belgium. This included people who had already been evacuated from other communes earlier in the war, old people, invalids, and women with young children. If the number of one thousand was not reached, others would be sent by force.

Decisions about children and adolescents in public care continued to be difficult, and Dr Hamel, the Inspector of Public Assistance responsible for their care in Lille, was frequently in trouble with the German authorities. In October 1917 one of the youths in care, among a number sent on work gangs, rejected the work to which he was allocated; emaciated and suffering from tuberculosis, he refused to work on the railways. He was beaten with sticks and the flat of a sword, and shut in a cellar. Despite medical advice he was returned to the work camp but escaped to his children's home where he was sought by the military police, who complained to Dr. Hamel. The local *sous-préfet* had authorised Dr. Hamel not to report the return of wards who suffered ill-treatment or were assigned to work prohibited by the Hague Convention, but Hamel, who struggled throughout the war to look after children without families, was briefly put in prison.

By the summer of 1915 he was having difficulty in visiting orphans placed out in rural communes; after several months when permission was easily granted, visits were now almost impossible and, with over 4,000 abandoned children to supervise, the doctor was increasingly anxious. His work covered health, nutrition and general care for orphans, and the recruitment of wet-nurses. A year later he was still not allowed to travel; the reason finally turned out to be his support for those who refused to work for the occupying forces.

Control over daily life was detailed and rigorous. In Le Nouvion, the little market town in the Thiérache region of small fields, woodlands and thriving communities near Mormal forest, every eventuality was covered, as recorded by M. Leduc, the head teacher:

12 April 1916. Any balloon found or caught coming down in the occupied area must be taken to the nearest military installation, without delay. This also applies to any newspapers, publications, flysheets or other objects attached. If no military establishment is accessible without special permission, all such objects must be handed over at the nearest *mairie* in return for a receipt showing the date and time of deposition. The *mairie* is required to transfer them without delay to the nearest German authority without informing anyone else.[5]

Two other long paragraphs specify similar instructions for dealing with illicit French material, followed by the penalties for infringement.

Attitudes towards civilians appear in the following day's diary entry:

Permission is given to the inhabitants of Le Nouvion to go for walks in the woods on Thursdays and Sundays between 3 p.m. and 7 p.m., in an area defined by official notice at the *mairie*. It is forbidden to walk round the lake. The slightest infringement of this order will lead to cancellation of the permission.[6]

Balancing modest diversions of this kind, infringements of regulations were punished by fines or arrest, recorded by M. Leduc in Le Nouvion. In November three people entered the woods on a day when such exercise was not expressly allowed, and were each sentenced to four days' imprisonment. Possession of a dog which was both undeclared and untaxed brought a 20 marks' fine and payment of the appropriate tax, while discovery of two bicycles brought fines of two weeks' labouring with a 50 mark fine for the man concerned and one week and 30 marks for the woman—whether the difference reflected an opinion on the level of importance that a mere woman's infraction reflected, or differences between the two machines, or perhaps a disparity in the two wrongdoers' ability to pay, is not clear! At a more serious level, M. Leduc recorded a death sentence early in 1916, when Charles Ancelin was condemned to death on 25 January and shot on 4 March. His offence was to have hidden weapons instead of giving them up as required.

Illicit correspondence was a frequent cause of entry in the crime record, with a particularly long list of offences around Christmas time. The level of the fine imposed varied from 50 marks—the standard amount—to an occasional punitive demand for 150 marks. Other offences included leaving the official roll-call parade without permission—for which several men were condemned to two weeks' imprisonment—to having a lamp lit after 9 p.m. (three marks). Poaching in the middle of December meant a fortnight in prison, while failure to carry a letter of permission to travel meant a week or two in prison, and a fine.

In October and November 1915 the inhabitants of Le Nouvion received reminders of what was and was not allowed. Correspondence was expressely forbidden: amongst themselves; with French residents in unoccupied regions; with German soldiers; with residents in other countries. The penalties were up to a year in prison, and fines of up to 15,000 marks. The possibility of more severe penalties was indicated.

The irritations of continual supervision, requisitions and regulations can be seen in M. Leduc's careful notes. All bicycle accessories must be handed in (pumps, lamps, etc); all livestock must be brought in for counting next day and the mayor and five men must accompany the soldiers in charge of the inspection. Afterwards, farmers are instructed to profit from the fine weather to put the livestock out to pasture.

It was not until after more than a year of occupation that Le Nouvion was required to do what had been imposed on Lille in its earliest days. Aline Carpentier records on 25 November 1915 that a clerk had visited every household in Le Nouvion, recording all names in full—with their ages. Henceforward this information was to be posted up on the front of the house; as Mme Carpentier records, 'old coquettes' knocked ten or twelve years off their age, while those who feared the Germans too much to do this did their best to nudge the offending figure behind the window frame or shutter.

She also notes that during the autumn of 1915 the whole town of Le Nouvion now appeared Germanised: all the streets had been renamed, generally with translations of their French names ('Bahnhofstrasse' for the 'Avenue de la Gare', etc.).

It was in mid-December 1915 that Madame Carpentier first mentioned the possibility of evacuation to non-occupied France. The suggestion from her young son, in response to a general appeal for volunteers to leave in a few days' time, was unsettling: so much to settle, loans to repay, possessions to distribute, arrangements for the journey, addresses and messages to be assembled.

Those who decided to go were overwhelmed with messages, letters, urgent words from a community cut off from its nation; but they were sent off like criminals, between ranks of gendarmes with numbers on their chests. Their fellow-citizens who were remaining were forbidden to watch or wave, or see them off.

The journey was deliberately very long and slow, so that any information they might take with them would be out of date on their arrival in France; they spent several days on each stage, travelling first into Belgium or Germany and then to Switzerland. Only when they reached the frontier of their neutral Swiss neighbours could they relax, and here they were met by the Red Cross with good food, baths, fresh clothes and sympathy. On their arrival in France, families were dispersed across the whole of France, either to relatives or to hospitable strangers, or to special accommodation. Here, finally, those with family or friends fighting with the French army were able to find out whether they were alive or dead, and feel that life could begin again even in conditions of mourning and poverty. Many never returned to the north.

It was a serious moment, leaving home with very little money, and no knowledge of where and when they would end their journey. In Ors, Marie Polvent saw her younger sister Victoria hesitate, and then decide to leave, with her three children—twin girls of 17, and a boy of 15. The train was announced for mid-June, bags were packed, and an envelope containing a small amount of money received its official seal, not to be opened until they reached their destination. A deception was undertaken against the German government: as Marie prepared a tin of food for her departing relatives, she inserted some gold French coins into the waffles for which she was famous. Hearts were heavy, both in those departing and those who waved them off, and their leisurely journey gave time to worry—two days to cross into Belgium and reach the German frontier, where they were required to undress and undergo an attentive inspection while their modest baggage, left behind in the carriage, was searched by guards. Happily the gold coins passed undiscovered. They were allowed to continue, slowly, to Switzerland, where nurses met them with milk, hot drinks and fresh white bread rolls - they ate slowly, closing their eyes and savouring the unfamiliar taste. On again, across Switzerland, through the magnificent scenery. Here they had the status of internees and were not allowed to leave the stations; food was brought to them. Five days after leaving Ors, the family reached Evian, where the Red Cross greeted them and they were lodged in a hotel, free of charge, while their papers were put in order. A cousin in Paris confirmed that she would take them in, and another week later they finally reached Paris—a journey which would have taken perhaps three hours by car or train had taken two weeks.

It was essential to find work, quickly, for they could not depend on their cousin's charity. The twins were taken on by Paquin, the couture house, and made good careers, while their brother was taken on as an insurance clerk: because of the lack of food for the past three years he looked as if he was only 12, rather than his true 15, and had to pile up three large accounting ledgers to reach his tall banker's desk. The family found a small flat, and the girls learned polite city manners from their grand clients; but they were not impressed with the welcome they received from the Parisians—who laughed at their old-fashioned long dresses and long hair piled up on their heads, their high button boots, and François with his knickerbocker trousers buttoned beneath the knee; all contrasting with the modern city girls' short curled hair and short dresses. They felt that they had come from a different world, and resented the judgement of the Parisians: because the refugees came from occupied territory, no longer recognisably French, they were known as the 'Boches du Nord', the 'Boches' from the north. Others were more considerate, and they made a wide circle of friends, including relatives from Ors who had managed to join the French army. Gradually the girls' dresses were cut shorter and their hair rearranged, but the button-boots reaching half-way up their calves had to be worn until they were past repairing. Their father was a prisoner in Germany, and news passed through him from Paris to and from the rest of the large family in Ors. (After the war the family remained in Paris, and the twins and their brother made good careers there, an example of the spreading ripples of demographic change created by the war.)

The announcement that lay behind this upheaval and departure appeared in the *Gazette des Ardennes*, offering evacuation via Switzerland to residents in various categories: women and children with relatives in France and without independent means of support; children separated from their own family; invalids, particularly any suffering from lung complaints, unable to be properly cared for locally; people without employment who had exhausted their funds; men beyond military age without means and dependent on local assistance. They were invited to apply for permission to leave, subjected to medical inspection, and required to pay for their travel. No papers or letters could be taken, and any messages discovered meant an immediate return, Some, like Aline Carpentier in Le Nouvion, put their names down and then withdrew, fearful of what might happen. In the midst of her anxious preparations, Madame Carpentier learned addresses by heart so that she could pass on reassuring news from her friends and neighbours to their relatives. Some of those remaining criticized her, others were jealous at her escape. They recalled a German officer's account of previous evacuations, when the voyage involved spending a month in a military-style camp in Germany, sleeping on straw in bitter winter weather. But she was desperate to see the rest of her family, particularly her daughter who was on holiday in Brittany when the war broke out; her diary reflects on the bitterness of their enslaved condition, the lack of news, the petty rules and the enforced limitations such as a recent ordinance stating that gatherings of more than four people in the street were forbidden. The prisons were full of ordinary people who had infringed some petty regulation.

The journey to France and freedom cost 33.70 marks for third class, or 50.70 marks for second class, with no gold to be taken. She spent an anxious few days, wondering whether to go second class—for comfort—or third, to avoid suspicion of possessing further wealth for which she could be retained. On 2 January 1916 she promises her favourite saint, St. Antony of Padua, a fine donation if she and her son are accepted for travel ... and she waits:

> ... and the good news is here with the new year. Wednesday 5 January 1916: Oh! what a marvellous day, this beautiful winter's day with our good friends at Barzy [four kilometres away]. I went for a travel pass, from the rough and bad-tempered soldier clerk who kept me waiting for an hour.
> Sunday 9 January 1916: we leave tomorrow, a stream of visitors, I am taking away 100 addresses in ... my head. I can't say any more. We are leaving, praise God![7]

The evacuation train was also welcome forty miles away in St Quentin. Elie Fleury, the journalist who later published his war notes, knew some of those who wanted to travel, such as a young girl on her own who had seven brothers or first cousins at the front: but she had no family to go to, and her house left empty would soon be pillaged. She stayed. Another woman calculated the cost of departure—36 marks each from St Quentin, travelling 3rd class; but with nine children she had no hope of raising the total for the family. She remained.

In the spring of 1917, the French had cause to be concerned on this side of the war-front, for deliveries of flour failed for a while (a consequence of the unrestricted submarine warfare) and further deprivation of food stuffs caused increasing difficulties for an already half-starved population. Although Madame Delahaye-Théry does not mention the fact—being presumably unaware of it—the all-out submarine war declared in February was disrupting food imports to Holland for the C.R.B. Schools were still closed, although the terrible frost had gone. and more people were leaving the city in a fresh sequence of evacuation trains.

The picture from contemporary records is one of a dark, cold, miserable and malnourished city, and Madame Delahaye-Théry's black notebooks seize with delight on the one piece of good news that reached the cowed French that spring: she reports the news in a Belgian newspaper that the French and British allied troops had recaptured Bapaume, Péronne, Roye and Noyon.[8] The requisition of possessions continued unabated: more copper was needed, a large quantity of beds, clocks, candle-sticks, above all kitchen equipment. She expresses her fierce indignation that French-owned goods were being taken to be used to kill other French people.

By mid-April she has some good news to report—that Vimy Ridge has been taken, and she hears of Germans retreating in the Somme; although she does not say where the news came from, this is evidently the Battle of Arras, with Lille well within earshot of heavy bombardment. 'Reassuring news' comes from Champagne - though not, of course, of the mutinies within the French armies, which were successfully concealed not only from the enemy but also largely from other French troops and their allies. Parts of Lille are being evacuated, and she hears (but without explaining how) from a friend who left on an evacuation train six weeks earlier.

Military history records 1917 as a year of disappointments and continuing effort. On the Western Front, the triumph of capturing Vimy Ridge in April, and the limited successes of the Battle of Arras, were accompanied by the wide-spread mutinies in the French forces after their failure in the Chemin des Dames attack, and the collapse of the British attack near Ypres into the rain-soaked muddy wastes of Passchendaele.

For the French in the occupied northern zone, who were kept in ignorance of any Allied gains and fed news of German victories both real and
invented, it was a year of increasing misery:

> Lille, 11 February 1917: Every day it felt as if we had reached the
> pit of human wretchedness, and then the next day we saw that
> there was more to come.
> For two weeks now we have suffered terrible cold. The poor coal
> ration that the occupying forces allow us cannot reach the city,
> because the canals are frozen. No coal, no water. The bread ration
> has been reduced. The indigent—that means almost everyone—
> have to go to bed at five in the afternoon because there is no light.
> And they have to live on a bit of bad bread, 15 grammes of rice and
> 25 grammes of salt pork. All you see in the streets are yellow faces,
> shrunk by privation and tears.

The requisitions continued. From June 1917 a description survives of a
visitation in Lille:

> The copper-thieves came round today. A warrant-officer with a
> folder under his arm came first. Inspection. Two soldiers, one
> shrinking back and looking like the poor relation who gets the
> rotten jobs, who laboriously drags along the clanking bag. He peers
> about sadly as he contributes to the devastation of the apartment,
> and follows his comrade—a tough type who must have been a
> rogue in private life and who runs through the rooms tapping on
> suitcases, stamping on the floor, opening cupboards and inspect-
> ing the panelling. They don't speak. This thief operates in silence
> and pretends to be unaware of his victims' presence ... He
> unscrews the curtain loops, cuts the hangings, pulls off the curtain
> hooks and throws them to his friend ... The man looks furious, he
> hasn't got much, it's a poor haul. The two soldiers depart, the bag
> bouncing down the stairs after them. Downstairs the warrant-
> officer enters name and address on a neat register, signs, and care-
> fully applies blotting paper to his signature. This is a tidily organ-
> ised theft.[9]

Out in the villages and the countryside, farm life was hard work. Men were taken for enforced labouring and basic equipment was requisitioned from the household, the dairy and the farmyard. Those who remained, women, children, and the older men, worked under pressure to keep up supplies, with constant demands for milk, eggs, butter and all other produce, while struggling with shortages of all kinds; and, in many households, a constant stream of soldiers and officers billetted in their living rooms, bedrooms and farmyard buildings, insisting on meals being provided and their quarters kept clean. Some of these unwanted guests were reasonable, prepared to take an interest in the farm or talk about their own families, but others were less easy to live with. In either case, the resident families felt harassed and uncertain, oppressed and exploited.

In many places their lives were complicated by an underworld of clandestine visitors—men avoiding German labour gangs, escapees from prison camps, a few who had managed to evade the original census and who remained hidden. A few managed to survive the whole war in hiding, causing great strain for their hosts or families—not least because of food shortages, for such secret mouths must be fed.

The secret diary written by Marie Polvent not far from Le Cateau shows that the traditional image of the late nineteenth-century life on a small and successful farm was completely disrupted. The picture that she draws is one of constant disturbance, unremitting hard work, fear for absent members of the family and uncertainty.

In Lille, occasional shelling from the direction of Mount Kemmel was not the only danger. In January 1916 a large ammunition store in the city ramparts exploded in the middle of the night. The toll of dead and wounded, both French and German, was enormous, many houses were destroyed or rendered uninhabitable, and all windows in the surrounding district were blown out. All supplies of glass were immediately seized, to replace the windows for the occupying forces, while many inhabitants were left without shelter in this coldest period of a bitter winter. The cause was never traced, although espionage was of course suspected.

Every French account of the war years in Lille gives an extensive description of this explosion, whether or not any personal acquaintance was affected. One diarist expressed fervent hopes that no word of it would reach the press in free France, for it would cause great distress and anxiety among friends and relatives there. The mass funeral of the

French people killed in this accident marked a sort of truce: all French people who wished were able to follow the long cortège, with French and German wreaths carried in the procession, full attendance of the cathedral clergy and twelve funeral vehicles each carrying ten coffins, German officers (including two generals), the mayor of the city and his council and staff; Von Heinrich, the German governor, wished to address the crowd beside the graves, but Monseigneur Charost (Bishop of Lille) and the mayor succeeded in stopping him.

Madame Delahaye-Théry, who gave this account of the great explosion, began her fourth notebook in January 1916 with a heavy heart. When she first began her account in the autumn of 1914, she was convinced that the war would end before she reached the end of the first notebook: and, she thought, if the length of the occupation had been known in advance, many would have given up hope long since.

A year later, 1917 opened with sad comments in her journal, as she recalled the gaiety and celebration of more normal times among her large family, and on 2 January she recorded an official announcement: in a fortnight's time there would be no more light. This was closely followed by news of proposed peace negotiations, then of a new evacuation train into free France, and news that the neighbouring town of Roubaix could have no fresh supplies of meat.

Four thousand people registered their names for the next evacuation train. All fresh food was very expensive, as ever, and the official prices were honoured only for German customers; eggs cost 1.10 francs each, meat between 22 and 26 francs per kilo, a kilo of potatoes cost 2.25, of ham 28 francs and of butter 23 francs. Two days later, eggs reached 1.25 francs each, and it was snowing heavily. She thought with sadness of French soldiers holding their defences, out in the snow and the bitter cold.

The hard frosts continued and the Kaiser's birthday, celebrated with such vigour in 1915, passed in silence in 1917. Lille is a sad city by now, with its dark houses and ruins; perhaps fortunately, there are fewer people in residence, for the population has dropped by nearly 8,000 in twelve months to less than 150,000: an overall decrease from 216,000 in July 1914. Food is short, although a little coal is available—100 kilos for each household every two weeks. This is not enough to do more than some very simple cooking, and many houses were without any form of heating throughout this period. Early in February, as the exceptional cold continued, schools were closed and their coal supplies taken to heat German-occupied houses and offices. News came in from Haubourdin, just outside Lille, that all stoves had been taken and sent to keep the German troops warm in their trenches - information that would have come as no surprise to Allied troops, who frequently expressed rather irritated admiration of the comforts and high standard of installation in German trench systems.

Petty fines and detention continued to plague French inhabitants who were found guilty of all kinds of minor offences:

- being slow to respond to a normal summons from the military police, and then being offensive, 3 days' detention;
- for throwing ashes on a ruined house, 5 marks or 1 day's detention;
- for being rude to a French woman because she worked for the Germans—7 days' detention;

and sundry offences regarding behaviour in trams. Food regulations were strictly enforced—selling above the set price, or importing goods from Brussels without authority.

All kinds of behaviour was equally strictly regulated. When some small boys in Loos wrote a brief and moderately insulting message about the Germans on a wall, the whole population was forbidden to go out except between 9 a.m. and 2 p.m.

Early in March 1917, all farm wagons were to be drawn up in the town square in Le Nouvion, to be inspected, with all donkeys, mules, horses and ponies, large wagons and light two-wheel vehicles used for transporting water containers. Agricultural management seemed to cause difficulties that spring, for once again the command went out that molehills needed flattening, the supply of milk to calves was strictly controlled, animals must not wander away from the farm, dogs found wandering would be killed (with the exception of sheep or cow-herding dogs), hedge-cutting was late; and—not for the first time—vehicles *must always keep to the right of the road*. No one was allowed to travel to another commune to attend school or church there.

After the war the returning French administration recorded that all farm-land and buildings were in very poor condition, and it is clear that food production diminished for a variety of reasons: land management was controlled by German authorities who were ignorant of local conditions, equipment and livestock had been requisitioned, and no supplies of fertilisers were available—essential chemicals were cut off by the blockade, and the manufacture of explosives had far greater priority. Perhaps for these reasons, in the spring of 1918 rabbit-breeding was authorised, provided that each time a rabbit was killed the skin must be deposited at an official centre. The rearer was paid for the skin.

The balance between residents and occupying forces became no easier as time passed and the weariness of war accumulated. Early in 1917, three small industrial towns on the outskirts of Lille were each fined 50,000 marks because residents were considered to have shown too much sympathy for two hundred French prisoners passing through. In addition, all travel passes were withdrawn and residents ordered to remain indoors between 5 pm and 5 am. Other fines rained down on all sides—as did bombs, dropped by French aircraft.

In mid-May of that year the severe weather of the winter is still making itself felt, for the lilac is still not out and the trees are as bare as in a normal early April. Meat is extremely hard to find, butter costs 29 fr/k, potatoes 4 fr/k. sugar 14-16 fr/k, flour 8-9 fr/k and chocolate 46 fr/k. In addition to these difficulties, and no doubt because of them, Madame Delahaye-Théry is diagnosed by her doctor as having anaemia, no doubt the cause, as she remarks, of her great feeling of sadness and weakness, and her longing to see her family.

No one's feelings are improved by a new announcement: a full inventory is required from all households, of all possessions - linen, clothing, furniture, food stocks, etc. The cost of everyday life gets higher by the day, with ham costing 36 fr/k. No eggs to be had, and the cost of butter has risen by three francs within the last week.

More and more residents are being evacuated from Lille, to other parts of the occupied zone, and a new proclamation forbids people from buying anything at all, with the exception of a few items of haberdashery. In Tourcoing, all the remaining textile factory looms are being dismantled, and a German is reported as stating that the invaders would not be staying much longer but will seize everything possible first, and what remains will be destroyed, so that the city will be completely ruined.

It was inevitable that the local civilian population would be required to work under the occupying forces' direction, and it was natural—and sensible—for the invaders to make the best possible use of all resources in their new territory. The aspect which strikes perhaps the greatest chord in later reactions is not necessarily the physical and moral coercion, the fear and the loss, but the simple unfairness of being required, as an unwilling and unqualified civilian, to undertake heavy and unfamiliar labour for the benefit of the aggressor nation, and to be treated as a form of industrial resource.

Truth is universally recognised as an elusive commodity in war-time. All civilians have to interpret the news dispensed to them with an eye to the need for governmental propaganda, but French residents in the occupied zone had to contend with a doubly distorted image: what little news reached them was the German propaganda version of a mixture of genuine war events and of French propaganda news, without any counter-balance of neutral interpretation or comment. The growing strains in civilian Germany—shortages of food, clothing and industrial raw materials—might be referred to lightly in broad terms by the *Gazette des Ardennes*, the French-language but German-produced paper distributed throughout the occupied zone, but any such reference would be in terms of the effect of the wicked British blockade, the weakness of the French army, and the high morale of the German people. The French readers in their humiliation and discomfort would accept none of this, and would always assume that their harsh treatment was a deliberate choice by an all-powerful occupying force. It was not part of their view of the war that the German nation might also be suffering, or that the troops who ruled their lives so strictly might themselves be suffering from poor supplies and the knowledge that their families back home were desperately short of food, clothing and fuel.

German soldiers and officers were frequently billetted in ordinary French households, where conditions would depend on the good nature or otherwise of both sides of the transaction. The occasional exchange of news or comment with their German 'guests' in a moment of cautious collaborative relaxation might enlighten the French about domestic conditions back in Germany, but it is not part of human nature, in circumstances of suffering and oppression, to feel instinctive sympathy for the oppressors' complaints.

Secrecy and danger continued in the midst of deprivation and discomfort, with a spirit of resistance still in evidence. Antoinette Tierce, a spirited music teacher living in Lille, responded with great spirit to the needs of the moment. Faced with two British sailors who had escaped from a prison camp in 1917 and were trying to get back to their own lines, she knew the risks in helping them: many French people had been shot for such help—but she lived alone so would not compromise others. She took them in, hoping to pass them on across the frontier.

In the end, the men stayed in her care for many months. She was supported by practical friends—an acquaintance did his best to betray her. Fortunately his accusations were wild and inaccurate, and the investigating German officers were careless. Madame Tierce was able to place one of the men elsewhere, and then talk her way out of trouble. She was imprisoned for four months for failing to declare the presence of the remaining Englishman, but, she convinced her interrogators, although he was indeed English, he was her lover and had nothing to do with the Allied forces. The denunciations that she suffered were probably typical of the time.

It is possible, at times like this, to sympathise with the men charged with administering this large and hostile city. Although they lived in considerably greater comfort than their oppressed 'subjects', and found varying degrees of collaboration and companionship in some French households, it is clear that the bulk of the population made their resentment as visible as they dared; and presumably some of the occupying forces must have found it disagreeable, at the least, to be living at the heart of a large semi-starved and hostile population. Charges against individuals may often have been time-wasting exercises raised out of personal grudge or supposed wrongs and had more to do with deprivation, anxiety and boredom than genuine wrong-doing.

Notes

1. Unpublished journal kept by M. Leduc, Le Nouvion-en-Thiérache
2. Leduc, journal
3. Eye-witness's 'Narrative of the War', from *Eye-Witness Accounts Presentation GHQ*
4. Report of Dr. Ducamp, Director of Public Health, to the Mayor of Lille
5. Leduc, journal
6. Leduc, journal
7. Carpentier, diary
8. Rather than a 'recapture', this was the German withdrawal to the Hindenburg Line.
9. Martin-Mamy, *Quatre Ans avec les Barbares, Lille pendant l'Occupation allemande*, Paris, La Renaissance du Livre, 1919.

5

Secrets

Resistance is a feature of all hostile occupations. By the nature of such activity, many of those who engaged in active secret work in northern France in the First World War are now unknown; some names reached public attention after the war, in both France and England, others remained obscure. Virtually all the resistance activity depended on colleagues or families who continued their efforts in quiet disregard of the dangers surrounding them. After some more or less successful individual feats of ingenuity and concealment in the early days of the war, coordinated resistance developed quickly and quietly. It was more easily organised in large cities than in small towns where strangers would be noticed and inhabitants might be almost outnumbered by the occupying forces.

The border between Belgium and France was soon protected by sentries, and electrified and barbed wire barriers, but secret traffic continued: food came in, and humans and information passed in both directions but generally out. Most were French soldiers left behind in the confusion of retreat in the late summer of 1914, but many British soldiers still hid in cupboards or lurked around farms, hoping to escape capture.

During the autumn Marie-Jeanne Dentant, a widow in Lille, came to hear of several men who were determined to take action. A French officer, Major Caron, and his motorcyclist Jobert, both from Lille, began by helping other fugitives with money and moral support, but it became obvious that more aid was badly needed—if only to avoid the danger of betrayal. The *préfet*, Félix Trépont, (who was also to distinguish himself in the Red Cross in the Second World War) was quickly involved, businessmen provided financial support, a butcher and a baker supplied meat and bread. Other contributions in kind—vegetables, dried goods, wine, clothing—poured in to Mme Dentant's flat, which conveniently had a second exit on to a different street, minimising the apparent number of visitors. Caron and Jobert risked discovery by German patrols each evening as they delivered food and other goods to their 'clients', but a new system was needed.

Madame Dentant, who was evidently an independent and decisive woman, collaborated with the Plouvier brothers, wealthy businessmen who effectively financed most of the operation. Further organisational support came from Emile Vermeersch, Lille's deputy municipal financial director, and from two other staunch supporters: a businessman, Georges Maertens, and a territorial officer, Ernest Deconinck. From early March 1915, the daily administration was taken over by Deconinck.

Trépont brought in Eugène Jacquet, a wine broker active in radical, socialist and pacifist movements whose name came to be attached to the secret committee. With the outbreak of war he rejected his Franco-German links with pacifism, turning towards the new allies and human-itarian aid. In October 1914 he had helped a young sergeant who col-lapsed outside his house, after active reservist activity defending Lille against the invasion. The man returned a few days later with his com-manding officer, saying that there were at least fifty reservist soldiers in the city, probably many more, and that they were destitute; money was needed, and Jacquet approached his friends for funds, adding 15,000 francs himself to form a fund to supply food and a little money, as required. Major Caron supplied pass documents and more money.

By March 1915, when Caron left Lille to escape into Holland, there were at least 200 men receiving nine francs per week each, or the equiv-alent in food supplies. Jacquet carried on the aid system, helping men who had been discharged from the army, those who had never served, pregnant women, old people without support, and large needy families—all, in fact, who needed it.

A regular escape network developed. The first step towards crossing the frontier was to be checked out by the committee, with confidential enquiries guiding the small group who had access to money, clothing and guides. Each candidate was questioned carefully, then examined medically to assess his physical condition. The cost to the committee was approximately 120 francs per head - and the constant danger of inform-ers. Committed colleagues passed the soldiers on towards the frontier, handing them over to the *passeurs*, the local guides who knew how to evade border controls and where to negotiate canals or wire barriers, which might be electrified; sometimes small folding canvas boats were used, rope-hauled across canals.

Some guides were professional smugglers, already well used to surreptitious frontier crossings. One, Van Heuverzwyn, was credited with three hundred successful escapes, singly or in groups. Discharged from the army, he was in Lille in August 1914 and built up his own network and route for passing men across from France, mainly active between April and July 1915. When one of his best guides was killed during an escape, Van Heuverzwyn was able to retrieve the hollow walking stick in which military documents were carried.

Inevitably, the occupying Germans knew that Frenchmen of military age were in hiding and being helped to escape, and in May 1915 Jacquet was arrested and then released. He knew that he was under surveillance, and was soon under arrest once more with others, this time over one of the disturbances where factory workers refused to continue working on sandbags to be used at the German front line against the French. Jacquet and his colleagues were released once again after four days' isolation; but now their names were on the list of hostages required to report together twice daily at the Citadelle, Lille's military fort.

The Comité Jacquet was finally brought down by an initially light-hearted episode involving an English aviator. On 11 March 1915 an English aircraft suffered engine failure and landed near Lille, followed by German threats of death by firing squad for anyone who helped the pilot, and offering rewards for information. Robert Mapplebeck, the young pilot, was sheltered by the Jacquet Committee and given the only civilian clothes available—which were noticeably too small and included a pass drawn up for a man of 50 who was a foot shorter than his distinctive 6'4". Mapplebeck was passed from one safe house to another, until two weeks later he was taken by Sylvère Verhulst, a Belgian sergeant, Jacquet himself and a colleague named Maertens, to Tourcoing and on across the frontier. He reached his unit again safely; and for weeks afterwards took a childish delight in flying over the heart of Lille, weaving patterns in the sky to thank the citizens for their help.

One day he singled out the Governor of Lille, Heinrich, and sent down a package with a long tricolor banner attached. The letter inside read:

12 April 1915

To the Governor in command of the German Forces in Lille
Lieutenant Mapplebeck presents his respects to the Commandant
of the German forces in Lille and regrets that he was unable to
make his acquaintance during his agreeable visit near him.

Mapplebeck[1]

This cheeky message was typical of the man: Jacquet's wife wrote of him
that he was 'a great gangling lad, casual, smiling, cheerfully unconcerned'.
The Governor was not amused, nor was he impressed by the guards who
had failed to notice the tall young man whose clothes and pass were at
odds with his size, physique and age. On his way to the frontier
Mapplebeck had crossed Lille—plastered with notices of his presence—
by tram, wearing his strikingly ill-fitting clothes and relying on a pass for
a man nearly thirty years his senior and a full foot shorter.[2]

Jacquet's success in organising escapes owed much to his boldness;
but the corresponding drawback was a tendency to excessively casual
self-assurance. He routinely stood his ground when passing German
officers in the street, for example, while others stood aside as officially
instructed. Mapplebeck, astonishingly, had kept a journal of his brief stay
in Lille which he left in Jacquet's hands; this was not destroyed, but
hidden down the side of an upholstered armchair.

The occupying forces' opportunity to break up the committee came
through a minor member of the group, Louis Richard, an unreliable idler
whose inadequacies were noted but not taken sufficiently seriously.
Jacquet mistrusted him, and it seems that he was finally despatched with
an escape group in order to be rid of him.

The route to the Netherlands regularly passed through a hotel in
Antwerp. On 9 July 1915 Verhulst arrived from Lille with a group and
found Richard, who should have moved on earlier. Verhulst waited for
their Dutch guide—but he had been seized earlier that day. In his place,
German police swept in, revolvers at the ready and further armed with a
compromising letter captured with the guide. It showed clearly the connection between the escape network and the Jacquet Committee.

Eugène Jacquet and his family were rounded up next day. The news
spread rapidly, compromising material was hastily cleared, papers passed

from hand to hand to evade the searching patrols, committee activists fled and hid. Disastrously, the upholstered armchair was seized, complete with the incriminating papers tucked inside, as nervous conspirators tried to carry it through the streets to safety. Old pay-books were discovered, some notes written by Jacquet's wife—and Mapplebeck's diary. This was catastrophic: it gave details of his crash-landing and all that happened after it, including the names of Jacquet and his wife, their colleagues Maertens, Deconinck and Verhulst, and various other compromising comments and bits of information.

Deconinck was seized in Ghent three days later, together with a British engineer normally resident in France who intended to join the British army, a guide, Léon Vestens, and others involved in the network. Delfossé, an important organiser, and Georges Maertens had already been captured.

Twenty-seven men and one woman were imprisoned in the Citadelle in Lille. Jacquet realised that he was unlikely to get away with his life and made sure that others who were less heavily implicated would look after his wife and children. A confirmed agnostic, he immediately specified a civil funeral for himself, even before interrogations began.

By the end of July a large area of Lille had been closed off for a detailed search and some two hundred people were arrested. One, Jeanne Leclercq-Bourgeois, was responsible for distributing money and essential items to the many aspiring escapees hidden in and around Lille. With the arrests, she warned them that she was in danger, and indeed she was arrested on 26 July, in the middle of the night. She was tried, declared she had done nothing beyond her duty as a French citizen—and was acquitted, for lack of evidence. Her records were safely hidden and never discovered.

By 8 August some men had already been tried in Antwerp and deported to Germany (where one died in prison). The twenty remaining captives included the chief activists of the Jacquet committee, their guides, and an Englishman, William Forrest. The men played cards, sang, read, and talked while plans were drawn up for their trial, and good humour and practical joking helped to pass the time. One man was suffering from great mental anguish and confusion; he made an attempt at suicide, was rescued, and committed to a mental hospital - from which he soon escaped. As the case against the group was prepared, Jacquet insisted that he alone was responsible: 'If anyone is to be shot, it must be me alone'. The men discussed their case and its presentation, inconsistencies noted by the investigators, the best way forward. A note written partly in Greek letters mixed with Flemish *patois*—which contained important information - was treated by the detectives as a kind of scribbled joke. Mapplebeck's diary, however, was the real give-away, and the magistrate's questions concentrated on the dates, times and collusion involved in his concealment and escape.

The hearings continued into September 1915, complicated by confusion over the identity of some of the accused. One man refused to answer questions put to him in his real name, stating only his assumed name and otherwise talking in a muddled and incoherent way. None the less, he was condemned to fifteen years' imprisonment in Germany. William Forrest, the Englishman seized with his guides, persuaded the Germans of his relative innocence by pulling out a photograph of his girl-friend and explaining that he did not want to leave such a pretty girl alone too long. The court laughed, and he escaped with two months in prison and a 500 francs fine.

In mid-September Jacquet was summoned to the prison governor's office and returned with a sombre expression. 'I have just learned that I am to be condemned to death, and shot.' One of the group commented that this was merely a possibility. 'No,' replied Jacquet, 'my lawyer was clear: "I will do my best but I can't get you out of this. I must warn you that your death is settled, so that you can make all your arrangements with your family"'.

The verdicts were announced. Eugène Jacquet - four death sentences; Ernest Deconinck, three death sentences; Georges Maertens, two; Sylvère Verhulst, one. The defence lawyers put in their pleas, in vain. Finally, Jacquet himself spoke up: 'I have acted in accordance with my conscience, with my rights, and my duty as a French citizen. I regret nothing of what I have done and I do not fear death. I make only one request: that the lives of my colleagues should be spared.'

His co-defendants responded: 'We all acted together, we have the right to the same sentence, that we should die together.' Jacquet's statement, that he had never given money to help escapes, simply to support the needy, was designed to cause confusion, by mixing truth and falsehood, and proving that he had only acted out of humanitarian sympathy. He had been noted before the war for his philanthropic activity—he could not refuse to help those who were in difficulties, even if they were soldiers.

The case was concluded on 17 September, and next day Jacquet wrote his final letters to friends, commending his family to their care and sending his farewells to various colleagues. He wished for no revenge. On 21 September, Jacquet's wife and four daughters were allowed to visit him; braced against a possible refusal of this final visit, the prisoner had already written to his wife with fond advice to his children and thanking his friends, including the British consul in Lille.

In his final wishes Verhulst expressed support for Jacquet and pride in what they had achieved together. Maertens was visited by his wife, with a priest, and in a letter to her later that day he begged her forgiveness for causing her such grief. Deconinck saw no one, but wrote to his wife in a spirit of proud patriotism on 21 September. He stated that he would 'cease to exist' at 5 a.m. next morning and added firmly beneath his signature, 'Shot in the ramparts of Lille, Wednesday 22 September, at 5 a.m.'.

Half an hour before the execution was due he wrote again to his wife, describing how he had spent the night thinking of her and of their two sons, of his parents; he had 'talked' to each of them and embraced them in his mind, and felt strengthened.

Jacquet too wrote to his wife from the Citadelle in the evening after her departure, a letter of praise for her courage and devotion which reveals his own qualities of endurance; and then another letter, in the early hours of the day of execution, with loving messages for his children, describing how he and his condemned friends had dined together cheerfully. They had agreed together how they would meet their fate, eyes uncovered, hands unbound.

A final document, signed by all four men, has survived with Jacquet's other letters:

> My dear friends and comrades,
> We have reached the end! In a few moments we will be shot.
> We will die bravely, as good French and Belgian citizens. Standing firmly, our eyes uncovered, our hands free. Farewell to all, and take heart! Vive la République! Vive la France![3]

Descriptions of their last moments vary, with legend asserting that they proclaimed 'Vive la République' (Jacquet), 'Vive la France' (Deconinck), 'Vive la Liberté' (Maertens) and 'Vive la Belqique' (Verhulst). The priest who supported Maertens at his request stated that they all shouted 'Au revoir mon général'. The words are not, ultimately, important: the spirit in which they acted, and in which they stood before the firing squad, is clear.

Jacquet's widow was allowed to leave the occupied zone for free France and received a pension. The other widows remained under German rule and received tiny pensions. The drama was revived after the war, when Louis Richard, who had betrayed the group, was tried early in 1919. He was found guilty and condemned to deportation, with the court's regret that the death penalty was not available, and died of tuberculosis soon afterwards.[4] The tombs of the dead heroes are covered with wreaths each year on All Saints Day. The large and eloquent memorial set up in Lille in their honour in 1929 was damaged in 1940, during the fresh Occupation, but after 1944 it was fully restored.

'Lille, *The Monuments aux fusillés*'

The memorial to Jacquet and his colleagues shows not only the four who worked together, standing boldly upright, but also a figure lying at their feet. This commemorates another activist who worked entirely separately from the Lille group but in the same spirit. Léon Trulin was a sickly youth from an impoverished background, forced into months of inactivity by injury; long hours of solitary reading fired his imagination and left with him with a determination to study and improve himself, and wild ideas of adventure and overcoming dramatic obstacles. He recovered his health, and on the outbreak of war plunged into a personal crusade which brought his dreams to life. He managed to reach England in June 1915 and offered himself to the Belgian forces based there; refused by them—because of his poor physique—he convinced the British army that he could provide them with information and returned to occupied France. Having accomplished his first task, he visited England again and set off on a further mission, using the false name of Noel Lurtin (an anagram of his own name). Living rough, without any support except a small group of friends, he gathered and passed on information about German troops, strength and movements. In the summer of 1915, while the Jacquet Committee waited in prison, Trulin visited Lille twice—and was betrayed, probably by one of his colleagues. In October he was captured with reports and plans of trenches, airfields and ammunition dumps. The consequence was inevitable: although his friends were sent to prison in Germany (and one acquitted), Trulin as the leader was sentenced to death. The touching note that he wrote in the last hours before his execution stated that he was dying for his country and without regrets, that he forgave his enemies, that he had done his duty. He asked for his mother's forgiveness.

Trulin, who was still only 18 at the time of his death, seems to have been an idealistic adolescent who was eager to sacrifice his life, while the members of the Jacquet Committee were experienced businessmen and organisers, risking the lives and freedom of others as well as themselves and their families. In the light of events later in the century their approach to subversive activity and security seems naive—yet they were inventing new methods for dealing with a new way of life. Memories of these episodes and these responses must have been recalled by the next generation, who lived through the next war. As in that later conflict too, there were collaborators who cooperated with the invaders while others again managed to stay clear of both resistance activists and the occupying forces, protecting themselves, their families and their way of life as best they could.

As the invaders took over their new territory they were concerned to prevent communication with the outside world. Radio receivers were rare and the new authorities immediately declared that anyone in possession of a set would be executed. There was of course no television—indeed, even the cinema was still a recent innovation—and telephones were very limited in number, installed in a few business premises (which came under German control) and a comparatively small number of prosperous private households. The written or directly spoken word was generally the only means of communication available. News of a kind soon appeared in the shape of the *Gazette des Ardennes*, a magnificent French-language newspaper produced as propaganda by the occupying Germans. Glossily printed, it was lavishly illustrated with fine photographs—showing French villages, and especially churches, that had been shelled and destroyed 'by the British allies'. These contrasted with pictures of unspoilt German landscapes, magnificent undamaged churches, towns and villages. The underlying message was unstated but clear: Germany was clean, beautiful, a fine place, while France's sufferings were the fault of her interfering allies. Fasol, the attentive note-taker in Péronne, wrote of the *Gazette* (which soon became known as the *Gazette des Menteurs*, the 'liars' paper') that it was:

entirely poisonous ... everyone swore they would never read it again, but still they rushed to read it, there were never enough copies.[5]

It was the only way to receive news of men held in Germany, for lists and photographs of prisoners appeared regularly.

The lack of hard news and these favourable images of German life offered a powerful contrast to the weary life of war-time, with factories closed and many urban residents out of work. This was the passive side of the occupation, with an atmosphere described by one commentator:

Apart from the inevitable assortment of shirkers and collaborators ... it could be said that the army of occupation and the population of Lille constituted two worlds which operated alongside each other but never blended.[6]

There were attempts among the Germans to overcome this mute disdain. For Christmas 1915 the Governor of Lille decided on a ceremonial opening of the new theatre, postponed by the outbreak of war; invitations were sent out to everyone of importance in the French population and a grand reception was announced. To substantial German annoyance and French satisfaction, no one came. A German officer remarked that:

> The city of Lille does not let us see her true face. She wears a mask. Many of us would like to feel the pulse of her former liveliness, but she remains hostile and inward-looking.[7]

The feeling of isolation began to take hold by the late autumn of 1914, as the war of movement came to an end. The death penalty was proclaimed for hiding or helping French or allied soldiers, for releasing carrier-pigeons, making signals, ringing bells, or using radio transmitters.

The prohibition against keeping pigeons, or against having anything to do with carrier-pigeons found by chance, was well-known and continued throughout the war. When in May 1917 a youth of 17, Charles Bisiaux, discovered a basket of pigeons tied to a balloon near Mormal forest, he took them home. That night he, his father and Fabien Mennechet carefully answered all the questions hidden in the birds' leg-rings, about ammunition dumps and gun emplacements at Cambrai; next day the pigeons were released, and a few days later the railway lines and guns at Cambrai were bombed and put out of use by French aircraft.

This use of pigeons to gain information was effective but extremely dangerous for the French who responded, and executions continued despite the dangers. Two women were shot for this crime in October 1917, at Tournai, and another at St-Amand in March 1918. Very occasionally, aircraft dropped newspapers from England or free France, but they were scarce and such news reached very few people.

A Lille businessman took the dangerous decision to provide a news service. Firmin Dubar, a substantial textile manufacturer well-known for his good works, went into partnership with a young priest, Abbé Pinte, who taught chemistry at Roubaix technical institute and Joseph Willot, a doctor of pharmacy at Lille University with his own laboratory in Roubaix. The priest assembled a radio receiver in his own small rooms, storing it behind the panelling round his bed with the opening disguised by marks and smudges. A telephone wire on the roof served as aerial, bringing news from the Eiffel Tower transmissions, denying wild rumours, and confirming the state of stalemate along the Allied front line. Willot's teaching took him into Lille every day; as the senior pharmacist for the health service he also saw Pinte daily, since he too worked for the health service in Roubaix, and it was agreed that he would distribute news in Lille and Dubar in Roubaix. In Tourcoing, the third town in this triple-centred conurbation, the dangerous mission of collecting news every day from the pharmacy department and passing it on was undertaken by the chief of police and head of French information services, M. Lenfant, who also became involved in other important forms of resistance.

Dubar, Pinte and Willot met each morning in Willot's private office above the pharmacy department. The radio news was spread by word of mouth, through apparently casual street contacts and whispered information and to the bishop Monseigneur Charost, Félix Trépont (the *préfet* of the Nord department, who had helped with the initial stages of the Jacquet committee), the local senator, the director of the health service, and several industrialists. All undertook to disseminate information wherever they had influence and were sure of discretion.

Dubar soon began to plan a regular newspaper; he contacted a friend, Joseph Delespant, whose private office housed a Roneo machine capable of producing eighty copies of a document, and on New Year's Day 1915, the first secret news-sheet appeared called *Le Journal des Occupés ... inoccupés* ('the newspaper of the idle occupied'), it declared itself to be:

> As resolutely hostile to the foolish optimism which is blind to truth and transforms the most obvious failures into victories, as to the destructive pessimism which, for fear of being surprised, can only believe in depressing news.[8]

The eighty copies were distributed in envelopes by hand or pushed under doors to the most important citizens of Roubaix and caused great mystification and delight. The second issue, a fortnight later, had less impact because of a severe bread crisis, but the third issue, on 24 January 1915, was well received. It gave military information, comment on official communiqués, and articles designed to sustain morale. Sketches of unpopular German officers offered the great revenge of laughter; the occupying forces themselves were perplexed and suspicious in the face of cheerful and well-informed citizens, and made great efforts to find out the source of news in Roubaix.

Joseph Willot was anxious to establish a similar paper in Lille. After discussion with Pinte and Dubar, the first issue of *Patience* appeared there on 23 February, with 19 pages carrying the same news as the *Journal des Occupés .. inoccupés* in Roubaix. Paper was not always easily available: all supplies were requisitioned, and each issue of the two newspapers required 1,000 sheets, but another industrialist came to their aid with a significant quantity.

Late in February 1915 the church bells were rung in Lille on German orders, to celebrate a tremendous victory over the Russians—there was even an improved supply of bread, as a reward. However, the news received from the Eiffel Tower failed to confirm the victory; it seems that the inconclusive German encounter with the Russians in the winter battle of Masuria was being presented as a success in order to demoralise the occupied zone. The 'great victory' was convincingly denied and the French population heartened.

Patience aimed to encourage and entertain its privileged readers: in March it printed a philosophy for trapped civilian population: 'Despite the troubles of present times, to show unwearying patience, invincible confidence - that is the means of serving modestly but not without distinction the greater interests of *Patience*'. Each issue bore instructions at its head:

We earnestly beg our friends:
1) not to enquire into the source of this information;
2) to make use of it only with great care and discretion;
3) not to keep these pages, but to destroy them carefully when you have read them; tearing is not enough, they must be burned.
To our readers: If, dear readers, you wish to follow these recommendations, you will help us greatly in our task and you will reduce our risks to the minimum. You do not know us, and you will not know us. This is essential, for it completely relieves you of any personal responsibility. (signed) VIDI[9]

The *Journal des Occupés* carried a similar notice, with the observation: 'under the régime of terror which we are undergoing, we must understand how to *dare*, but we must *dare* with *caution*, with *moderation*, and without rashness'.

Copies of the papers circulated quietly, hidden in books or bags, inside chocolate boxes, one in a man's cap, another tucked inside a belt. As requisitions and searches were carried out ruthlessly, with or without an official pretext, and teams of specialised investigators with trained dogs searched and stripped houses, lifting floorboards and digging in gardens, Dubar prepared a hiding place in the chimney flue of some disused steam-driven machinery. Located behind the large flush water-closet, it appeared to be a drain and successfully escaped observation.

By mid-March an official proclamation forbade the reading of any paper except the German-controlled *Gazette des Ardennes* and *Bulletin de Lille*. Willot and Dubar agreed that since their activities met with official disapproval, they must undoubtedly continue, and preferably expand— particularly as the Germans were announcing further demoralizing news. The best way to avoid detection was to combine the two secret papers, reducing the amount of activity and the work of production, and after March a single edition was prepared for the two cities.

Pinte, Dubar and Willot continued to meet daily to prepare the issues, which sometimes covered more than 20 pages, containing military news, extracts from French papers, practical suggestions and encouraging advice. When 400 French inhabitants—old, poor, or women with large families of young children—were evacuated from Roubaix, at a time of diminishing food supplies in March 1915, the next issue of the paper carried 'Von Heinrich's Ten Commandments'. The list gives a good picture of regulations and restrictions to be dealt with in everyday life. (Heinrich was the heartily-disliked German governor of Lille, and 'KK bread' was the famously indigestible official bread.)

KK bread shalt thou eat
and painfully digest;

No badge or banner shalt thou wear
boldly upon thy chest

From 5 p.m. shalt thou stay indoors
on pain of imprisonment

Thou shalt not join in any group
to create a public gathering

Thou shalt not speak to any prisoner
When we kindly take them out.

Thou shalt give us all your money
without protest, with docility

All Germans shalt thou treat
On all occasions with thy best behaviour

The worst of falsehoods shalt thou swallow
Without the least reproach

Thou shalt accept the situation
or else look out for retribution![10]

Production of the paper became more difficult: the roneo process was inadequate, with gaps and poor quality reproduction, the master copy fell apart after about 80 copies, and paper supplies were dwindling again. Joseph Willot offered a small room behind his laboratory, large enough for a proper printing press, and Madame Reboux, manager of the *Journal de Roubaix*, agreed to help. A typesetter was found, Edouard Dutrieux, capable of working alone as compositor and printer on an awkward proof press; then Madame Reboux produced a pedal-driven press, production was increased, and the paper expanded. Articles and news were gathered locally or copied from French newspapers dropped by aircraft, acquired from prisoners passing through, or thrown away by German officers. A Brussels trader received Paris papers daily via Holland, and used them to wrap goods sent to Lille.

On 1 April 1915, as the team worked on the current issue for distribution later that day, four German officers arrived. Dubar rang the special alarm bell to warn printers and folders to hide everything, while the concierge took his time answering their knock. Dubar appeared and led them up and down the building, avoiding the printing room, for half an hour, while the printers hid their equipment inside the steps of a small flight of stairs. The letterpress went into drawers, while papers were hidden behind account books. The newspaper production line went undiscovered, but next day an official convoy of fifteen four-horse wagons and forty soldiers 'requisitioned' more than a thousand lengths of fabric from Dubar's textile stores.

Three weeks later, Madame Reboux's printing press was set up in Willot's house in Tourcoing; some ten metres away, German soldiers were installed in a *Landsturm* barracks. The press was established between the Red Cross laboratory and the German barracks, with nothing to hide it; the door was open, everything inside was visible. The usual distributors were used; one, Henri Soubricas, avoided tram searches by walking from Roubaix to Lille.

The next issue was to be the last with 20 pages; henceforward, it would consist of only one or two pages, but with more frequent issues, containing only French news from the Eiffel Tower signal, and some foreign news. At first this version had no title, then it was changed frequently; from April to June 1915 it was *Nouvelles*, then for some time *Patience*. By the end of 1915 it had also appeared as *Nouvelles Françaises, Echo de France, Voix de la Patrie, L'Hirondelle de France, Courrier de France*, and finally *La Prudence*.

Abbé Pinte continued to listen in to the receiver in his tiny apartments with German sentries patrolling outside the door, along the corridor linking the military prisoners' rooms in the technical institute. He decided to move the equipment to a space behind the altar in the chapel at the far end of this corridor, and transferred it in a suitcase, carrying it calmly past the sentries. The young priest managed to continue receiving the news for two years, although the Institut Technique was under suspicion and was searched eleven times.

A women's page was added to the publication, and Henri Soubricas, who was an artist and sculptor, provided dramatic and amusing illustrations, maps of the front, and caricatures of all the most important German officers stationed in Lille. (Later in the war Soubricas also helped Antoinette Tierce, who sheltered two British soldiers for several months after their escape from a German prison camp.) The continuing aim was to sustain and encourage, and to preserve the pride and confidence of the oppressed French population.

There were increasing German demands for money from the French citizens, and for labour—which included work of military relevance. Refusal meant ruin, increased misery and tighter rationing. Willot addressed the problem in *Patience*:

By refusing to carry out the military tasks imposed by our enemies, you are within your rights and are fulfiling your duty as French citizens ... those unpatriotic people who take on work of immediate or remote military relevance will be guilty of unpatriotic behaviour ... we will suffer in silence, to achieve true greatness ... We leave it to the Germans to oppress a defenceless civilian population, while we wait impatiently for the day of deliverance.[11]

The paper's triumvirate announced to the mayor of Tourcoing and to the region's leading industrialists: 'We will not work, we cannot work, for the enemy'.

Madame Willot helped her husband, who was suffering from the physical labour and mental strain involved, while he continued his teaching work in the university. While supposedly busy in his laboratory he was free from suspicion of clandestine work, and he pursued academic contacts with German professors in order to sustain his alibi. Meanwhile, his assistant Marguerite Nollet worked with Abbé Pinte, and another member of the team, René Wibaux, called at the Willot pharmacy every morning, passing straight through to the family's living room where he picked up the latest messages received overnight, tucked under a candelabra.[12]

Conditions towards the end of 1915 were deteriorating noticeably in Lille. Levels of oppression and the cost of living were both increasing, private correspondence (allowed within the occupied zone) was more closely supervised, houses searched and sometimes emptied. Interrogation, fines, and imprisonment increased, and prisoners—men, women and children—accumulated in the Roubaix public baths, taken over to 'store' French civilians who came under German military or police control.

A few copies of *Patience* fell into German hands. Willot realised the danger, and the next issue stated that the paper was produced by French refugees in a neutral country, and sent into the occupied area. One of the secret distributors took care that a copy carrying this statement reached the Commandantur.

The affair eventually ran into greater danger when a French woman took a copy of *La Prudence* to the Commandantur. Lille was searched, although not Roubaix, but Willot decided to suspend publication, in October 1915. Thereafter there was silence except for a few bulletins for a few privileged people, under the name of *L'Oiseau de France*, a name suggested by Madame Willot. Copies bore a rubber stamp indicating 'French airmail', so that anyone found with a copy could claim to have picked it up from an air-drop.

In this form it continued through most of 1916. The demand for copies was tremendous; they were passed from hand to hand, reaching other cities (Douai, Tournai, Brussels) and on at least one occasion even read out from a church pulpit. On 9 March 1916, when all bells were rung by German order to 'celebrate the capture of Verdun'—which would open the road to Paris—the fabrication was denied next day in the *Oiseau de France*. A copy of this issue was pinned to the senior general's door in Roubaix and several copies put into officers' pockets. (Although the front line came very near to Verdun as its surrounding forts were captured, the city itself was never taken.)

The Somme offensive in July 1916 was reported, following the German version of the battle of Jutland, balanced by such items as a new census of guinea fowl and chickens, and orders to take one egg for each three chickens to the nearest police station. On 14 July 1916, Bastille Day, the paper bore a triumphal tricolor border. The French recapture of Mort-Homme and the Fort de Vaux, near Verdun, in the summer of 1916 was announced in the *Oiseau*, although—not surprisingly—it went unrecorded in the official German press.

In October 1916 Dubar, who had been detained under suspicion, was released from detention and destroyed compromising papers. He visited Willot, advising him to flee to free France with his wife and son, but Madame Willot was ill and he could not go alone, for fear of reprisals on his family. The police searched yet again, without success, but removed Dubar to the Roubaix public baths. He was interrogated, remained silent, and was put in solitary confinement; his prison number, 22,906, indicated that one-quarter of the citizens of Roubaix had been held there in the past two years. His assistant, Marguerite Nollet, was arrested.

Willot, free and unsuspected, decided on a final issue of *L'Oiseau*. A radio receiver was installed in his laboratories and he prepared a two-page issue of *La Voix de la Patrie*. When the Germans discovered a copy, they descended on the whole university. All the teaching staff were kept in one hall, although Willot himself was absent. A young assistant managed to disappear quietly with the receiver's headphones. The police arrived at Willot's house while the next issue was being prepared: papers were thrust into the stove, and in the haste a packet of printing characters was spilt, swiftly gathered up—and hidden inside the piano. Upstairs, Madame Willot hid the receiver, and all other equipment was safely hidden in prepared places inside the laboratory.

Abbé Pinte was under suspicion, and the Institut was searched once more. Marguerite Nollet and his other assistants hid material—some in their pockets—and escaped through the back door, hiding equipment in the lavatory cistern as they went and throwing other items into the drain. Dubar was seized at the Institut and searched, together with a friend—in whose pocket a copy of *L'Oiseau* was found. Madame Devivoise, one of the Institut team, hid the incriminating headphones on her head by cramming her hat down over them while she accompanied German investigators through the building for several hours. A complete set of the papers was found, hidden by the cook in the face of express instructions, together with notes of communiqués in the handwriting of Pinte and Mademoiselle Nollet, and a photograph of the *Oiseau* team, taken on Bastille Day 1916.

Finally, towards the end of October 1916, the printing press itself was discovered, and the team was tried in April 1917. Apart from Pinte, who denied everything but was none the less sent to Brussels prison, all involved were sentenced to long terms of imprisonment in Germany. Marguerite Nollet was sent to Siegburg, near Bonn, where she encountered other French women convicted for their resistance activities. Although all survived, Willot died soon after the Armistice from the effects of prison life.

The team's work continued even when they were in prison, for their young electrician helped Madame Willot to set up the radio receiver inside a table top. When the police arrived at the Willot house while he was in prison, Madame Willot was entertaining young visitors; the young cheerful party was a good disguise and the investigating Germans retreated, convinced of their innocence: but the shelves of jam in the pantry hid boxes of print characters and a panel above the window hid documents. Her house was searched frequently and she was forbidden to receive visitors, but she was free from regular supervision and was able to visit a friend two or three times each week, in Lille; while there she passed on radio messages to reliable friends. This continued until 17 October 1918, when the captured cities were released.

After the war, Madame Willot and Mlle Nollet were awarded the *Ordre de la Nation*, and Mlle Nollet (who was only 18 at the time of her capture), together with Willot, Pinte, and Dubar received the *Croix de la Légion d'Honneur*. In 1920 the Académie Française awarded the Prix Buisson to the *Oiseau de France*, thus honouring all those involved.

Despite the repeated instructions that the news-sheets must be destroyed, copies have survived. The text is written in sober literary style, giving genuine news of the war's progress and comment on the different German and French attitudes. There are quotes from Russian, German and French communiqués, and news from London.

The first issue, dated 30 December 1914, describes how France has had a fairly peaceful day from the North Sea down to the River Aisne. Two French trenches have been blown up but an attack on the French was repulsed. By the end of January 1915, the journal has grown to 8 sheets - printed on both sides - for its third issue. It tells of Allied success on the River Yser, and gives detailed accounts of fighting around Soissons: the ground lost and won, the problems of the river in spate after heavy rain.

Political news appears too: Millerand, the Minister of War, has received a cheque for four million francs to buy war supplies. News of the battle of Jutland tells of the sinking of the German warship *Blücher*, a serious loss for the Germans. American accounts of the battle proclaim the German defeat at sea as one of the most brilliant and decisive events of naval warfare, and recognise the supremacy of the British fleet in the North Sea. There are some of the jokes that appeared in the previous issue, and an extract from the Times of 9 December 1914, on Schneider and Maxim factories, also a stirring martial song.

The newspaper stresses the need for patience, the importance of being able to wait.

Other secret radio receivers were put to good use in passing information. Near Le Cateau, and near Mormal Forest which provided shelter for many French and British soldiers in hiding, the young priest François Polvent was active in his village of Ors. His most daring activity was to go fishing—but with a difference. For anyone to go fishing in the canal, the many streams or the marshes around Ors, when food was so short, was a natural activity, but in this case the fishing line had a double purpose. While one line was conventionally employed in the water, a second rod was flicked to send its hook high up into the overhanging trees along the canal bank. The line was linked to a portable radio trans-

135

mitter—carried in a case for the Abbé's requirements for officiating at Mass, but with a false bottom. Sitting quietly among the reeds, François Polvent sent out his information on military movements by morse code to the British forces. At the same time, his sister Marie enjoyed a few quiet moments in the open air not far away; leaning on a gate, she took off her large sun-hat if a German patrol approached, and wiped her brow. At this warning, François Polvent quickly brought down his antenna, closed up his case, and carried on fishing until his sister's hat went back on her head and he could begin again. He came under suspicion several times, although not for sending radio messages, but was never convicted.

Notes

1. Lorédan, Jean, *Lille et l'Invasion allemande 14-18*, Paris, Perrin, 1920
2. Mapplebeck's delight in flying 'stunts' eventually led to his death in a plane crash a few months later, still aged only 22. He is buried in one of several First World War military graves in a South London municipal cemetery.
3. Deruyk, René, *La mort pour la liberté, l'histoire du comité Jacquet*, Lille, La Voix du Nord, 1993.
4. Richard wrote to the wife of the President, pleading for clemency; the response is not known, because the papers are held in military archives and not open to enquiry until 100 years after the verdict.
5. Douchet, Henri, *Péronne sous l'occupation*, Péronne, 1928
6. Pierrard, Pierre, *Histoire de Lille*, Paris, Mazarine, 1982
7. Pierrard, *Histoire de Lille*
8. *Patience*
9. *Patience*
10. de la Forge, Henry, *Feuilles françaises dans la tourmente*, Jean Mauclère, Paris, Eds. Berger Levraut, 1932
11. *Patience*
12. Wibaux, who was also actively engaged in other subversive activity, survived the war and produced several books about these and other episodes of resistance.

6

'My Girl Guides'

Women were in a minority in some resistance activities, such as the Jacquet Committee, but in most forms of anti-occupation activity—for example, the clandestine newssheets—they played an important part. Although memoirs written by women are in the minority, it seems that in general—particularly in the more prosperous or better-educated classes—women may have been able to achieve certain tricks of subterfuge that would have been impossible for men. It is sad that we do not know more about the ordinary women's lives in the war years, for as mothers, wives and housekeepers their daily lives became drastically more complicated during the occupation—the food shortages, the difficulties of feeding and clothing the children, caring for the sick and the old. Published post-war memoirs generally give us the men's voice—the few women who have left us their experiences were the exception, those who acted independently or who enjoyed social distinction. It seems likely that social status affected the occupying forces' attitude to women with whom they had official dealings, while within the household the attitude and relationships depended on the individual owners and housewives, and the soldiers or officers billetted on them. Those who took charge of their lives as far as possible, or who met the challenge of the situation calmly, seem to have been treated with greater courtesy.

What is generally unknown or forgotten is the extent of espionage and escape routes which developed in the First World War, an area in which women could operate effectively and often pass unobserved where men would come under suspicion. Among those who risked danger, Edith Cavell was the most famous activist and, eventually, victim—her name is rightly and widely remembered for her courageous resistance to the war.

When war broke out, Edith Cavell refused to leave her clinic, the Institut Berkendael, in Brussels, and sixty of her nurses remained with her. Their patients included men who had suffered industrial injury, so that a fairly constant movement of men in and out of the buildings was normal. At one time she sheltered as many as 35 escaping soldiers at once, hidden or disguised as patients, and their identity was concealed from most of her nursing staff.

Most of the fugitives were brought to the institute via the large houses just across the frontier in France, with the heavily-used escape route from Mormal forest based on the château of Bellignies as a staging post. Both the Prince and the Princesse de Croÿ, whose house this was, were recruited by Edith Cavell who knew of their hospitality and their generosity in looking after wounded men after the battle of Charleroi: her work in rescuing French and British soldiers and passing them on to free France or to England depended on them and their network, and dozens of others who contributed to their efforts at great risk to themselves and all their families.

Louise Thuliez was a teacher in Lille when the war broke out, and spent the summer of 1914 in the area between the Belgian frontier and Mormal woods; she saw the Belgian peasants as they fled from their burning villages, heading southwards with livestock and possessions. After the Battle of Charleroi (23 August 1914), the retreating British army loaded up its wounded men and left some behind 'to be collected next day'—but in the panic and confusion the remaining half-dozen men were missed out. These six men were nursed and fed, and the invading Germans left them in the women's care. In September a count was made of French and British men in local hospitals, but the six were overlooked once more and remained unnoticed and uncounted. The women in the village managed to gather enough food to feed them. By October, German notices were posted up, stating that all Allied or French soldiers still in the area must give themselves up, under pain of severe penalties for them and their protecting communes if they remained in hiding. Louise Thuliez turned to her neighbour, Prince Reginald de Croÿ, who put at her disposition an isolated house at Obies, a village a few miles away on the edge of Mormal forest: an English soldier had already been in hiding there for two months.

Once the temporary dressing station had left Bellignies château after the Battle of Charleroi, the Croÿs retained a large room for the use of clandestine temporary guests. Beds were made up, and Louise Thuliez knew where to find keys to the château so that she could let the men in when they arrived in the small hours of the morning. On one occasion, news of a German inspection arrived too late for the newly-arrived escapees to be removed from the château without risk of discovery. The emergency hiding place was a narrow corridor between a panelled ground floor room and an old defensive tower: after three hours' sleep they were hidden in the corridor, the camp beds removed and the door to the corridor concealed behind shelving full of old shoes and an untidily laden table. As they explored the château, the German inspection team passed to and fro in front of the panelling while the Princesse de Croÿ did her tapestry and her friend Louise Thuliez read her book. The visit ended and the men were released, cramped and dusty. Generally, the escape parties stayed only one night on their way through from forest to freedom, although sometimes they had to remain longer, a source of anxiety and of difficulty over providing them with food. When they departed, their route onwards took them along winding country tracks and across fields for two hours, to an empty house by the Belgian frontier whose owner allowed it to be used. The frontier was no great barrier for those who knew the smaller and quieter country roads, and on occasions the two women used children who were particularly familiar with such routes.

Many families looked after the soldiers in hiding in and around villages on all sides of Mormal: one farm sheltered more than 30 men over a three-month period without discovery, despite a few narrow escapes when searching German soldiers made their rounds of all houses. Descriptions survive of men hiding in all kinds of spaces in old farm-houses, sometimes for hours at a time, of cigarette ends left carelessly which required respectable elderly women to 'confess' to a secret passion for smoking.

Louise Thuliez' autobiography tells of large numbers of men, hiding in ones and twos or little groups, cared for by ordinary sensible people who passed them on when it was safe to move. Mlle Thuliez and her friends gathered them up, and took them via the curé of Salesches, a village near the western edge of Mormal forest. Whenever an official—i.e. German—visitor arrived to visit or search the curé's house, anyone in temporary secret residence disappeared into a special hiding place behind the altar in his church. No civilians were allowed out at night, there were therefore few late patrols—and so, paradoxically, this was the safest time to travel. Leaving an hour after the curfew began, it was possible to reach their destination by next morning.

Not all their charges were easy to care for; they might be careless of the danger to those who sheltered or guided them, or might jeopardise the security of their travelling arrangements. One, Thomas Hanley, caused great anxiety. He was part of a fairly large group which successfully crossed into Belgium—but he then broke away from the group and returned to the wandering existence in and around Mormal forest until he was arrested in 1916. Two other men—one English, one Canadian—refused to be helped to move on until they knew that the first of their group to use this route had reached safety. Once they had been persuaded, and had reached Edith Cavell's clinic in Brussels without any incident beyond the inevitable weariness and anxiety, their companions who still awaited their turn to travel to Brussels confessed that the Canadian had intended to shoot Louise Thuliez immediately if anything unexpected happened along the way.

The women were struck by the men's casual attitude to danger, both to themselves and for those who sheltered and guided them. On at least one occasion they had to take a quartet of whom three were very drunk; luckily there was no need, on this occasion, to hide in ditches or behind bushes from a passing German patrol, and the cold night and rain soon sobered them.

The system of taking men across the frontier into Belgium, to be passed on to Edith Cavell's clinic and from there to safety, extended to helping young French men, adolescents too young to have been called up to fight but who were required by the Germans to work in civilian labour gangs. Some had escaped from labour camps.

Inside Belgium, life felt different. While in France all men of military age and anyone remaining was at risk of being taken as a civilian prisoner, conscription was not obligatory in Belgium and men of all ages remained at liberty to continue their usual work. Travelling was much simpler in Belgium, since only an ordinary identity card was necessary, whereas specific travel passes were required for each journey in France. This, added to the density of the Western Front defences, made Belgium and then the Netherlands the main route for French and Allied men behind the German lines to return to freedom. Louise Thuliez speaks of hundreds of men on the move every day, using an enormous and discreet network of devoted patriots. Among the measures taken to prevent these escapes were landmine types of bomb and electrified barbed wire, as well as the usual patrols, roadblocks and police dogs and death sentences for fugitives and those who helped them.

In June 1915 Louise Thuliez heard of two French soldiers hiding in Cambrai. She acquired false identity cards for them, and took them to the civilian hospital: here she discovered that the matron, Mlle L'Hotellier, was protecting some 60 soldiers and officers, managing to feed them despite their lack of official right to food, and keeping their presence hidden from as many of her staff as possible. She continued this dangerous work until she was denounced and arrested in 1916; on arrival at the German women's prison at Siegburg she discovered many of those who had been associated with the same network.

The risks were obvious, and when the topic came up one day among those who brought in the escapers, Miss Cavell's comment was cool: 'If we are arrested, whether we have done much or little, we will be punished; let us go ahead, therefore, and liberate as many of these unfortunate men as possible'. If there were too many arrivals for her institution, the surplus was housed in friendly households prepared to accept the risk. One such friendly establishment caused a problem for the network: it was a neighbourhood bar frequented by working men and women, where well-educated women could not pass unnoticed. It was explained that she belonged to the Salvation Army and was seeking work for needy cases.

The women discovered that it would be extremely difficult to pass the men through the German lines to rejoin the Allied forces to their south, although they made contact with a group of 40 British soldiers hiding in the forest with their senior officer, Lieutenant Bushell of the Queens Bays. A failed attempt to blow up the railway nearly gave away the existence of the camp. They also made contact with a Captain Preston, who was already hiding in Bellignies château a few miles to the north. Early in November, the German army discovered the huts and hiding places of the large group in the forest, although the men themselves managed to escape—thanks to an ingenious electrical alarm that they had rigged up. They scattered throughout the area and many did not manage to find their friends again.

Louise Thuliez led some of them the twenty kilometres to Obies, where they joined the original little group, and took on the responsibility of looking after the group, bringing in food every day from the neighbourhood. The 30-odd men constructed huts close to the house and passed the time in smoking, playing cards and chatting quietly. Local families helped with food, clothing and books.

The forest was being searched systematically, and the German troops were discovering British and French soldiers in hiding. Although close to the forest, the Obies site was not actually in it, and the men hoped that the search would not reach them; but Louise insisted on careful screening of their little encampment, and took care to hide her tracks in and out. The danger increased day by day, and when the searching party reached the nearest houses it was decided that the English group must leave immediately.

They put socks or strips of carpet over their boots, to prevent noise, took up their rifles and packs, and set off in two groups to reach the château. Heavy rain protected them, and they arrived safely; beds were ready for them, and next morning the beds were folded away while the men hid within the ancient stone walls. Next day, Louise Thuliez and Mlle Moriamé, another independent-minded woman determined to save the men, walked the twenty kilometres to the Belgian frontier, and back again. They thought that they would be able to smuggle the men across the Sambre canal; the railway lines were closely guarded, following an English attack on the line near Landrecies. But when the women returned to the Croÿ château, Bellignies, they were dismayed to find that most of the men intended to give themselves up: Louise Thuliez' autobiography uses the English word 'honourable' to describe their decision, taken to avoid endangering the women who were looking after them.

Giving themselves up was in itself a dangerous undertaking if the helpful French were to be spared; first, all uniforms were checked and smartened up so that there could be no risk of being 'captured as spies', (items of British uniform left behind during the retreat from Mons were invaluable), and a route planned to Bavay which would not betray their hiding-place. The manoeuvre was successful—but unfortunately the interrogating German officers did not believe that these well-fed and tidy men had been living in the forest for three months, subjected local villages to heavy fines and took as hostage the mayor who had 'found' them and brought them in.

Meanwhile, Lt. Bushell and Capt. Preston, the officers from the original two groups located by Louise Thuliez, still remained in hiding at the Croÿs' château; their disappointment at their men's decision to submit to the Germans was balanced by the first winter snow-fall—the system of bringing in provisions, or moving secretly across country, immediately became impossible because all movements were obvious.

At the end of December, 1914, however, news reached Louise Thuliez in Brussels that a possible escape route into the Netherlands had been found, and the two officers could use it. A few days later she collected the two men and the Princesse de Croÿ's maid from the château de Bellignies and took them to Montignies-sur-Roc, a few miles away in Belgium; here, the Comtesse de Belleville and her mother helped to make up false identity papers. Next day, a tram from the little town of Dour carried the two men, the Prince de Croÿ and Louise Thuliez into Mons to catch the tram to Brussels; while waiting, they had lunch in a restaurant where, escaping British officers and French guides, they were surrounded by German officers: for the rest of his life Lieutenant Bushell recalled his emotions when he found himself sharing a table with a friendly and would-be talkative German officer. This encounter, like their passage through an inspection point, passed without incident, and a week later they reached Holland in safety. Movement was more difficult in France than in Belgium, where the curfews were less severe and trains or trams ran by night as well as by day. The false papers prepared for the fugitives were very effective, and Louise Thuliez recounts how on one occasion, travelling with a group of men on the tram journey from Mons to Brussels, she was horrified to find German officers inspecting all identity papers; fortunately although a dozen or so were taken off for irregularity in their documentation, none of her false travellers was discovered.

Now that Louise Thuliez and her friends knew of a reliable way of crossing the frontier, they set out to trace the many British and French soldiers left behind the German lines after the battle of Charleroi. Conveniently, German regulations allowed local families to go into Mormal woods to gather fuel on certain days; a farmer agreed to let his vehicles be used to bring out one or two soldiers each time from their hiding places, then to be guided along quiet tracks to Bellignies château. Eventually, a warning came from a soldier from Alsace serving in the German army that suspicions were aroused—informal talk showed that the numbers of men going into the woods did not match those leaving.[1] A young Paris artist, Schneider, was among the first to leave the forest, and drew sketches of himself being allowed over a level crossing by a

German guard.

The Princesse de Croÿ, whose mother was English and who had been educated in England, had complete confidence in Louise Thuliez and her tireless fellow-guide Mlle Moriamé. In her memoirs of the war, she describes them as her 'Girl Guides'—a nickname which sounds like a fictional nostalgic echo but which reflected genuine admiration and affection for real people sharing an all-too-real danger.

Although many people risked their lives for the escaping soldiers, the men themselves were often less than discreet and could be overhead in public discussing their movements and their route to freedom. The length of their stay in Brussels depended on the readiness of the *passeurs* to get them across the frontier into the Netherlands: the passage required nerve and courage, and, as Louise Thuliez remarks, it was sad that after the war no official honour was granted to recognise them, to match the *Medaille des Evadés* (the Escapers' Medal) for those who were successfully passed on. Some of the men who escaped through the Brussels network brought their rescuers into great danger by writing to them, expressing their enthusiastic gratitude; one such letter from England helped to convict the Princesse de Croÿ in the German courts.

By May 1915, Edith Cavell began to feel burdened by the cares of her double life, and begged for fewer fugitives to deal with. As a result, a Brussels architect, Philippe Baucq, who had already set up his own escape network, took on greater numbers even as the level of German control intensified. By the end of July 1915 it was clear that Edith Cavell was being closely watched and no more escapes could be managed by her. Louise Thuliez and the Princesse de Croÿ had already arranged the departure of two groups of mechanics and metal-workers from occupied France to help them through Belgium to freedom, and Philippe Baucq promised to arrange lodging in Brussels for the two women. Louise Thuliez reached his house, but the expected travellers did not arrive; and late in the evening a party of German soldiers arrived instead, and arrested Baucq and Mlle Thuliez.

Inevitably, after several weeks in a Brussels prison, they ended up in court, along with Edith Cavell and 33 others. The hearing in October 1915, before a military judge, was brief and centred on the systematic organisation centred round Edith Cavell; defending lawyers were appointed for the accused but were not allowed to meet them—their part in the trial was simply to see that court regulations were followed.

As the trial was conducted in German and not translated into French, the accused had little idea of the proceedings; and as they were held in isolation, and conducted to and from the court in a police wagon with individual cells, it was impossible for them to discuss their circumstances together.

The prosecuting lawyers demanded the death sentence for eight of the accused; in the event, 17 of the group were condemned to forced labour or prison for between two and eight years, the Princesse de Croÿ to ten years' hard labour, four defendants to fifteen years—and five were condemned to death, including the architect Baucq, Edith Cavell, and Louise Thuliez. Louise asked Edith Cavell whether she would appeal: 'No,' she replied, 'it is pointless. I am English, there is nothing to be done!'

Louise Thuliez and Jeanne de Belleville—also condemned to death—did appeal, and were allowed to share a cell, a great source of comfort to them in the month which elapsed until the result of their appeal; but Edith Cavell and Philippe Baucq were held in isolation and executed the morning after the verdict.

The international outcry was loud and prolonged, particularly when it was known that the execution had taken place after less than the minimum 48 hours' respite specified under German law. There were severe recriminations from the United States' ambassador, Brand Whitlock, who acted on behalf of British citizens in Belgium, and Edith Cavell's final expression of her faith and determination became universally known:

> I feel no fear nor apprehension; I have seen death so often that I do not find it strange or terrible. … In the face of God and Eternity, I realise that patriotism is not enough. I must have no hatred, no bitterness against anyone.[2]

In preparation for her execution, she pinned a small Union Jack over her heart.

Philippe Baucq was allowed to see his wife before his execution—provided that he hid his imminent death from her. He spoke to her of being sent to prison in Germany.

The other three people condemned to death waited sadly and quietly in prison. The Spanish ambassador, responsible for French interests in Belgium, protested on behalf of the Comtesse de Belleville—until, some time later, Louise Thuliez' French nationality was reported to him by her sister and he made loud protestations on her behalf and for the German concealment of the fact that she was French. He arranged for the King of Spain to intervene on their behalf, an action without precedent; the arguments raged to and fro between the Spanish representative (the Marquis de Villalobar, who was heavily embroiled in the difficulties of food supplies) and the German representatives. The Pope also intervened with the Kaiser on their behalf and the French ambassador to the United States persuaded Wilson, the American President, to plead with the Kaiser too.

The result was that the remaining death sentences were commuted to hard labour for life, and the women were sent to Siegburg prison in Germany—where, a few months later, they were joined by Louise de Bettignies, similarly condemned to life imprisonment after an initial death sentence.

Louise Thuliez' description of life in prison is spirited, and reveals her strength of character and endurance. The long hours of darkness—with a lamp allowed in the cell for only one hour each evening—meant that all the prisoners suffered long dark periods alone, without occupation or distraction; during winter months the scanty evening 'meal' had to be dealt with by groping in the darkness once the cell door was closed. The conditions and staff were harsh, the food grossly inadequate, and Louise Thuliez remarks that women without education or inner resources suffered particularly cruelly.

Her account of her three years in prison tells of many deaths; and she remarks that she could well understand how long imprisonment, with each prisoner isolated during the tedious hours when they were not in the workshop, could lead to a future of anarchism and bitterness.

In prison, their only source of war news was, naturally, what they saw in the two French-language *Gazettes*, designed to depress and demoralise French people in all the occupied zones. A typical news item stated that the French had handed over the city of Calais to the British.

She found solace in doing her piles of sewing—her forced labour—as badly as possible, sewing buttons on to military tunics so that they would come off almost immediately. While the women worked at their stitching, they were able to talk and she discovered the wide range of society that they represented. Several nuns were imprisoned, one for having helped the men shot in Lille (Maertens, Verhulst, Deconinck and

Jacquet) and another for having hidden soldiers and helped them onwards to freedom. In some cases several members of a family were there, one woman with two daughters, another with four; and ages ranged from 15 to 70. This was where she met Marguerite Nollet, condemned for her collaboration on the secret newspaper *L'Oiseau de France*.

This 'community of misery', as her autobiography calls it, created bonds which survived into the years of peace and led to regular meetings of the 'Siegburg women' in Brussels. A number of the women were recognised with gratitude after the war by French and British soldiers who escaped.

Another of the leading figures in this resistance world was as distinctive in her field of action as Edith Cavell was in hers. Born in 1880, Louise de Bettignies was an active, determined and independent-minded woman from a Lille manufacturing family, whose cosmopolitan education included a period in Oxford and considerable foreign travel. Sporting and energetic by nature, she also spoke English and German very fluently. Although by 1914 she was seeking spiritual guidance and considering entering a Carmelite convent, the war offered her a different sense of vocation. She escaped from the occupied city to Holland, then crossed to England. In Folkestone she was interviewed by the British military Intelligence Service, who were taking advantage of the arrival of thousands of Belgian refugees to select people who might be able to help them. She described being under attack in Lille, and how she had helped the wife of the British consul to escape. When one of her English listeners commented on her good fortune and boldness, she remarked that her refusal to accept discouragement was a great advantage.

Her competence and independence impressed the British officers, who asked whether she was prepared to help the war effort: she would not be required to bring over information herself, but to establish contacts across the Lille region—to set up a network of observers. She agreed to cooperate, to collate the information and send it on to England.

In February 1915 she reached Philippine, the last village in the Netherlands before the Belgian frontier, found a guide, and slipped beneath the wire barrier that same night and made her way back to Lille. Depending on her wits and a disciplined pattern of life, she set up her network of informers who supplied her with news, or who were smuggled through to the Netherlands. Her *nom de guerre* was 'Alice Dubois', and her chief aide was 'Charlotte', Marie-Léonie Van Houtte, from Roubaix. 'Charlotte', her brothers and three others travelled secretly to Holland, where she set about establishing a network of Belgian hoteliers who helped with the escape route. An important link in the route consisted of crossing the railway line as the German sentries relieved each other and the way back into Belgium led through a house backing onto the frontier, where the roof of a low pig-sty provided a launching point for a leap across into the beleaguered and occupied country.

The two young women travelled throughout the occupied region, recruiting observers and messengers. They adopted various false identities: 'Alice' was a cheese merchant, a teacher or a sewing maid, while 'Charlotte' was a lace-seller or dress-maker. Louise, always smartly but plainly dressed, was skilled at flirting with patrols and guards. It would be interesting to know how much her more educated style and manners helped her cause.

'Alice Dubois' contacted more important and prosperous men and women, with the leisure and means to move around the German-occupied zone a little, even in wartime conditions. Information would be gathered in their rural estates or in Lille itself, with market days used as convenient occasions to pass on verbal or written notes. The location of artillery batteries, the scale and contents of supplies of ammunition, or information about troops culled from staff officers in the city—all such scraps of detail were gathered and passed on.

The information was written out carefully, on the finest paper available, to create tiny documents that could only be read with a magnifying glass. Copies were despatched by more than one messenger, to make sure that the information passed through successfully, and the hiding places used make the enterprise sound like children's adventure stories: slips of paper would be hidden in umbrellas, skirt-hems, under the candles in vehicle lamps, in suitcase handles, round corset whale-bones, even in an elaborate hair-style. Concealing letters in the heels of shoes soon had to be given up, as this was a well-known hiding place. Another method of passing information was for two of the women to sit together on a tram or train and say their rosaries—but passing information instead of repeating their prayers.

Monsieur Lenfant, the senior police officer in Tourcoing, joined forces with a substantial industrialist, Louis Sion, whose son became responsible for passing letters in Tourcoing and on into Belgium, to Ghent and Brussels. The records show that the information network was built up on lines that have become familiar to modern spy story readers: messengers and safe houses were chosen with care, and none of the agents knew who directed the system. At frontier crossings, distractions were set up: children squabbled or an apparently unconnected traveller delayed the sentries in a lengthy search for a mislaid passport. Louise de Bettignies was adept at travelling with a large number of packages which she would helpfully untie and unwrap herself, chattering and gossiping cheerfully with the sentries. Dangerous documents were concealed in false-bottomed cake boxes, with the cakes set carefully in place.

'Louise de Bettignies'

Major railway junctions- were of great importance. In Roubaix the 'Service Alice' and the German police were both in constant attendance; but when the police called at the railway loading yard they were not concerned with the woman who sat by her window, perpetually knitting with the window wide open to gain the best light. They were not aware of her heel tapping on the floor, heard and recorded by her sons sitting at their books below, in a code which recorded the number and type of railway wagons that passed after loading. Some of these activists continued their work throughout the war, such as Madeleine Doutreligne, who established an information network based on railway level-crossing keepers. They observed and reported on trains and their contents; in April and May 1918 the Allies were kept informed of their numbers and loads, and the wounded men who were transported by the Germans from Mont Kemmel. This was added to the knowledge of the divisions engaged provided through Louise de Bettignies, so that the active enemy

149

strength could be calculated. As the German trains passed, French eyes watched and counted. None of these railwaymen betrayed their leaders.

Elsewhere, postmen were enlisted; one, feeling aggrieved, betrayed a number of secret workers, including two in the 'Service Alice'. Fortunately, the system of ensuring that agents knew as few as possible of their fellow workers prevented a major disaster.

In Lille the service operated an information bureau for those who wished to return to free France. Louise de Bettignies herself took only two escapers, one of whom, Captain Marguerie, had evaded capture after the occupation of Douai and had acquired civilian clothes. Hiding in the Lille Art School—which was occupied by Germans—he wore a cleaner's uniform and swept the stairs, working until the next trip which took place in the guise of joining a major pilgrimage. Dressed as country people, the captain and his companions were smuggled through the customs post by sympathisers, collected false passports and travelled on to the Netherlands.

The danger of *agents provocateurs* was inevitable, and considerable alertness was required to avoid discovery. The German police force released a few carefully-chosen civilian prisoners who were prepared to betray their fellow Frenchmen; among their successes was the betrayal of the network leading to Edith Cavell in Brussels.

Two different means of identification were needed: an identity card, which had to be carried at all times by everyone living in the occupied area, and a passport to travel from one town to another. 'Alice' had several sets of papers in order to move easily between Lille, Mouscron, Ghent, Tournai and Brussels. A specialised household developed which was expert in creating the necessary papers: identity cards, passports, documents from judicial files, stamped and initialled, with photographs certified by the Commandantur.

It seems that 'Alice' crossed into the Netherlands between 15 and 20 times, evading sentries who had orders to shoot, particularly at night, electrified wires at ground level, and other traps. Her destination was Flushing, where she contacted the British representative, M. Courboin, handed over her messages and received instructions. Four or five trips to Folkestone have been recorded, although she never visited London; twice she travelled to free France. The official British records show that her work achieved more than any other information system throughout the war, in terms of the amount and quality of material.

In August 1915, under pressure from Major Cameron, in Folkestone—'Uncle Edward'—she agreed to extend her network further to the south-east. She was also in contact with Abbé Pinte in Roubaix, whose invaluable radio receiver brought news from all the belligerent nations into the occupied zone. He agreed to transmit and receive telegrams in code from the British secret staff. Little record survives of these transactions, apart from the directional coordinates required for an English aircraft to drop homing pigeons in an aluminium cage, for information to be flown back.

Louise de Bettignies and her network were finally captured in September 1915 when she tried to bluff her way through a sentry-post without a passport. They were tried in March 1916; Léonie Van Houtte ('Charlotte') received a sentence of fifteen years' forced labour and Louise herself was condemned to death. The sentence was commuted to life imprisonment and she was sent off to Siegburg women's prison in Germany; in the harsh conditions there (cold damp cells, heavy work, frequent solitary confinement, semi-starvation, lack of medical care), she died in September 1918, probably of cancer. But she was in the company of other French women there, including Madeleine Doutreligne and Louise Thuliez, who had helped escaping soldiers to find their way out of the occupied zone, and Marguerite Nollet, of the radio receiver and newspaper production network.

Correspondence in prison was heavily censored, and Louise Thuliez writes of the women's frustration and rage at finding details of family news heavily blacked out; but they managed to establish a code whereby news could be passed through the prison from those in free France to those in the occupied areas and back again—since direct correspondence between the two communities was impossible. When any of the women came to the end of her sentence, or was granted an early release, letters were sewn into her clothes or hidden between the layers of cardboard boxes in which they took their possessions. Louise Thuliez used this method to smuggle out copies of a complaint about munitions work required of the women prisoners, and about Louise de Bettignies' treatment in prison. Their official 'ration' for letter-writing was limited to two sheets of writing paper and four cards each month—always sent, but rarely received. Similarly, in order to receive the two parcels allowed each month, families had to send off many more to allow for disappearances en route. Food formed the main item in the packages, and was generally looted so that the prisoners received little or none of their families' contributions; the women were relieved when they were added to the list of 'prisoners of war' and became entitled to a ration of two kilos of biscuits each week. This was particularly welcome for the younger women, for the adolescents among them were suffering from malnutrition, and women with babies needed the extra food so that they could breast-feed and nourish their children properly.

Two of the young prisoners were given work to do which aroused suspicions: small steel caps were to be trimmed with a thin layer of aluminium, with an instructor coming into the prison specially to show how the work was to be done. The older women recognised the pieces of metal as part of a grenade. Louise de Bettignies and Louise Thuliez advised the girls to refuse the work, and the former, when named as the source of resistance, was punished with isolation and reduced food supplies. News spread through the prison and another woman, Marguerite Blankaert, decided to make a more public protest.

She chose the end of their chapel service: the chapel was arranged so that each prisoner had her own 'compartment' with seats boxed off from each other along the pews, so that the women could see the altar and the priest but not each other. The arrangement also meant that, once inside her box, each woman was out of reach from the end of the row. At the end of the Mass, Marguerite Blankaert stood on her seat and addressed the company: 'I beg you not to undertake the work required of you: it has a military purpose and you have no right to work against your brothers …' The women guards tried to stop her, but the prisoners kept the doors to their own boxes tight shut, pushing their feet against them, until she finished. She was put into a punishment cell, and the metal pieces continued to be presented for work. Louise Thuliez insisted, with some difficulty, in writing and sending an official protest to the Minister of the Interior in Berlin, while the Princesse de Croÿ wrote to the prison director and the Comtesse de Belleville to the Spanish ambassador. The work stopped, and Marguerite Blankaert and Louise de Bettignies, already suffering from the illness that was to kill her, were returned to normal prison life.

After the war Louise de Bettignies's body was returned to her family through French governmental intervention. On 20 February 1920 she was buried with full military honours; she was awarded the Médaille de Guerre, the Croix de Guerre and the Croix de la Légion d'Honneur by the French government, and the Order of the British Empire by the grateful British government.

Louise de Bettignies has a memorial in an unexpected and otherwise severely masculine setting; among the many private and official memorials to individual men or military units in the French memorial chapel of Notre Dame de Lorette (visible from the modern motorway from Calais towards Arras), a large display cabinet shows her as a youngish woman with thick brown hair piled up on her head, and a determined expression. The wooden cross with German lettering, from her original grave, looms over assorted documents and a list of her achievements.

The list states that the British awarded her the Military Cross. This is inaccurate; but there is a file on her in the Public Record Office which shows how highly her services were valued, confirming that she was awarded the Order of the British Empire (instituted in 1917). In November 1915 General Sir William Robertson wrote from his staff office in the field as Chief of the General Staff to General Huguet, Head of the French Military Mission:

> ... This young lady ... has crossed the Dutch-Belgian frontier many times, bringing information of great value, thus risking her life on several occasions. Neither asking nor accepting any reward, she organised and directed an extensive and most efficient service of intelligence in the Lille-Roubaix area, sending complete records of all troop movements for many months past, and by her ability, courage and devotion surmounting all the obstacles inseparable from such an undertaking. ... The difficulties which awaited her are shown ... as also the unflinching courage with which she was prepared not only to face them but to accept added responsibilities animated purely by feelings of the loftiest patriotism. I regret to say that she has been arrested recently by the Germans. What the evidence is against her I cannot at present say, but it seems possible that she may make the supreme sacrifice for her country.[3]

The rest of the file shows the exchange of letters between British military and civil departments and French officials three years later, beginning in October 1918.

The British Army wished to award her the O.B.E. - but she had died in September 1918, and this award could not be granted posthumously.

It was therefore necessary to establish the date of death (not simple, since the war was only just coming to an end, and the information was held in Siegburg Prison), and then to announce an earlier date for the award, under the Foreign Decorations Section of the Orders of Knighthood. A minute from Military Intelligence stated:

> I cannot speak too highly of the bravery, devotion and patriotism of this young lady. Her services to the British Intelligence ... were simply invaluable. She sent us much information from Lille and Tournai and braved the greatest dangers...⁴

The same minute makes it clear that O.B.E. awards were available for immediate reward to Allies, for secret services; no names were to be reported and the lists of awards would not be sent to the Foreign Office until after the war.

After some debate about the mechanics of avoiding duplication and confusion between various departments and their awards, the Order of the British Empire (4th class) for a French civilian was despatched 'under an arrangement known to the Foreign Office and approved by the King'. It was to be presented to Madame de Bettignies for her daughter.

A further difficulty arose: the Central Chancery of the Orders of Knighthood pointed out that 'Your request was one O.B.E. Badge for a French Civilian, consequently we sent you a Badge for a gentleman. The ladies' O.B.E. Badge is suspended from a bow.' It was supposed that 'in the circumstances' (in other words, because the recipient was already dead) it was unnecessary to change the insignia.

Sir Douglas Haig had intended to present the award himself to Madame de Bettignies; but she fell dangerously ill, and to save further delay it was presented by a senior member of the General Staff in France, as reported in a note dated 1919. The King's office sent a warmly worded letter to Madame de Bettignies, expressing great sympathy and appreciation, and acknowledging her daughter's valuable services to the Allied cause.

Ironically, we know much more of the discussion about this award, and the arrangements to present it to the heroine's mother, than about the precise information that won her the decoration.

The end of the war, foreseen for some weeks, was in the end a sudden and unexpected moment for the prisoners, who were despatched unceremoniously to freedom. Told of their imminent release and departure, the women scrambled to retrieve their civilian clothing and possessions, and all 600 of the French and Belgian women in Siegburg were despatched by train. Despite the revolution in progress in Germany, they found the outside world calm, and were escorted back to Louvain which they reached on 10 November.

Among those whose names did not become known outside their own circle is Marie Polvent, of Ors, the village east of Le Cateau better known to English readers for the death of the poet Wilfred Owen in the Allied attempt to cross the Sambre-Oise canal in November 1918. Marie Polvent was a farmer's daughter, part of the intensely active household which made up a prosperous and efficient dairy and arable farm before the First World War. Intelligent and educated, and unable to pursue her chosen career of secondary-school teaching because she was needed at home, Marie spent her life in Ors. When the Germans arrived in 1914 she continued to keep a diary, even when the house was crowded with refugees and with German soldiers and officers who were billeted on the family. The family had to give up their better rooms to the occupying officers, and Marie used a small room under the eaves. Here she slipped her notebooks into the rafters, where they remained undiscovered and survived the war and the damage caused by shelling and bombs in the final days of the war. Marie's description of the day-to-day activities of the farm and the village brings the individuals to life and shows more clearly than any official history how difficult and wearisome the occupation became.

By mid-1916, Ors was recording the same kind of experiences as every other occupied town and village. None of the inhabitants was prepared to work voluntarily for the Germans, and numbers of men escaped from labour camps and hid, fed with difficulty by their families or friends who could draw no C.R.B. rations for them. In the autumn of that year 78 men were taken to work on the Hindenburg Line, leaving very few to work the village farms. When, two days before Christmas 1916, Marie Polvent's brother Alcide was demanded for a labour gang, he hid in a silo of sugar-beet in their barn; Marie was taken in his place, and put in prison. Considerable numbers of men were in hiding by then—one lived more or less underground, in a hole in a field on the outskirts of the village. He and a friend killed cattle in the fields. Another young village man spent long periods hiding in a well

Ors is not far from the forest of Mormal, and lay within the area covered by Louise Thuliez' rescue network: and not far from Ors, at Le Favril, Jeanne Contesse, a young mother whose husband was captured early in the war, hid three Irish soldiers in November 1914 before passing them on to Belgium. In prison after refusing to pay a fine at a later date, she was horrified at the wretched condition of the 600 civilian prisoners—particularly the Russians—held in the establishment that she was sent to, inside the military barracks at Landrecies; on her release she gained permission to bring them food, clothing and shoes. To the German commandant's surprise and displeasure, she arrived outside the prison at the end of April 1916 with two large wagons, piled with 600 items of clothing and personal linen. Such efforts were forbidden in future. Undismayed, however, she took in three French soldiers later in the year and hid them for three months before they could move on to the Netherlands. Two other local men joined them, and all five were able to gain their freedom and join the French army. She also passed on important information about enemy movements, until she escaped to Switzerland in the summer of 1917.

In Ors, Marie Polvent's brother François, a priest, was active in many ways. In August 1915 he led a young man out of Ors to join Louise Thuliez' network, on their way to Belgium and to Edith Cavell: betrayed at the frontier, captured and sent to a civilian prison camp in Germany the enterprising young man doctored a urine sample with fruit juice, was diagnosed as having severe diabetes, and was sent to Switzerland.

Meanwhile, Abbé Polvent began smuggling letters in and out of prison while on pastoral visits. This was discovered, and stopped; but he was able to continue reporting maltreatment to the Red Cross, and when one of Edith Cavell's organising network realised that he was about to be arrested, he was able to pass on his portable radio transmitter and secret code to the priest. This was the origin of his fishing expeditions which he used as cover for his radio transmissions to the British army, and continued to take food to civilian prisoners and pass on escaping soldiers to freedom. The active resistance work undertaken by Louise de Bettignies and Léonie Van Houtte, like that of many other secret activists, lasted only a few months—although it must have felt a great deal longer at the time. After 1915 most organised resistance diminished, with only the clandestine newspapers continuing in one form or another. Other forms of defiance consisted of individual attitudes and actions. After the war, some victims' families received compensation, with 500 francs going to each of the Jacquet, Trulin, de Bettignies and Maertens families, and to Verhulst's companion Madame Ployart.

Notes

1. Mormal forest seems to have been full of unexpected temporary residents: before all the trees disappeared into saw-mills, a circus elephant was used there for hauling timber.
2. Whitlock, Brand, *Belgium under the German Occupation*, (2 vols.), London, Heinemann, 1919
3. PRO WO32/S406 2718
4. PRO WO32/S406 2718

7

'The Will of the German Authority'

Of all aspects of the occupation, the world of work was perhaps where the two cultures confronted each other most sharply in terms of each community as an identifiable social entity. Perceptions outside the domestic circle were based firmly on normal peace-time habits, income and social standing. The personal accounts that survived into post-war publication record the reactions, in general, of the middle classes - people with a reasonably comfortable life (or better), a good education, and the independence that came from an assured commercial, professional or *rentier* life. This applied particularly to the women who kept the diaries drawn on here; however hard they worked for their families and households, they were supported by the social structure of the day and were not familiar with life in a factory or as a domestic servant. Hierarchies of respect and order were recognised even where they were resented: more than three-quarters of a century later, the great gulf separating 'us' from 'them' represents more than merely the passage of time. The occupation created two kinds of confrontation: between the German forces and the French civilians, and also between different classes in French life who found their normal social relationships distorted. People who were accustomed to being in charge of their lives, and of other people, did not take kindly to a subordinate situation and forced work.

The system for managing labour developed quietly but inescapably. First came administrative instructions for specific tasks to be carried out locally, then military orders of a more general nature. Typical of these was the instruction as early as 29 October 1914 at La Fère, directing that 'all men capable of working should work in the fields' while a month later another district instructed the population of Sissonne that 'all men who are not working in the fields and who have no other full-time work will be sent to labour gangs and will be obliged to work there'. An order in Valenciennes stated that all men between 17 and 55 were subject to military service, i.e. army-directed labour.

Manpower was an important commodity, to be controlled and directed by the German administrators. A pocket-book left behind by mistake in La Capelle by a German administrative officer at the end of the war gives an inventory of inhabitants similar to a list of livestock. It shows the nine communes in his district, with separate columns listing the men and women fit for work, children, and men and women who were not fit for work, and he carried it with him at all times as an aide-mémoire of his human resources.

In October 1914, workers were recruited in Lille, to receive board and lodging plus 1.50 francs per day (a skilled worker would expect around 8-10 francs per day in 1913). Men were needed for digging trenches; the notice attracted very few volunteers. Two years later, in November 1916, it was the unemployed who were sought for all kinds of construction and factory skills: blacksmiths, metal-workers, locksmiths, turners, electricians, tool-makers, etc.

French mayors refused to produce lists of men who were out of work, but from the age of 14 each inhabitant was required to carry an identity card validated by the mayor's office. By the beginning of 1917, all French men between the ages of 16 and 45 were required to work, and six months later the ordinance was extended—all men, of any nation (French, Belgian, Russian, British, Italian, Rumanian or American) between the ages of 14 and 17, and 52 and 61, were added to the roster.

In Saint Quentin, a large centre at the headquarters of an administrative District and a distribution centre for C.R.B. food, Elie Fleury as editor of the *Journal de St.-Quentin*, was making the notes which he later turned into his published account of the war. When the occupation began, boys and a few old men were directed to help in cleaning up troop billets—a simple measure of public hygiene. By mid-November 1914 these human requisitions had proliferated as the German *Étape* administrative system was established. Notices appeared, demanding a specific number of men at a specific place and time, and in January 1915 the tasks for this civilian labour force expanded. A vast construction site developed on the edge of the town, with a civilian prison camp with its own laundry, saw-mill, etc. Carpenters built sheds, and mechanics, metal-workers and blacksmiths were busy in the electric tram factory. In February the first orders came in for French workmen to make barbed wire entanglements, man-traps, iron-clad truncheons, etc. Men who resisted were directed to other labour.

Grain brought in from the surrounding farms was stored in large warehouses, and stocks of cotton thread and fabric was cleared from local factories; other manufacturers and traders saw their stocks of starch, or iron, or old clothing and rags, requisitioned, while there was a constant search for wine. The great textile mill was cleared, and turned into a convalescent and disinfection establishment, in April the fine linen works was stripped and in May mechanical engineering workshops were invaded, all their supplies broken or thrown out to make room for ambulance vehicles with a maintenance workshop near by. The German engineer who was promoted from the ranks to take charge was nick-named *Le Roi des Pilleurs* ('The King Pillager') for his success in stripping other people's workshops and making use of their tools. French workers were appointed to work in all these establishments, and a day missing meant three days in prison. The wages, paid by the city, were two or three francs per day, depending on ability, and the German civilian supervisor ruled with blows and threats of his revolver.

The women worked too; the military laundry employed 200 women (as well as 30 men), and in season the preparation and drying of apples occupied at least a thousand women for two months, paid 30 centimes per day. German officers made sure that French women who were prepared to sleep with them were appointed to this lighter work.

Elie Fleury calculated after the war that in October 1915 the occupying forces in Saint Quentin were managing 91 establishments employing 875 men and 1,079 women in a wide range of work. In June 1915 he saw a trainload of local citizens returning home. There were 460 of them, civilian prisoners brought back because of illness, reaching the end of their prison sentence, benefiting from official intervention, or simply displaced persons caught up in the war away from home. As a journalist he questioned them; he quotes Henri Leblay, a mechanic by trade before the war, who had been working at the municipal poor-house; when, ill-advised, he responded to a German notice in November 1914 which was intended for members of the French armed forces, he found himself despatched to Wetzler camp in Germany with a group of French soldiers and civilians. Forty-two men were crowded into a cattle-wagon, without food or a latrine bucket for their thirty-six hour journey. Life in the German camp for these conquered civilians and soldiers was harsh, as Fleury reported later:

> The camp was enormous. They were searched, and all smoking materials, knives and money taken from them. Living quarters consisted of bare board barracks each holding 200 hundred men, with a bag of wood-shavings each to sleep on.
>
> They were woken at 5 a.m., given a mug of coffee, and a 4 lb loaf of bread per 10 men, per day; at 10 a.m. and 6 p.m., a broth of barley, flour, beans, oats, turnips, a little bread—a scattering of these ingredients in water with occasional potatoes and often drowned mice. Once a week the soup was replaced by macaroni, boiled without salt, or a little salt herring. On Sunday the soup had rice in it with a few dried prunes, grapes or apples.
>
> Anyone who reported sick was punished by four days in prison before a medical examination. The work consisted of stone-breaking for roads, including the deep muddy tracks in the camp. Punishment, for the slightest misdemeanour, was always the same: no food for a day, blows and kicks. Industrialists asked for labour from the camp, and at first, no doubt hoping for better food, volunteers came forward; they received a wage with which to buy food but were so ill-treated by other workers or local people that they asked to return to the camp; where they were punished 'for laziness' with two weeks in prison.
>
> On one occasion a group of officers visited the camp, handed out a cigarette to each man and set them at a table with (empty) bottles and glasses. They were photographed, for propaganda purposes, then kicked back to their barracks without the cigarettes.
>
> When prisoners were moved to another camp in Germany, local citizens were warned, and the French civilians were greeted by hostile and jeering crowds.[1]

Inevitably, it was the worst features that were most widely reported and remembered later, and not everyone had such gloomy memories. Some were luckier, like the Saint Quentin lawyer who on his return, while still held by the Germans, not far from home, managed to pass a letter to his family. Life in Holzminden camp, he said, was not too bad—

the camp was run by the French themselves under German supervision. The worst feature, he said, was boredom and the separation from his family.

Perhaps he was reassuring his family; most of the 460 civilian prisoners who returned, aged between 15 and 50, had a different experience. They had not been convicted of any crime, but their ragged clothing was striped with red paint, they had not been able to wash for months, had lost all human dignity. Some were released in Saint Quentin, and given food and fresh clothing by a committee of local citizens, but others were sent on to camps in Ham, Bapaume or Roye to work on roads. They were to be maintained by the local population, for Germany wanted to reduce its civilian prison-camp numbers.

When Commandant Schöttl in Cambrai was refused a list of the unemployed by the mayor, he issued an order for all men to be rounded up; inevitably, many went into hiding, particularly the younger men. Protests were met with a disclaimer—'It is all the mayor's fault; who will go in your place?' Anyone picked up in the street without good reason for being there was held with others, until there were enough (500 or 1,000 men) to form a convoy. The round-ups brought in civil servants, the professional classes, fathers responsible for large families. The German commandants put the blame on the French authorities.

It was a feature of this group, forced into the work, that the men wore a red armband with the initials Z A B - *zivil arbeiter* (or *zwangarbeiter*) *bataillone*, civilian labour or forced labour battalion. The hours were generally from 7 a.m. - 6 p.m. with a two-hour mid-day break. In the autumn of 1916 the system was extended so that the gangs could expect to be sent anywhere in the occupied zone; and they were required to help in case of emergency or public disaster, with fines imposed in case of refusal.

The conditions and pay offered to volunteers were good - free lodging and clothing, and skilled workers earned a minimum of 5 francs per day, with eight francs per day for specialist workers on heavy, or especially dangerous work (it is not clear whether the danger was inherent in the type of work or whether it was a consequence of the war conditions). Another 0.50 francs per day was paid to foremen. Women received 5 and 3.50 francs for skilled and unskilled work respectively. Workers were charged for board and lodging, although free medical treatment was officially available. In March 1917 workers in Roubaix were tempted with offers of better wages and lodgings, and 'encouraged' with threats of forced employment if they did not volunteer. In the same month a demand for boatmen on the Lille canal was recorded, offering 'good pay'. Lille was short of workers, and pay of up to 9 francs per day was noted for labouring work or the dazzling sum of 11 francs per day for skilled men.

Their contribution to the enemy war effort was recorded in many places, but always in small numbers: forced labour was the inevitable answer to the German need for workers. Post-war memoir-writers commented that those who accepted the offers were generally from the least desirable part of the population, almost all of them 'trainards', idlers, or 'mauvais sujets', unreliable or shifty types, 'whose trade was to do nothing respectable'.

When forced labour gangs became inevitable—because of insufficient volunteers—some men came forward before they could be drafted so that they might have some small choice over what they might be required to do. Many young people were sent to 'discipline battalions'. There were official denials, but public statements actually indicated the possibility:

Cambrai, 28 November 1914

The government of Lille needs workers for undertaking fortification work. The male population capable of bearing arms must be ready to be sent to Germany if there are insufficient numbers of workers. The commune of ..... must inform the Cambrai commandanture how many workers will be available for this work. Signed, Schöttl, Cambrai Etappen Commandant

In the winter of 1916-17, the German decision to shorten the front line by withdrawing troops to a new fortified line had considerable implications for residents in the occupied territories. This new Siegfried Line, known to the Allies as the Hindenburg Line, was to be defensive, and immensely strong; it occupied the greatest single body of forced labour gangs, with men of all backgrounds, students, shopkeepers and professional men as well as experienced manual workers from over five hundred French communities. Once more, those who refused to undertake this military labour were imprisoned, sometimes in cellars, on bread and water—although in Cambrai they were simply left without food until they agreed to work on the intensive construction of defences and fortification of the villages; the Germans denied putting pressure on the French civilians and stated that 'only volunteers' were used. The men were set to work on various heavy tasks: digging trenches, mining, building shelters and blockhouses, new communication trenches, gun emplacements, munitions depots, light railways.

Throughout the occupied region, work could be divided into four groups: for the commune; in factories (or demolishing them) under German control; agricultural labour; and civilian prisoners, the *brassards rouges*, directed to any task regardless of danger or international convention.

Names and ages were recorded from the beginning of the occupation and wages were be paid in 'bons' with a face value representing no genuine funds. It was therefore simple and cheap to call up local men who were not absent in the French army and form them into labour gangs. There were two categories of civilian workers: work contrary to the Hague Convention, and work in line with international agreement. The former was the fate of the recalcitrant and those who only accepted forced labour under fierce constraint, the '*brassards rouges*', (referring to their red armbands).

As the war continued, boys who were initially too young to be used in this way could also be added to the labour force as they reached adulthood. The potential labour-force was reviewed regularly, by categories in large centres or as a whole in smaller communities. In Douai in 1916 all the men between 17 and 60 were summoned to parade together, and 4,000 men appeared. Cambrai had monthly parades of men between 17 and 50, while in the villages all men were summoned each month and sometimes the whole population. At first these general summons applied every week, then fortnightly, later monthly or at two-monthly intervals.

Local work began with specific tasks such as street cleaning, unloading goods, setting up road barriers or cleaning and decorating offices for the German authorities to use. Soon, however, it changed in nature and became a permanent obligation. In some cases Russian prisoners were replaced by local inhabitants, in others the work imposed was railway and road maintenance or construction. It was heavy work and when the men were worn out—because they were poorly fed and housed—they were sent home and replaced by others. When any individual failed to appear as demanded, a replacement was taken at random; or, as happened with bakers, if a specialist trade was required to work for the authorities, the skilled workman was replaced by any local inhabitant, with or without experience. Cambrai had insufficient unemployed men to supply the labour required; each man had to bring his identity card to the weekly roll-call with a card from his employer if he was in work. Anyone without a card was allocated to a labour gang for land clearing, road or railway work, woodcutting or engineering workshops repairing guns and other weaponry.

By its nature, farm work could not be kept waiting, and workers must be found whether or not they knew what to do. Resistance was firmly repressed. Roubaix, in the industrial north, records frequent resistance when labour was imposed, with fines and imprisonment the consequence for any gathering of more than five people near factories. When the whole population of a village tried to resist forced labour, 80 men were put in prison, and when their wives tried to force their way in to release them, they too were imprisoned. All areas seem to have experienced some form of resistance, and many men spent some time in prison. In the villages everyone between the ages of 16 and 60 worked in the fields, except those with a trade or profession which was directly useful to the German authorities; when necessary, particularly at harvest time, the age limits were extended in both directions, and sometimes everyone in the area capable of working, including tradesmen skilled at other crafts, had to turn out to the fields. The work was supervised by German guards, and grain threshed as soon as it was brought in.

In the towns, the labourers operated in teams, directed to tasks as the need arose. In Masny, in the coalfields, a hundred miners continued to bring out the coal while all other men were sent out to the fields and in Raismes, near Valenciennes, most of the men were directed to tree-felling in the surrounding woodlands, as the German soldiers who had begun the work were replaced by French civilians.

In Valenciennes the town council was required to supply cleaning squads; the constant movement of troops left barracks and billets in very dirty conditions. In 1915 the Germans set up squads of workers to be used on railway construction, with direct recruitment via round-ups of youths who were 15 or 16 in 1914 and were taken into the squads as they reached the age of 17 or 18. Men arrested in Valenciennes were sent to Solesmes to work on railway construction, to Maipent to a supply depot, to Locquignol, to work in a sawmill and timber works. Young men were brought into Valenciennes from Saint Quentin and the Aisne, and set to work in vehicle repair shops, making beds and coffins, factory demolition, or removing material after demolition or war-damage. In 1916, workshops were requisitioned which had imagined that their machinery was safe, and German soldiers were installed with forced-labour French gangs.

Women's Work

Although most men were forced to work for their enemy occupants for at least part of the war, many others were of course absent in 'Free France', having joined their military units before the invasion turned into occupation. All the women remained, however, and they too were required to contribute their labour. At first they were set to work locally, after individual call-up, but gradually the system was extended and they were sent to work away from home under general mobilisation orders. Some women volunteered early in the war; in Denain a group agreed to make sandbags for the trenches, although others denounced them for this unpatriotic effort. The German staff, administrative and military, needed many women to undertake all kinds of domestic work - cleaning, washing, cooking, sewing, etc., to sort the wool from requisitioned mattresses, or for farm work. Demands were sent to the mayor, who allocated the tasks. Women who worked on the land were paid 3.50 francs for a ten hour day, with overtime rates of 45 centimes per hour, and five days' leave with free travel after eight weeks' work. They were offered free lodging and good food. In Valenciennes, for example, some 300-400 women worked in this way, about half at home and the others in workshops where they were paid 6 francs per day.

This did not attract enough volunteers and forced labour was introduced. Beginning in 1915, all women living in villages were required to work on the land under German supervision and for German benefit, and anyone missing was punished. In many places, women who did not usually work on the land were initially allowed to find a replacement, and one woman was allowed to remain in each household with young children, while all others had to work in the fields. It was generally the grandmothers who looked after the children while the mothers went out to work, but they were not exempt from other work, washing clothes, cooking and cleaning for German soldiers billetted in the house.

Girls from the age of 14 and women without dependent children were required to work throughout the occupation at all kinds of labour. The youngest were required to work for three or four days each week, then every day including Sunday; one village noted that the only two who were allowed to stay behind were teachers of young children. All the others worked in the fields, making hay, digging or tending potatoes, putting them in clamps, working throughout the day from 5 in the morning until 6 in the evening in summer and from 7 until 5 in winter, with an hour off at mid-day.

The women were generally expected to be as productive as the men, without regard to their background or physical strength, pulling up beet, cutting cabbages or threshing corn. In areas of pasture land and livestock the girls were generally employed on the less heavy work around the stables and farmyard—although where one man was usually expected to look after 10 cows, teams of two women were expected to walk out to the fields twice a day, starting at 3 am, and milk thirty cows each. Other types of work might include unloading barges, working in the communal wash-house, washing linen for the local grand houses, or bandages for casualty stations.[2]

By the end of 1916 women were being called on to undertake all kinds of work that was useful to their enemy occupants. Although the orders officially applied to women up to the age of 45, it was extended beyond that - in effect, all women were required to work. Any who could not work or contribute to the economy in some way were encouraged to leave on the special evacuation trains to unoccupied France - when an evacuation train was made up on 1 January 1918, only girls of under 14 or women over 60 were allowed to go, together with mothers with young children; all others were retained in order to work. By the summer of 1917 the order was extended to teachers, nuns, and women in hospital as soon as they were fit enough to walk.

General roll-calls were held for all women, when they were paraded for inspection, to see if they were physically fit, to assess their probable usefulness and to assign work to them. In Roisel the German officers took photographs of this human flock; records survive of these parades, and the women's departure to their labour. This public display was con-sidered a great indignity by the French, and did not seem necessary, since most of the women were assigned from lists in the town halls.

In reports written long after, the indignation at this forced war con-tribution reflects above all the misery of the physical conditions. For the many women whose health was poor for much of the time, medical treatment was almost unobtainable. An effective way of reducing the number of applications to the doctor in authority was to insist on all women reporting sick to undress completely before he would examine them: the offence to physical modesty was increased by harsh and insulting attitudes, and the women would not seek attention unless they became seriously ill.

In Saint Amand, one young girl triumphed over the system. Summoned to join the labour force in 1917, she refused consistently through half a dozen sessions in prison, lasting several weeks on bread and water and sleeping on boards without mattress or blanket. In the end the commandant despaired of her stubbornness and she was allowed to look after small children.

It was in the spring of 1916 that the most notorious of these 'exports' of labour took place, in Lille. Worried about food supply problems, the governor decided that a large number of residents of the Lille-Tourcoing-Roubaix conurbation should be evacuated to rural areas, to help with agricultural work. On 20 April, the notice was put up, warning residents to be ready to leave with 30 kilos of luggage, and the next day was spent in anxious waiting. At 3 am on 22 April, troops surrounded the Fives district of Lille and set up machine-guns at street corners. Rifle butts banged on doors and everyone was ordered out into the street, to be counted carefully, the numbers being checked against the official list beside each door. Then the victims were selected, almost at random, with a preference for girls and young women. As they were dragged from their parents at bayonet-point, screaming and terrified, the Mayor and the Archbishop protested in vain at the central Commandanture. Rank or status had no protective value, although one young wife was spared: her strikingly pale and fragile appearance raised fears that she would fall ill and cause problems. (The 'consideration' shown in this one case was frequently quoted by the occupying forces as proof of their general kindness and concern for their workers.)

Street by street, night by night, the round-ups continued over Easter, until by the end of April some two thousand civilians had been taken, part of a grand total for the whole area of about 25,000, most of them women and children.

Young girls who had led very sheltered lives, ignorant of the world and protected from harsh realities, were crowded into wagons with prostitutes and criminals. All were taken out to remote rural areas, unloaded late in the day and directed to walk to villages 'where there would be food, shelter and work for them'. In most cases the farmers who were supposed to benefit from their labour were told that all the new arrivals came from criminal or immoral backgrounds; no accommodation was provided and the girls in their light city boots and clothing had to do their best to find shelter in sheds, barns, dilapidated empty houses or stables. They were all city-dwellers, and even those used to hard factory or domestic work had no understanding of agricultural labour. Five months later, after an unprecedented intervention from King Alphonse XIII of Spain, the deportations ceased until the final months of the war.

In October 1916, women were sent out in train-loads from La Fère to a variety of places and tasks, living in empty factory buildings or barrack huts and sleeping on straw. Local residents often took pity on them and brought in tables and chairs, and curtains for privacy. These groups stayed for two months before being replaced by the next group, but their successors, after the German withdrawal to the Hindenburg Line, fell prey to a new complication; by now their home town had been abandoned to the Allies and lay out of reach beyond the front line—so they were treated as evacuees and retained until the end of the war. It might also happen that while women were away labouring, others would arrive to take their place and work in their home town; the number of women workers in each place did not necessarily change, but they were unknown and disorientated and therefore more humiliated and easier to manage than in their own ground.

From *Le Bulletin de Lille*, 27 September 1917:

> Dressmakers and laundresses are required immediately. Pay: three francs per day, 7¹/₂ hours per day. Adequate food from the Spanish-American Committee, supplemented from the military depots, is guaranteed, for which approximately two francs will be withheld. Lodging will be in groups of between 10 and 20 women. Leave of two weeks will be granted after three months' work.

The oldest primary school children (in their early teens) were sent off on forced labour gangs, some to look after horses (one report refers to a large establishment near Laon), others to look after cattle. In Charleville, a schoolmaster was 'called up' in October 1917, and despatched early next morning, together with eight more men, in charge of 200 children aged 11, 12 and 13. Divided into groups of fifty, they were lodged in empty houses left by other deportees, and provided with straw palliasses to sleep on. In three teams, they worked from 7 a.m. until dusk, with two hours off at mid-day, picking apples and pears, climbing the trees and slaving to complete the allotted task. In Armentières, children who rebelled against bad treatment were assembled in a field, surrounded by soldiers and threatened. When they still refused, they were bound to stakes for hours without food or drink, forbidden to speak or turn the head. The slightest movement brought blows with a rifle butt. Other places recorded similar episodes.

Men who were used to dig trenches, put up barbed wire, carry munitions, died of 'wretchedness, weariness and exhaustion, or killed by Allied shells'.[3] It was virtually impossible to keep any record of this kind of abuse, for the workers were not able to make notes and no official orders survive. Instructions came from Berlin that the inhabitant of occupied territories is not an enemy: he has rights, but under certain restrictions:

> The enemy who occupies inhabited territory has obligations. He should see that the people can feed themselves and not fall into indigence ...[4]

However,

> ... most of the civilians requisitioned by the Germans were taken in more or less direct defiance of international convention ... in all cases, these workers were exposed to being killed or wounded by shells from the other side of the front line, or by bombs ...[5]

Work of direct military purpose was also assigned to young women, such as assembling ammunition belts and making sandbags or gasmasks. Refusal, as with the men, meant imprisonment in oppressive conditions.

The Hague Convention stated that 'work could be demanded from residents if it did not require undertaking war work' (article 52), but many of the French groups were forced into sustaining the war on behalf of the German forces, with penalties set in the form of prison or fines for refusal to work. The long-running controversy over French workers being required to make sandbags—a direct contribution to the German war-effort—came to a head in June 1915 in Lambersart, near Lille, when arguments were running about all work required of civilians. Penalties were imposed in cases of continued refusal:

1. No right to leave the commune
2. Passes already issued to be given up, fine of 50 francs for non-compliance
3. Curfew from 5 pm—8 am
4. No right for residents of other communes to visit Lambersart
5. All bars to close
6. No more than two people to gather together in the street
7. Heavy fines imposed on the mayor because he has not persuaded women workers to work for the Germans

(The mayor refused to pay the fines, and the money, 375,000 francs, was taken from civic funds 'for bags to be bought elsewhere'.) In Haubourdin, the mayor and his assistant were fined 10,000 German marks, plus one year in prison, while in Roubaix a one-thousand franc fine was imposed on any workshop which refused to start work again, while all the inhabitants were forbidden to use the trams for a while. The commune of Wattignies was fined 150,000 francs and five local dignitaries suffered individual fines of 30,000 francs.

Halluin (near Lille), June 1915, Commandant Shrank, to the Conseil Municipal:

There is a difference of opinion about the interpretation of the Hague Convention over work (Article 52) We shall never come to an agreement since neither of us is competent to decide, nor shall we agree. Today, it is exclusively the interpretation of the German military authorities which is valid, and therefore we demand that everything that we need for the maintenance of our troops must be produced by the workers of the occupied territory. It can be assumed that the German military authority will not shift in any way whatsoever from its demands and its rights, even if a town of 15,000 people has to be annihilated for it. Today, and perhaps for a long time to come, Halluin has neither *préfecture*, nor French government, there is only

one will, and that is the will of the German authority.[6]
All civil rights were withdrawn; but manufacture of the sandbags was
halted.

After the war, the U.S.-based Carnegie Foundation investigated the ways
in which civilians were organised for work during the occupation, and
recorded a typical experience. On 24 April 1916, a train load of women
was sent on a twelve-hour journey from their homes in Lille to Ligny, via
Vervins and Laon. On arrival the women were assembled in a field and
conducted by military escort to a nearby village. When the house to
which they were taken—empty since the outbreak of war—proved too
damp, they were locked into the local mill. Next day, twelve were taken
to Montigny, near Marle, where they were greeted by hostile jeering,
showing that an evil reputation had preceded them. They were given
shelter in a completely empty house. The group consisted of a sewing
maid, a dressmaker, four ladies' tailors, a household linen maid, a
children's nurse and one without any trade or profession. As at home,
they were required to salute all Germans of any rank, not to leave the
house after 8 p.m., and not to leave the area without a pass. Each day they
were roused by an early call and taken to work in a neighbouring hamlet.
Getting to work usually took an hour or more, on foot, wearing heavy
clogs. They were taken back for their mid-day meal and returned to work
all afternoon; four hours a day could therefore be taken up in getting to
and from work. Their labour consisted of all kinds of agricultural
tasks—planting potatoes, hoeing, loading and unloading firewood,
fodder and manure, cleaning up farmyards and barns, weeding in the
cornfields. The worst task was threshing the corn and using the mechanical hay compressor, for long hours in very dusty conditions. It caused
surprise in the area, for women never normally undertook this type of
work—it was seen as heavy, even for the men.

Otherwise, they were required to sweep and clean roads, particularly
when important German officers were in the area. There was no rest, and
no time off on Sundays, so that it was barely possible to attend church.
The outdoor work continued regardless of the weather.

The guards were coarse and boorish, with some of them inclined to
punch the women in their charge or hit them—as recorded when one
gave apples and bread to starving Russian prisoners (any such kindness
to prisoners was always harshly treated). Or there were comments such

as Lieutenant Bleyhoeffer's remarks to women and girls sent to work in his district of La Capelle, 'Off you go! And don't forget that all of you, whoever you are, you are available for our officers and our soldiers'.

The local administrative officer based nearby would drive round the area to look at the women working, and talk to any of them that he liked the look of: 'Very hard work, miss! Your clogs are very heavy, very ugly! It's up to you, you could easily have pretty little slippers and nicer work!' The account of these women's experiences does not record whether any of them took up the offer of making themselves available to the enemy, but they were often harassed by the guards bursting in on them, on pretext of surveillance, while they were washing or if ill in bed. Language and manner made the sexual advances clear.

After several months without pay they were given one franc per day, with a portion held back for food. After six months some returned with 15—20 francs, while others were actually in debt. In October and November 1916, two thousand women worked in this way for four months, and others for two months.

At Chauny, between Saint Quentin and Soissons, 1500 men between the ages of 18 and 50 were sent to Germany while others were organised into labour gangs and set to work digging trenches, against international conventions which outlawed civilian work for enemy forces in front-line areas. They were paid in bread and meat, but their conditions were very poor. In Lille, 400 schoolboys were sent to the front line zone to work on ground-levelling and in Laon, Belgian worker gangs were lodged in bare barrack buildings, fed the barest starvation rations and provided with no clothing beyond what they wore when they left home. Hundreds died, particularly those who tried to protest, and civilians who tried to give them food or clothing were beaten or fined heavily. It seems to have been a matter of principle that men rounded up for work gangs were sent well away from home so that they would be less likely to try an escape and there would be less likelihood of families trying to find and feed them. The workers were also moved fairly frequently, and were consistently undernourished; they lost any interest in escaping, hoping only to survive—which many did not, particularly in the severe winter of 1917-18. The labour contingents were large; one camp took in 14,000 men, of whom 1,200 died within a year.

Town councils tried to use as many people as possible in their administrative and food offices, but this subterfuge was noted and staff taken.

In October 1916 the mayor of Douai was asked for a list of young men without work. He pretended not to understand and provided a list of those already employed by the Germans—who were regarded as out of work, since they did not have independent French employment. The irritated German commandant, who wanted a group of 800 workers, called in a number of local men and then had pedestrians brought in off the streets and despatched to work with groups from other towns. After several days' work some 100 miles away they were required to sign a declaration that they were working voluntarily, and those who refused were forced to continue work under harsher conditions.

The Germans in Péronne

From 1917 this became the regular pattern, with men forced to work after signing a declaration that they had volunteered. In Valenciennes a total of 60 per cent of men between 18 and 50 were forced to work, with genuine volunteers representing 4-5 per cent among them, while in Charleville all the men were working for the Germans by 1918. Men of military age, between 20 and 48, were treated as prisoners of war and subject to martial law. Many were sent to work in Germany, although they were brought back to France after varying periods.

One group of men, reported to be snipers, was held in September 1914 and sent to Germany. Together with about a thousand other prisoners from all areas, they were set to work on roads, railways and drainage, sometimes forced to walk eight kilometres carrying sections of steel railway line on their shoulders. Sent to another camp, they were required to work building canal embankments without barrows, passing the soil from hand to hand. Food was so inadequate that the men scraped the grease off the sides of the camp boilers. With no water available in their camp, they were allowed to wash their clothes in a river some distance away, once a week. After two years they were sent back to occupied France, and either signed a 'voluntary' agreement to work - so that they could work near home—or were sent to the Z.A.B. as battalions of forced civilian labour.

In younger age-groups, youths of 18-20 were called in and despatched without advance warning to an unknown destination. In Douai, school-boys were summoned to work in April 1917; 28 who tried to resist war work under the terms of the Hague Convention, like others elsewhere, were put in solitary confinement in prison, the window covered to exclude daylight, and were fed on dry bread. Their only attendant was an officer who came to see if they were ready to give in, beating those who continued to refuse. Eventually all gave in and were sent to dig trenches at Oppy Wood, where several were killed or wounded. Adolescents were generally allocated to local work, including in at least one case a muni-tions depot; elsewhere, groups were set to work repairing railways within range of British guns. Others were then sent to dig trenches, where they worked under armed supervision and some were killed and wounded. They were ragged, starving and stinking. As resistance grew among the civilian population to this slavery and destruction of their men-folk, the dawn raids increased and men and boys were seized from their scream-ing families and dragged away with blows from rifle butts. The death rate among these slave gangs remains unknown; they will have been easy victims in the severe winters and then the Spanish flu epidemic.

It is hardly surprising that many of the youths who did survive such treatment turned into what one book calls *des apaches*—young savages. Unheard of at the time, these conditions were a dreadful forerunner of later decades in other countries' *gulags* and concentration camps. (At least one German commandant knew of a precedent, for he quoted to prisoners the conditions in British camps in South Africa, during the Boer War.)

In the spring of 1918, Gaston Prache was one of these 'called up' in

Cambrai, to work in a labour camp. Perhaps he knew about the great German advances sweeping westwards, which so nearly broke through the Allied lines and almost won the war; his forced personal contribution to this effort was to be marched twenty kilometres to a military-style camp behind barbed wire. There the youths were numbered and provided with a small enamel basin to use for the thin soup which formed most of their meals and also as a washing bowl. They were directed to street cleaning, or maintenance work in the military camps. Occasionally a few who lived locally managed to slide under the wire and return home for a few hours, returning at dawn exhausted and damp with dew. Then their work changed and they were required to transport cases of explosives in small wagons, from the special light railway to lorries. They were only 600 metres from the front line.

A month later, Prache escaped and reached home, but gave himself up three weeks later to spare his family from threats that they would be seized and sent to Germany.

Labourers were moved from one camp to another, so that no personal friendships could develop with local residents who might try to supply food or help with an escape attempt. Georges Gromaire's 1925 account of the the German occupation provides a picture of distress and confusion:

> In this occupied land, where no one had the right to leave his own place without a rarely-obtained pass, there was a constant movement of people, coming and going to meet all the needs of the occupying forces. Those who lived near railway lines saw trains passing every day full of men, youths, women and young girls, packed in all together on their way to some work or other. They went from the north to the Somme, to the Escaut, to the Ardennes, and from the Ardennes to other places. It was a continual cross-country chase for no apparent reason.[7]

Civilians were strictly instructed not to offer food or help of any kind to French labour gangs or to Allied labour gangs. The penalties for disobedience were vividly illustrated in Guise in March 1918, when a youth of 18 gave a piece of bread to a line of captured French and British soldiers. The boy was immediately pursued by one of the guards, shot and killed without hesitation.

The Z.A.B. 6, disciplinary forced labour gangs for ex-prisoners—to which others were also allocated—were given the most demanding and dangerous work, usually close to the front line and exposed to Allied fire. They were lodged at night in ruined barracks, schools, workshops or factories in evacuated villages. Dirty and hollow-eyed, they were identifiable by their red armbands and other identifying stripes on trousers and jacket, and by an individual number-plate fixed to their cap. Their clothes wore out until they existed in a jumble of ragged and torn garments, lucky if they could find a scrap of blanket or sacking to cover their shoulders.

Girls were also used for work in dangerous conditions, and a number were killed by an ammunition depot explosion. The fear of explosions caused by sabotage or carelessness brought an ingenious solution: prisoners and labour-gangs would be lodged inside the depot, at personal risk from any careless or deliberately risky activities!

Most of the men taken to work in civilian labour gangs were sent home after nine or ten months, as they became exhausted; a number of them never recovered their health and there were certainly deaths from tuberculosis and other illnesses or general debility afterwards. As soon as one batch of men was returned home another took its place, and it seems that the number of men who served in this way was not less than 100,000. The gangs returned when their tasks were finished, arriving by rail or in long grey columns of marching men, weak and ill and ashamed of their enforced slavery. Many died—succumbing to flu, the severe winter weather or ill-treatment or punishment when they tried to escape—or of electrocution when they tried to escape across the frontier into the Netherlands.

The few men who volunteered for work were treated well and shown off proudly to residents of their assigned work-place. It was perhaps fortunate for them that these volunteer groups no longer existed by the time the war ended: there seems to have been no settling of old scores on the same scale as at the end of the Second World War—in different circumstances and in a war which affected the whole country—but the wretched conditions at the time of the 1918 Armistice left little room for easy forgiveness towards those seen to have colluded with the oppressors.

How many civilians were forced to work for the Germans? It does not seem possible to answer this; sometimes the number in any one camp, on any one date, of Z.A.B. workers is known, but not the numbers elsewhere on the same date, to establish a total. There were however a great many civilian prison camps along the front line, and some held several thousand men. In the Verdun area alone, some 68 camps held only Belgian workers; another 78 camps were located between Lille and St Quentin. In December 1916 at least 4,000 men were being held in camps around Laon.

On 17 June 1917 Charles Delesalle, mayor of Lille, wrote a letter of enquiry to General von Graevenitz (Governor of the city) about a rumour than men were being taken to Dourges, Don and Hénin-Liétard, only 8 - 10 kilometres from the front line. These villages had already been evacuated—an indication of the danger—and there was an official Franco-German agreement that prisoners should not be used within 25 or 30 kilometres of the front; the workers seized from home—old men or boys of 14-17—should therefore not be used there. The protest was brushed aside, but renewed, based on sworn testimony from youths who had managed to escape, possibly with help from sympathetic German soldiers.

In Harnes 500 such workers were used to build troop shelters, some within two kilometres of the front line. In Courrières, men and boys unloaded barges of sand, cement and gravel from the Rhine to build troop blockhouses. Workers slept in the local distillery and slept in barrels with doors cut in the sides. Some men were taken to the Aisne, with 300 established near Laon, working on the railway. Under the régime of maltreatment and severely inadequate food supplies, within a few months their number had dropped to 180 through death and illness.

For farm work or heavy labouring, the workers were formed into 'columns'. The farm groups were lodged in hostels, usually for lengthy periods, with teams of horses requisitioned from neighbouring communes kept in vast stables, often a factory which had been dismantled. A typical 'column' would consist of a non-commissioned officer with an aide who was exempt from military service, in control of about thirty men, sixty horses and thirty vehicles. As with all such labouring groups, payment was in vouchers and food came from the C.R.B., the American supply line, supplemented by local potatoes. When the inhabitants of Saint Quentin were withdrawn ahead of the strategic German withdrawal to the Hindenburg Line, the electricity works was transferred to Maubeuge and its French workforce with it. In Maubeuge they were allotted to accommodation in abandoned houses and given American food with pay of 2.50 francs per day. Punishment for inadequate work was loss of pay, and stubborn cases were sent to the Z.A.B. Late in 1917 the factory was transferred again, and as the war came to an end it was identified for despatch to Germany, but the French workers were able to escape in the general confusion. Most Lille workers were sent to the Douai - Lens area; others went to Cambrai, Moeuvre, Marquion or Havrincourt. A few were sent to Laon, where there were already some 20,000 Belgians. Men from Saint Quentin were sent to Quesnoy sur Deule, Perenchies, Santes, Allenne-les-Marais.

'Groups of civilians photographed for identification before evacuation from Péronne'

Apart from workers who signed up voluntarily, very few were employed close their homes. It was easier to keep men under control if they were exhausted—and as to providing nourishing or even adequate food, no one could be certain of that towards the end of the war, whether German or French, soldier or civilian. Living on cabbage or turnip soup, housed in rough lodgings where they might often sleep on the floor, the men and youths of the labour gangs were more concerned with simple survival.

Survivors' accounts of this aspect of the war include many descriptions of attempted resistance when the orders involved excessive work or ill-treatment, and beatings or lack of food were commonplace. In the end all resistance was overcome, and the work columns were encountered everywhere throughout the occupied region.

In view of the conditions under which they set to work, it is not surprising that their living arrangements and facilities for the sick were inadequate. When wagons arrived to clean up after troops moved out, the work-gangs rushed to look for any left-over scraps of food, for they were generally very poorly fed. They slept on straw which was changed three times in nine months, and in the sick-quarters the beds were black with vermin. Other gangs, working out of town, were lodged in tents without straw or blankets.

Some of the camps had a particularly evil reputation. At Moeuvre, men who refused to work in October 1916 were ordered to undress down to their shirts and trousers and were left standing out in the rain all day. At night they were crowded into pig-sheds, too many to sit or lie down, and nothing was available to drink. The work required of them, when they finally gave in, was to carry baulks of timber and rolls of barbed wire, and their housing was in tents or abandoned houses with leaking roofs or no glass in the windows. As their shoes wore out they were given clogs, and most went bare-foot; many suffered from frost-bite in the terrible winter of 1916-17. Since their food consisted of thin 'coffee' morning and night and a meagre soup at mid-day, they did their best to seize potatoes and beet from the fields, despite beatings with rifle butts. Hundreds of men died.

Anyone living near a large agricultural feature was at risk of been seized and sent to work there: the Forest of Mormal, for example, demanded large numbers of men to cut and clear timber for use in the trenches. Timberyards were set up in the wood, with a special railway loading ramp, and men were brought in from the neighbouring towns and villages—Landrecies, Le Quesnoy, Ors, Maroilles, etc. Two shifts were organised, with the first one leaving at 5 am and returning at mid-day and the second taking its place for the afternoon session. This group was lodged six kilometres from the wood, to be covered on foot each way, while civilian and military prisoners and men evacuated from distant cities were housed in the wood itself in rough wooden barracks and never left the wood. For all the men, their only 'proper' meal came in the early evening. It consisted only of C.R.B. supplies which were inadequate as the sole source of nutrition for an ordinary adult diet, even without the heavy labour required of these workers. In the towns and villages, the knowledge that any of the men in the area could be taken at any time, for unknown work over an indeterminate period in exhausting and ultimately dangerous conditions, was a constant drain on all families. The labour system was recognised as one of degrading slavery which had no concern for fitness, stamina or aptitude, illness or personal circumstances.

Yet even these men who were subject to this enforced labour were better treated than prisoners of war who were brought from camps in Germany to work in France. A few were French or English, men who were taken back to the camps in Germany when they were too worn out by overwork and poor food to work effectively, and numbers were not great; the far greater numbers of Russian and Romanian prisoners, on the other hand, remained until the war ended and were treated worse than any others. Their sufferings, from lack of proper food and clothing, terrible living conditions and very harsh treatment, aroused the pity of the French population who saw in them the worst form of slavery and smuggled bits of food to them where possible. Any such attempt was savagely repressed, and many of them died. Once Russia had been defeated, the Russian prisoners were of no concern and could be neglected, starved and maltreated without risk of retribution.

Several personal accounts of this labour have survived, and the young electrician who was taken from Saint Quentin in December 1914 appears to be typical. All men between 18 and 48 were summoned to parade, and 1,000 were taken immediately. He was sent to work on the roads around Péronne, living in barracks and rarely receiving his parents' food parcels or letters. He worked on the front line, frequently exposed to shelling, from 5 in the morning until 7.30 at night with a mid-day break of 90 minutes. The roads crossed the Somme marshes and the men worked waist-deep in water, filling shell-holes, breaking stones and mending the roads. No more than five men could be off sick at any one time, and resistance meant beatings and harder work. The C.R.B. administrators recognised that there were substantial groups of men who were not registered for food supplies, and did their best to provide them with food.

Another account describes a worker's life between June 1916 and November 1918: Francois Leclercq was a head postman in Saint Quentin, born in 1866, who helped with the C.R.B. distributions. In June 1916 he was requisitioned for work, along with five colleagues, and sent away in a group of 2,400 men aged between 14 and 60. Early in October, the six postmen, none of whom had volunteered, were sent to Cantin, and Leclercq was sent on to Denain and then Oisy le Verger where he refused to work, and was sent to prison for twelve days. As the German army withdrew he was sent to Gouzeaucourt, then Bapaume, and was taken with the German army as they withdrew to the Hindenburg Line, together with two British soldiers and one Belgian, to Mons. The system finally collapsed as the war ended and he returned to Lille on 20 December 1918, where he needed three months of hospital care to recover his health.

Hirson: 1915, hostages taken to guarantee bridge security

In their camp, the men were lodged in large wooden barrack huts surrounded by barbed wire, where the armed guards had orders to shoot any would-be escapers. Elsewhere, they were lodged in cellars or in the woods or open fields. Leclercq did not dig trenches or set up barbed wire, but saw others go off to work on defence construction. He worked in a saw-mill, gathered up munitions and supplies left by the British, cleared up dead horses, or helped to recover guns left in the battlefield. Men were used to build railways, transport timber, build officers' shelters, or unload gravel from barges for making concrete.

The discipline was backed by special sections for difficult prisoners. One form of control was through the food supply, which was inadequate and very poor in quality—the men became undernourished and needed all their strength to carry out the allotted work. The main element of diet was turnips, cooked into a thin stew. Weak coffee was distributed in the morning, a loaf of bread every two or three days, and the turnip brew. Occasionally no bread was available, in which case prisoners had to buy their supply from the Germans.

The men received 30 pfennigs per day and paid for supplements to their diet; Leclercq spent between 700 and 800 francs provided by his wife during his enforced work period. He made three attempts at escape; twice he was recaptured, but the third try coincided with the collapse of the German army.

Escapes were frequent, with young boys being more successful than the adults, but they were often recaptured when they went home—they had no identity cards, vital documents required at all times. The boys were taken back to the camp and paraded as 'deserters', or beaten. Of Leclercq's six colleagues, two—father and son—died of privation and overwork, and a third suffered a complete mental collapse and had to remain permanently in an asylum. As conditions became more desperate, a wider age-range was drawn on and men up to the age of 70 might be summoned if they had specialised skills.

Towards the end of the war there were unannounced round-ups. In the final weeks, in late October 1918, the village of Audigny near Guise was surrounded by soldiers and the mayor received instructions to assemble all the local men between the ages of 18 and 48; those already in the fields were brought back to join the parade. Identities were checked against the presiding officer's list and the men selected were despatched immediately to an unknown destination, in front of their distraught families.

Some men escaped, or disappeared before being rounded up for labour. As soldiers had discovered on the retreat from Mons early in the war, ingenious hiding places could be found in town and village houses or isolated farms. Without official existence, they could not draw on C.R.B. food supplies and relied on the secret generosity from households which were themselves already short of food. Some barely saw daylight for many months or even years, and lived in fear in their cramped and dirty corners: they were as effectively imprisoned by their circumstances as their brothers in the labour gangs.

There were some successful escapes, leading to an official order:

1. for any fugitive from a civilian work battalion, one male member of the escaper's family or relatives, or a resident of his last dwelling, would be taken to a work group and held there until the escaper returned;
2. anyone helping a fugitive with food, shelter or any assistance, or who immediately failed to report a fugitive returning home would suffer one year's imprisonment and a fine of up to one thousand marks.

A Cambrai nurse recorded that 'Many young strangers, civilians, were left in our civil hospital by the Germans after terrible ordeals: frozen feet, mutilation, tuberculosis, from bad treatment, lack of hygiene and lack of food. On some days we had nearly 700 such patients in our hospital.'

In a letter of protest to the German Chancellor, Bethman Hollweg, Monseigneur Charost, Bishop of Lille, stated that out of 500 adolescents taken from a single parish in the Nord on the first round-up of civilian workers, only 179 returned: 321 had died or disappeared.

Under the section of the Treaty of Versailles which dealt with compensation for damages payable to civilians for low-paid or unpaid work, nearly 305,000 claims were dealt with in 1921, relating to men, women and children who worked at some time, even for a few days, for Germany. A further note in January 1924 records that 80,000 Belgians and 250,000 French workers were claiming for wages not paid by Germany. Once more, an observer writing in the 1920s makes a perceptive comment:

It is hardly surprising that under such a régime of slow and persistent administrative oppression, which increased its hold rather than slackening as time passed, the French population diminished alarmingly.
The strongest and most energetic, the mobilised men, had gone; evacuations to free France removed two hundred thousand, forced labour and deportations killed many, while anxiety and distress overwhelmed anyone who lacked stamina. The birth-rate dropped, almost to nothing in some areas.[8]

The birthrate in France had been dropping for some time before the war, and the war years themselves intensified the trend. During the 1920s and 1930s, the period was referred to as 'les années creuses', the empty, or hollow, years; it had serious implications for France, particularly when the Second World War approached. This aspect of the war was one of the elements which had long-term effects; in France and in other countries, suffragettes and supporters of women's rights demanded an inquiry and compensation for victims. Five million American women signed a petition to Clemenceau for protection of women in international legislation.

Notes

1. Fleury, Elie, *Sous la Botte, Histoire de la Ville de Saint-Quentin pendant l'Occupation Allemande, Août 1917*, St-Quentin, Elie Fleury, 1925; Noyon, Les Éditions de la Tour Gile, 1996
2. The occupying commandants were said to take pleasure in ordering girls from the most sheltered backgrounds to distasteful work, such as repairing soldiers' dirty and vermin-ridden shirts and underwear; it is not clear whether this was an accurate observation, or a reflection of the writer's expectations and own standard of living.
3. Blancpain, Marc, *Quand Guillaume II Gouvernait de la Somme aux Vosges*, Paris, Fayard, 1980
4. Blancpain, *Guilluame II*
5. Blancpain, *Guilluame II*
6. Martin-Mamy, *Quatre Ans avec les barbares: Lille pendant l'occupation allemande*, Paris, La Renaissance du livre, 1919
7. Gromaire, Georges, *L'Occupation allemande en France (1914-1918), Collections de Mémoires. Études et Documents pour servir à l'histoire de la Guerre Mondiale*, Paris, Payot, 1925
8. Gromaire, *L'Occupation allemande*

8

Liberation

'It feels like a victory to me, because I am alive at the end of it'
Dorgelès, *Les Croix de Bois*

Georges Gromaire concludes his extensive account of the occupation, published in 1925, with the comment that it was characterised by two main innovations in European history: the removal of all natural or manufactured products, and forced labour imposed for the sole benefit of the invaders. As the fourth anniversary of the war approached, these features were felt with increasing insistence as requisitions of all kinds continued to afflict and strip every household. The cities suffered earliest and most severely, but no one escaped entirely. Some areas were treated more lightly, such as Longwy in the industrial belt in Lorraine: it was due to be formally annexed as part of Germany and its mining was vital to the German war effort. All possible objections were dealt with; when a town responded by saying that items demanded were not available, the instruction came in return: 'Buy it somewhere else—buy it from Germany'.

This brisk alternative was becoming increasingly difficult. By the final stages of the war conditions in Germany and Austro-Hungary were often little better than in the occupied territory, and morale was collapsing. The Central Powers suffered increasingly severe problems of resources, affecting food, manpower, and industrial production, and by the summer of 1917 their reserve troops were malnourished, and horses were being slaughtered because there was insufficient fodder for them. Austro-Hungary had only one-third of the petroleum that it needed, wool and cotton were blended with paper or nettle fibre, and paper was used to make bandages or underwear. German production of aircraft and munitions was dropping sharply, and although more than two million men were freed from internment camps by the collapse of the Russian empire in 1917, a quarter of them died of hunger and disease. Hunger was a problem for soldiers in the front line, although they received more than civilians (100 g of meat per day for Austro-Hungarian troops early in 1918, against 23 g per head for Austrian civilians and 33 g for their Hungarian counterparts. Even potatoes were in very short supply—the ration was 70 g per person per day, compared with 357 g in Germany and reduced from 493 in 1913. Vienna was reduced to meatless days—three every week—and had to go without milk, fats, eggs and vegetables. Essential industries, such as car and aircraft factories, suffered from strikes. By the end of the war, the German home front had effectively collapsed, with people in rags a commonplace, and rotten food dug out of rubbish heaps to alleviate starvation; food supplies, at 1,000 calories a day, were adequate for a 12-year-old child, instead of the 2,500 considered the minimum for a working adult.

A description of one of Lille's poorest quarters shows how the inhabitants were living:

> In what could be called a district of the true people, about 150-200 people are waiting in a queue, bowl in hand, for their soup or vegetable stew, under the steady rain of a January day.[1]

These soup-kitchens opened at 11 a.m., but queues began to form from 8 a.m. or even earlier. Similar queues waited in patient desperation outside the offices where grants for the unemployed were paid out. Along the streets ragged children, chattering among themselves in a mixture of Flemish, German, French and local dialect, peddled cigars, soap or postcards to the Germans. In the poorest district, where many houses had no glass in the windows, the unemployment hand-out was inadequate and families lived off rice and cabbage, and whatever could be made from selling rags and rabbit skins. Requisitions had stripped away household belongings - a large family had one big iron bedstead with a single threadbare covering - and wooden fittings or furniture were often burned to the stove for warmth or cooking.

By February 1918, the population of Lille was down to 129,000 people, three-quarters of whom were receiving some form of aid. 46,000 were registered for unemployment pay, nearly 2,000 received funds as *sinistrés*, and nearly 47,000 a military allowance. Families of French soldiers received an allowance, and there was aid for refugees from front line areas, or those who were separated from evacuated families, at the rate of 1.50 francs per person per day (1 franc per child under 16).

If the French population living under such conditions in the occupied area had realised the extent of their enemy's domestic difficulties, would they have sympathised? Fellow-feeling for the individuals, the increasingly hungry women and children at the bottom of the heap, perhaps; or where there were reasonably relaxed relations with German troops billetted in a French household, family photographs may have aroused interest and sympathy—but the diaries of the period do not reflect much concern for the occupying forces, however uneasy the German troops may have been about their conditions at home.

By now, the region was suffering not simply from the repeated requisitions, but from deep-seated exhaustion—the land had lost fertility to an alarming degree, the result of poor management and frequently of excessive cropping without the usual fertilizers. By the end of the war, large areas of usually productive land was lying uncultivated for lack of manpower, equipment and direction, and almost everything that belonged to the land had vanished—livestock, machinery and crops. Great orchards of fruit trees had been destroyed, rather as, earlier in the war, all walnut trees had been cut down—the timber was the preferred wood for making rifle butts.

The under-nourished and sharply reduced numbers of livestock could no longer be the source of future herds. Cattle, pigs, goats and horses gradually disappeared—near Laon a resident recorded the departure of the last goat in mid-June 1917. Gergny, a commune in the Aisne, recorded the reduction in farm livestock throughout the war. In August 1914, the village had 260 cows, many with calves; the number of beasts requisitioned at any one time varied between 15 milk cows (October 1914), through 26 separate demands for cows, bulls or calves during 1915—between three and 25 on each occasion—to a dozen demands in 1916, fifteen in 1917 and 23 in 1918. At the end of the occupation, 102 cows and 15 calves remained. Horses were important to both civilians and the armed forces: all the combatants needed them in large numbers for transport and for the officers, and farms relied on either horses or oxen to draw the plough. By the last months of the war, the few horses remaining in civilian hands were barely fit to haul the wagons or carts—which were also in poor and unreliable condition. Some communes had no horses or mules at all. Human muscle power—mostly women, children and old people, suffering from malnourishment—had to take over on both field and road. Fresh milk was unknown in many areas, and by the end of 1917 communities received only condensed tinned milk for children and the sick from the Commission for Relief.

None the less, life somehow continued and the civic framework staggered along on paper transactions. Allowances of various kinds were paid, with most towns giving a regular allowance to the wives of mobilised men, the unemployed, the old. Money was needed for taxes; even dogs were taxed, with the exception of working farm dogs, and several observers record that owners sadly and bitterly had their pet dogs killed rather than pay such a tax.

In Le Nouvion, school closed at mid-day in August 1918, so that the children could go out in teams with their teacher to pick raspberries and blackberries, and clear brambles. Instructions were issued on how to gather the fruit and deliver it in the best possible condition. They were also required to gather nettles: the plants should be cut or picked carefully and bunched tidily—the stems would be sent back to Germany to make fabric, while the leaves would be fed to farm animals. After the short summer break, classes began again early in September—but ceased, for lack of premises; the abattoir had been destroyed by shelling, and the studio previously used was occupied by ever-increasing numbers of evacuees.

Later that month, prisoners were evacuated from the school building and civilian prisoners, billetted with residents, were removed from Le Nouvion and taken further east. The approaching end of the war began to be apparent. In mid-September, and despite the lack of direct news, rumours of retreat were confirmed and civilian prisoners were prepared for transfer to an unknown destination. Late in September, and continuing in early October, evacuees arrived every day and space for lodging was running out. The town hall staff arranged for hot cocoa to be delivered each night to people lodged in the church which was bitterly cold because all the windows had been blown out. The consequences of four years of oppression and poor nutrition were apparent in the high death rate.

For two years all civic records (births, marriages, deaths) had been kept in triplicate; the Germans had taken a register in 1916 and failed to return it, and the mayor therefore decided that henceforward a triple record of registrations would be kept—one for the occupying forces if required, one for the central record and one for the town hall itself, as usual. When shelling threatened the town in mid-October, all these civic registers and other important documents from the town record office were put into a heavy chest, taken down to the town hall cellar, and walled in. Afterwards, all records were registered in ordinary notebooks, to be added to the official registers after the liberation.

By mid-October the regular bombardment showed that Allied troops were approaching and, as in the summer of 1914, the residents took to their cellars to shelter. On 3 November 1918, the German Commandant in Chief wrote to the French chief of staff to point out that there were still a large number of French civilians behind the German lines, presumably as a warning about the approaching bombardments. Two days later a doctor in Le Nouvion recorded in his regular daily notes that they already knew of the Austrian and Turkish decision to lay down their arms, reported in the German newspapers; and that Germany had overthrown its régime and was now in the hands of a democratic civilian government. Armistice discussions were under way in Paris—but meanwhile, Le Nouvion was being shelled, with both French and German shells falling in the town and in the surrounding woodland. The doctor and his assistants organised cellars to take in the wounded.

Outside, rain fell steadily and the familiar tide of mud increased, inside as well as outside as refugees arrived from neighbouring communes affected by the fast-moving front line. Most of these refugees, like their equivalents in Péronne in the Battle of the Somme two years earlier, arrived on foot carrying or pushing their meagre belongings, while two German vehicles brought the sick.

Through the summer of 1918, the infamous *Gazette des Ardennes* appeared less frequently and less prominently. Its wide circulation was replaced in Lille by copies posted up in front of the telephone exchange, the general pattern of German movement in and around the city gradually changed and some soldiers talked about departure.

The style and subjects of demolition also changed, and the railway lines round Lille's fortifications were destroyed. Buildings were smashed or blown up, and those with windows intact found it safer to keep them open, to prevent blast damage to the glass. One of the worst episodes of this final burst of damage in the city took place on 10 October, when the railway lines near one of the city gates were blown up and pieces of shattered lines blasted into nearby houses. Careful lists survive of the numbers of window-panes broken, the floors splintered, the furniture destroyed. In some households at least, evidently, traces of civilised surroundings had escaped the repeated requisitions, for the lists include lamps, blinds, mirrored wardrobes, decorative jardinières and glassware, and rugs. One piece of railway line caused a claimed 800 francs' worth of damage, other houses listed items totalling 120 francs or sought an expert's visit to advise on broken windows. More significant was the report from the Wazemmes gas company reported damage to its gasworks and street lighting installations amounting to 64,520 francs. As the Mayor of Lille pointed out politely to General von Graevenitz, the Governor of Lille, this break in power supplies meant that the bakeries which supplied the city—and which were almost completely dependent on powered machinery to knead and prepare the dough—would not be able to feed the residents. He made it clear that in such circumstances the Governor was responsible for feeding the city.

On 12 October a notice appeared, printed like so many before it in French and German. It announced that the German Government was to ask the enemy governments not to shell the three cities of Lille, Roubaix and Tourcoing, in order to preserve the cities and avoid victims among the residents. Such a clear expression of the approaching peace must have put fresh heart into the beleaguered and half-starved residents. By now most of the occupying German administration had gone, ahead of the approaching Allies, but on 16 October the town hall received yet another requisition demand: for 2,000 shirts and 2,000 pairs of underpants 'in good condition' to be delivered to the 63rd Infantry Regiment by 4 p.m. that day. The penalty proposed for non-compliance was to be a fine of one million francs—but by now the French staff in the mayor's office knew that the war was effectively over, and firmly showed the messenger out. On that same day, all shops were officially instructed to close, and all inhabitants to stay indoors between 8 p.m. and 8 a.m. In the middle of the night all the city's bridges were blown up and all the inhabitants rushed down to their cellars. Heavy trucks could be heard, passing all night long.

The next morning—17 October 1918—Lille woke up, startled to find the city quiet and free once more: the heavy traffic during the night had borne the occupying troops away, the long enslavement was over. The first British advance troops appeared in the city; Madame Delahaye-Théry tells of British aircraft overhead, and British soldiers in the streets, admired for their quiet polite behaviour. A Scottish military band, playing as it marched through, was described as 'funny, but nice', while another commentator noted, 'the phlegmatic British rendered the moment even more solemn'. The French army was represented by the 43rd infantry regiment—the same one which had left Lille on 24 August 1914. The first allied troops arrived in Lille to joyful excitement, and the weary citizens pressed round one of the Scottish troops. 'Have you any newspapers?' 'Can you post a letter for me?'—but mostly they were simply shouting, waving their arms, shaking hands wildly. In the Place de la Republique, three Scotsmen disappeared under piles of flowers. The advancing Tommies were surrounded, embraced, suffocated by the crowd, weighed down with packages, surrounded by women. French papers appeared the same day, and the *Bulletin de Lille* carried the mayor's greetings.

The French flag was flown everywhere and English and French aircraft flew low overhead. One landed on the central esplanade the same day: it was piloted by Captain Carl Delesalle, son of the Mayor of Lille, flying in from Dunkirk to greet his father. The mayor himself, Charles Delesalle, signed notices which appeared all over the city:

> The terrible nightmare is over ... we must show our recognition of the admirable soldiers who have liberated our land and who are marching towards the final victory ... The magnificent sun of glorious peace is already high above the horizon.[2]

On 18 October, more British troops arrived, then a group of French officers and journalists from the main Paris newspapers. Next day the Prime Minister himself, Clemenceau 'the Tiger', visited Lille, followed two days later by President Poincaré who pinned the ribbon of the Légion d'Honneur on to the mayor's chest.

Madame Delahaye-Théry wrote in the last of her 'black books' on 20 October:

> That makes three nights when I have woken up wondering if I am

not dreaming, if I am really here. We have lost the habit of this restful silence. Everything is calm. Can it be possible? What about the twelve hundred nights when we always heard the guns? Our joy is growing. Every day we are getting used to happiness again.'

She describes the atmosphere in the cathedral, when the Bishop of Lille conducted Vespers:

The great church was packed full more than an hour before the service began. The Bishop addressed us, magnificently. His tears of joy intensified his words. I cannot call it a sermon. It was a speech of unimaginable inspiration ... despite the majesty of the sacred setting, the crowd rose to its feet three times, applauding and cheering the Bishop ...
The streets are crowded, the people of Lille cannot stay indoors, they have to see their liberated city. I went to see an English military band playing, in the Grand'Place. They ended up with the *Marseillaise*. It was a triumph! The musicians were literally carried shoulder high in celebration.'

On 28 October Winston Churchill, as Minister of Munitions, was present when General Sir William Birdwood led a ceremonial parade through the city. The British Army marched through the streets, polished, gleaming, clean and victorious. The procession took two and a half hours to pass Madame Delahaye-Théry who, as she stood watching, regretted that her grandchildren were not there to see the fine sight ... and also expressed the hope that such an occasion would never arise again. General Birdwood, leading the British contingent, presented Charles Delesalle, the Mayor, with his commander's banner in memory of the British Fifth Army; the General was thanked, awarded the title of 'Citizen of Lille', and presented with the city banner (a silver iris on a red background), bearing the legend: 'From the City of Lille to its liberators'. Charles Delesalle expressed the feelings of the city during their imprisonment:

For four years we were like buried miners listening to the picks and shovels which we could hear far off, announcing our rescue ... and suddenly the dark pit opened and we saw the light.

In the final days of the war Madame's black notebook has some less welcome news to report: the Spanish flu epidemic has delayed the arrival of French troops, and orphan children are dying of flu. Material conditions are so difficult that for six burials only one hearse could be found, with one horse.

Practical considerations came to the fore as soon as the war was officially over. Reports came in of unexploded shells, collected at various points in and around the city, and the mayor's office established a list of the 39 bridges and footbridges destroyed by the Germans before they departed. This final wave of destruction caused no human casualties, although the material damage was substantial, and a policeman was posted outside the station to advise pedestrians. During the first week of November, before the Armistice but with the end of the war clearly in sight, a statement came from the Germans that the destruction in Lille was caused by British artillery. A British commission was set up to enquire into the events, and the scale of destruction during the final week of the enemy occupation.

A hundred kilometres away to the south-east in Le Nouvion, the firmest indication of the approaching peace was the official announcement that inhabitants could choose where to install themselves—but that from 5 November they must not venture out until after the troops' departure. Food supplies were sufficient for several days, and civilian doctors would care for the sick. The notice continued with instructions that when Allied troops approached, the mayors and a few other important residents should go to meet them, with prominent white flags waving.

Next day, 6 November, was Liberation Day, with no more enemy uniforms visible in the streets. French troops appeared quite early in the day, to tremendous enthusiasm and delight (though it was regrettable, as the doctor noted soberly, that it was a wet and muddy day). As part of their evacuation, the German army left some immediate problems, for Le Nouvion's road bridges over the river were blown up and the railway bridge, also dynamited, had collapsed into the main road. One of the explosions had also cut off the water supply. Everyone capable of the physical labour turned out with pick and shovel to clear the debris.

Shelling disturbed the next night, but this time it was the newly-arrived French army pursuing the retreating enemy. The people of Le Nouvion sighed, and went down into their cellars yet again; but the next night, 7 November, they were back in their own beds once more, secure in the knowledge that French patrols had advanced 15 kilometres without encountering enemy troops. Bags packed ready for a threatened evacuation eastwards were emptied out again, thankfully.

At the time of the battle of Landrecies in 1914 the Polvent family had left their farm in Ors after a warning from British officers that the village would be fought over. After three days they were able to return, and endured the four years of occupation without any further encounters with active combat. In 1918, the war reached their quiet and by now shabby village and shells began falling in and around Ors after the British army reached the River Selle on 10 October. On 13 October the German forces gave orders for evacuation and the inhabitants of the village had to leave their houses with their families, old and young, including many suffering from Spanish flu. They set out in ox carts, pushing hand-carts or on foot. One girl, ill with flu, was pushed by her parents in a hand-cart; the wheels had been stolen and her father had replaced them with wheels from a mowing machine. One young woman, gravely ill, was taken away on a cart by her father who had already prepared her coffin. She died on the way and was buried in a field. Marie Polvent's brother Henri departed with a neighbouring family for the Netherlands, but died of flu a week later in Belgium; the neighbours cared for him there, buried him, and returned later to bring back his clothes and tell his family about his final hours. Others of the Polvent family were already ill when the evacuation order arrived: Marie awoke with flu that day, her brother Alcide was too weak to stand, and the German general billetted in their house set about finding a wagon to take them—yet by the time it was found, the shelling was too heavy to risk movement. When it died down they departed to safety, drawn by a mule. Others insisted on remaining, and two villagers were hit on 3 November, the eve of the battle. Both died a few days later in hospital.

Preparing for the British onslaught on the canal along the stretch which ran through Ors, which the occupying German army could foresee as the front line shifted steadily eastward, a trench was dug on the west side of the village, linking the outposts with the canal which was provided with a temporary footbridge. When the last of the outposts was eliminated by the British, on 2 November, the footbridge was removed and the Germans dug in on the east side of the canal.

Marie Polvent returned to the family farm in the Rue Verte in Ors, on 8 November 1918. Two days later she wrote to her sister Julia (who was five miles away in Le Cateau, suffering from Spanish flu), to tell her about conditions after the battle.

'Woodland near Ors, 1912 and 1918'

The war, which had ignored them for so long and left them to cope with the awkward 'peace' of occupation, had swept past and left the kind of destruction which had become an everyday experience for many less sheltered communities. Marie describes the damage left by a shell which exploded against the stable, blasting away some 4 metres of the roof and part of the gable end and bringing down the barn and shelter behind it. Another shell had gone straight through the rabbit hutches, another had brought down part of the garden wall. The house itself was not seriously damaged, with simply a quantity of small holes in the roof - needing only a few tiles each - and the loss of all its windows. All the doors in the house - and from the neighbouring houses along the Rue Verte - were missing, and found in the ditches alongside the canal, together with doors from the sheds, stables, the outside privy, the wardrobes, and all the farm's corrugated iron. They had been used to make shelters and temporary dug-outs, which were further protected by a layer of turf on top.

Marie found quantities of household items and family clothing on the dung-heap or in the fields, and lists her sister's blouses, mother's skirt, father's trousers, piled up with empty jam tins, clogs, empty bottles, and a big basket. Everything must be washed, she asks Julia to send her some soap. The house was full of British troops, everywhere except in the parents' bedroom. They had lit fires everywhere, in the stables, barns, cellar, even in the henhouse, and everything was being used without consultation. Soldiers installed themselves in the cellar with beds, mattresses, table and stove—and a harmonium, so that once their meal was cooked and eaten, there was music for their leisure moments, drawing in passing companions. A stove was set up in Julia's bedroom, with the chimney pushed through the roof via the cupboard where beans were stored. The beans were gone, together with the potatoes and other vegetables, although some carrots, turnips and parsnips were recovered. Anyone who saw potatoes should buy them. Papa must collect up bits of iron to be used for rehanging the doors, and bring nails and tools, for all had vanished. And a saw was essential.

By now, (10 November), nearly 500 people were back in Ors and there would be Mass in the church today. Bread and meat were being distributed, free, but no other food was available. Marie asks her sister for sugar, clothing, a little flowered curtain to hang across the kitchen shelves— housewifely pride was quick to restore order and decent appearances; and sheets and a quilt, and kindling wood suitable to make matches which were totally lacking—the boxes used for C.R.B. food supplies would be invaluable, she notes. Papa will be able to build up a fine collection of rifles, bayonets and helmets, lying around all over the place. It was easy to get around the village again, there were at least six footbridges across the canal. The wild duck were returning, using water-logged shell craters to land in. Many of the apple-trees were damaged or completely blasted—and if Julia would like some shell-cases for flower-pots, there were plenty to be had!

This was Marie Polvent's last entry in her war diary, the practical and determined notes of a housewife anxious to return to normal life as quickly as possible, not hiding reality from her family but not allowing despair to creep in.

Lorraine, far beyond the Western Front for most of the war, came within range of Allied aircraft during 1918. Leaflets and newspapers dropped from the air, and stations and military convoys came under aerial attack. The occupying forces became less confident, as the tide turned in the summer and optimism grew among the downtrodden occupied zones. They noted that German officers no longer talked about conquest, that the troops were discouraged and casual, their rations reduced.

The Americans were coming: their attack on the Saint Mihiel salient finally shifted the line which had remained virtually static for four years. As the Germans retreated, they took part of the French population with them and active warfare reached many areas for the first time. Shelling intensified, with stations particularly targeted. German residents in Metz, not far from the modern German frontier, felt threatened, and departures for Germany, which had begun during the summer, increased sharply as families gathered up their belongings and moved out. French families, however, refused evacuation. News of revolution in Germany reached French ears on 9 November 1918, but it was not until ten days later (a week after the official Armistice) that French troops reached this far into their old pre-1870 territory.

Across the whole of the occupied area, the population was on the move ahead of the approaching Allies. In Douai the inhabitants were evacuated to Avesnes early in September, leaving their belongings. No food was supplied, and they took what they could from their meagre stocks. The flu epidemic was taking hold, and there were deaths along the way as old people were pushed on handcarts and children were lost. The sick were evacuated by boat to Saint Amand. As they travelled there were both deaths and births, while some of the nurses were forced to help tow the boats along the canal. Among many forced shifts of the population, this particular episode remained in the minds of those who experienced it as one of the most distressing.

Four days later, Cambrai was evacuated, an operation which lasted for three days, followed by deliberate firing of the town centre. In Guise and Sissonne the evacuation took place on 11 October. When the inhabitants returned after the liberation they found all their heavy furniture intact, but no linen, crockery, kitchen utensils or books - much had already been requisitioned, but the final departure of the enemy troops meant the final stripping of portable possessions. In some villages, transport was supplied to take people towards the French lines, so that they would be liberated by the advancing troops.

By the end of the war, many of the diaries begun over four years ago, to record the adventure, had been abandoned. Sometimes this signified a happy outcome—as for Aline Carpentier of Le Nouvion, who had successfully travelled through Switzerland to free France—and sometimes it indicated that the writer had not been in a position to continue writing, such as the schoolboy Gaston Prache of Cambrai who had been forcibly enrolled in a labour gang. Other diarists who are quoted in this book wrote triumphantly of how their war ended - Henri Douchet, 'Fasol', in Péronne, Elie Fleury in St Quentin, Madame Delahaye-Théry in Lille.

Among the numerous accounts of the liberation, the blend of joy and solemnity is still striking. In the northern industrial town of Avesnes, liberation came on 9 November, when the first British patrol arrived in the town:

> Everyone's heart was overflowing with emotion. We laughed and wept at the same time, everyone shook hands in a kind of wild delirium. Only those who lived through those unforgettable moments can really understand them.[5]

Notes

1. Martin-Mamy, *Quatre Ans avec les barbares: Lille pendant l'occupation allemande*, Paris, La Renaissance du livre, 1919
2. *Le Bulletin de Lille*, 17 October 1918.
3. Delahaye-Théry, Mme Eugène, *Les Cahiers Noirs*, Rennes, Éditions de la Province, 1934
4. Delahaye-Théry, *Les Cahiers Noirs*

5. Gromaire, Georges, *L'Occupation allemande en France (1914-1918), Collections de Mémoires. Études et Documents pour servir à l'histoire de la Guerre Mondiale*, Paris, Fayot, 1929

9

Rebuilding

'On the frontier of the living lands ... This is the dead land'[1]

On 11 November 1918 the stalwart Mayor of Lille, Charles Delesalle, wrote to the equally stalwart Bishop, M. Charost, requesting him in the name of the French government to sound all the bells in every church in the city. In his office, the *Préfet* of the Nord also ordered bells to be rung, and all public buildings to be decorated and illuminated in red, white and blue; and—in what may have seemed, in view of the long trials and dangers of the war, a less than tactful move— he ordered that salvoes of the heaviest artillery be fired.

The war was over and the Allies were victorious; but apart from celebratory bell-ringing and illuminations, it was hardly a fairy-tale happy ending. France's terrible human losses were reflected in the north by further totals - the material damage to cities, villages and landscape, and the many displaced, dispossessed, starving or homeless civilians. It would be hard to say which burden of the war was the worst affliction that they had borne. A Lille woman who lived through both world wars remarked that while civilians suffered greater fear during the 1940-44 occupation, in 1914-1918 hunger was the sharpest affliction.

Conditions in Lille were particularly severe. By February 1918 the population had dropped from 218,000 to just over 129,000; of these, 46,000 people—21,115 families—were on the unemployment register, and regular financial aid from one source or another was being paid to almost three-quarters of the city's residents. Despite the heroic efforts of the Committee for Relief, almost everyone was affected by the long-term food shortages. Dr. Calmette—the expert on tuberculosis whose experiments on pigeons so nearly brought disaster upon him early in the occupation—noted in April 1918 that the city had no fresh meat whatever, no milk, eggs, potatoes or fresh vegetables. The C.R.B. rations provided only two-thirds of a non-manual worker's daily calory requirement, and 15,000 young people were at great risk from tuberculosis, rickets, and heart or kidney problems. Between 1914 and 1918 the overall mortality rate had risen from 20.65 to 41.55 per thousand; for tuberculosis, the rise was from 3.05 to 5.75 per thousand. The proportion of deaths to births among the civilians was startling: during the bitter cold early in 1917 the city recorded 14 deaths for each birth.

Sickness had made great inroads into the weakened population, with a serious outbreak of typhoid at the end of 1915, followed later by cases of enteritis, beri-beri (caused by undernourishment), and, not surprisingly, the effects of the Spanish flu epidemic. By the end of the war all of Lille's children under the age of 6 years weighed less than they should, and 80 per cent of the 12-13 age-group failed to reach the appropriate height or weight for their age. Of 11,296 children examined by a medical commission after the armistice, 4,409 were normal but 6,359 were 'débile' (weak, undernourished or feeble), 116 suffered from tuberculosis and another 412 from the early signs of this dreaded disease. More than 40 per cent of adolescents (aged 10-20) showed some signs of lung disease. Fourteen-year-olds looked no more than ten, and girls of 18 appeared no more developed than their 13-year-old sisters; sexual maturity was absent or seriously delayed, and teachers noted emotional and intellectual backwardness among their pupils.

The one encouraging sign among all this misery and hardship was that mortality among the very youngest children had actually decreased. Breast-feeding had been encouraged, no doubt helped by the absence of factory work available to take mothers away from the household, and condensed milk was made available to nursing mothers.

Apart from breast-fed babies, the increased general mortality rate was caused by four years of undernourishment; despite the noble efforts of the C.R.B, their rations never attained the energy values needed for ordinary life, particularly during periods of growth and maturing. Dependence on these foodstuffs, poor in vitamins and other essential elements, and a lack of fresh food, inevitably caused outbreaks of scurvy and other symptoms of malnourishment. Sources for this information are French rather than neutral; but the figures they give, the extent of material damage to be made good, and the continuing need for C.R.B. food supplies, indicate the long-term physical and emotional effects of the war. They also emphasise how this northern experience of the war differed from that of the rest of the country.

Family life suffered enormously from the divisions, privations and unreasonable burdens of the war. One of the age-old consequences of invasion and occupation was evident—babies born to unmarried girls, or to women whose husbands were away at the war and could not have been the father. In many communes, the registers recorded children whose fathers were German soldiers, although the record often shows simply '*père inconnu*' (father unknown). It seems that most such births occurred where families were evacuated away from home and had much greater contact and closer dealings with the occupying forces. Although there were also many more abortions than in normal times, it seems that there may have been around ten thousand of these births. The children remained in France after the war, although as they left, some of the Germans offered money to the mothers to take their sons with them (rarely their daughters). Few such offers were accepted.

It is impossible even to guess at how many women had brief or longer liaisons with German soldiers or officers. The civilian population was wholly subordinate to the invaders, in miserable and uncertain conditions; and although six months or a year of occupation might have been bearable, the apparent permanence of the invaders' presence must have undermined morale and affected many women whose lives were effectively wrecked by the war. Nor should the effect of the occupation on soldiers fighting with the French army be ignored; one of the most striking images in Henri Barbusse's 1916 novel *Le Feu* shows a soldier making his way through the front line and back to his mining-village home near Lens, in the occupied region. Peering in through the glass door, he sees his beloved wife and small children contentedly chatting and laughing with the German soldiers billetted in his home, enjoying their company—they have evidently adapted to the changed circumstances and are making the best of them. Without making himself known, the soldier steals back in despair to his unit and, careless now of his own survival, is killed very soon after.

Although many observers comment on the high morale which was generally maintained in the French population, the future health, education and attitudes of a whole generation were profoundly affected by the war, for children were set to work from the age of ten or even less. These future workers, leaders and parents suffered physical, educational and moral deprivation; and those whose childhood in the 1920s was overshadowed by their parents' experiences in 1914-18 continue to recognise the longterm effect of those hard years. As one commentator wrote in the 1920s, 'part of this generation was cut down, while the other part was weakened, and ruined physically and intellectually'.[2]

Practical aid arrived, and was sorely needed; the resident who wrote in mid-December 1918 that her family was without clothing or household linen was typical of many. Lille's archives show distributions during January 1919, listing hundreds of beds, mattresses, blankets, sheets and bolsters. Some were broken or tattered, but the need was urgent and the distributions continued throughout the spring of 1919.

After forced immobility for most of the occupation, combined with large numbers of people absent as refugees, evacuees or forced labour workers, the release from oppression meant a burst of confused activity. As families returned from free France, having escaped as refugees in 1914 or on evacuation trains during the war, they discovered the extent of damage - or found strangers lodged in their houses. An urgent demand in December 1918 asked for French refugees to Belgium to be sent home, because their temporary wartime accommodation in unoccupied Belgium were needed once more by its rightful owners who had fled in 1914 and spent the war years in France. People were not only in the wrong city or country, many were in desperate conditions. In December 1918 a letter from a Lille resident begged the mayor to help in returning his wife and three small children to the family home; they were, he said, stuck in a tiny hamlet, homeless and alarmed at the approach of winter weather. Others were missing, with no record of their wartime lodging or the destination of their forced departure in a German evacuation convoy.

Food was still short, everywhere, and travel was virtually impossible. The Mayor of Lille's office received hundreds of letters begging for help, travel passes, information, support of all kinds. A Lille resident hoped for the return of his two brothers, deported to Lithuania, and his wife who had spent the war in Brussels. Another hoped for the return of one daughter with her two small and ailing children, penniless and destitute; and a woman sought her husband, a military prisoner of war, not knowing that he had died during his journey back to France. A family evacuated to Belgium wanted to return home to Lille. Six weeks after their liberation by the British army, they were turned away by both British and French authorities who each advised seeking help from the other.

Madame Delahaye-Théry's son Eugène (who was responsible for publishing his mother's newly-discovered notebooks after her death) spent the final months of the war in prison, and her diary reflects her worries about him. He did not suffer greatly, although in his final chapter concluding her account, he notes somewhat bitterly that he 'reached France early in January 1919, at Dunkirk, where we were looked after very badly by fresh young sub-lieutenants who had escaped the war'.

There were sick people to bring home, evacuees who needed transport and care: the official aid committee for the Nord sought urgent authorisation to direct patients to a hospital with beds available. Details of numbers do not survive, but the message scribbled across the letter approved immediate care and food supplies. Even before the end of the war, at the end of October 1918, a distraught mother of five children asks the Mayor to help her to be reunited with her daughter in a Tournai hospital after being injured by a German car; she wants to take her stockings and boots, and to bring her home:

I hope that you will concern yourself with my daughter as quickly as possible. I think of her every day and weep for her, because I hear that Tournai has been shelled, I don't know if she is still alive or not, that's why my maternal heart begs for news as quickly as possible ... I have five children, my husband went to the war in August 1914 and I have no news of him since then.[3]

The reply written across the letter records simply that 'the Mayor regrets'.

A lesser difficulty is recorded, a week after the Armistice:

I was evacuated on 2 October, and having been taken ill on the journey I lost my luggage. I've got nothing left except what I was carrying ... please help me find my luggage, or replace what is lost.[4]

Another letter, dated a week later, records that luggage had been deposited at Ath and could be reclaimed there—but there is no way now of knowing whether the petitioner was matched with the missing goods.

Similar claims and requests flooded in from people without clothing or bedding, and arguments developed over evacuees' belongings stored in Belgium. Taken singly, many of the requests seem trivial, set against the vast background of the long years of war: taken together, they represent a vast weight of distress and dislocation both personal and communal. A generation later the circumstances in this occupied area immediately after the armistice were to become familiar on a wider scale, in the European chaos following the end of the Second World War.

Basic supplies might be unobtainable, in short supply, or available but inaccessible because of the collapse of communications and the almost impassable state of many hundreds of kilometres of roads, canals and railway tracks. The Committee for Relief in Belgium, which had kept the enslaved populations of Belgium and northern France alive since the spring of 1915, continued to operate because there was clearly no other way of sustaining the liberated communities. In cases where men had been taken to Germany for forced labour, families were left without support, and when the men returned they were often ill and weak, possessing only the clothes that they had been wearing ever since their departure.

One of the most significant implications for the future of the region was the drop in population. Cambrai, for example, had lost four-fifths of its inhabitants, and the population of the triple city conurbation of Lille-Tourcoing-Roubaix had dropped from 606,000 in 1911 (the last national census before the outbreak of war) to 360,000 in 1918.

Although individual movement within the occupied area had been at best heavily restricted throughout the war, and at worst impossible, paradoxically large numbers of people were missing, or in the wrong place, by the later stages of the war, by which time the birth-rate had dropped sharply. The ancient cathedral city of Laon, with a population of 16,000 in 1913, had only 4,300 people by the end of the war, following many evacuations, while Cambrai dropped from 21,000 to 18,000. Births in Avesnes, with an average population of 5,000, dropped from 44 in 1914 to 20 in 1917. Nouzon, in the Ardennes, recorded its birthrate: 68 in 1915, 29 in 1916, 32 in 1917, 28 in 1918 (and 155 in 1920).

In many places, incomers—refugees from the front line, or from Belgium, or simply from elsewhere in the occupied regions—represented a large proportion of the residents. In Fourmies 12,000 local people were host to 5,000 outsiders, Guise had 5,000 strangers out of 8,000 people in the town.

The *départements* of the Aisne and the Marne suffered the most dramatic loss, with their populations dropping from 530,000 to 197,000 and 436,000 to 200,000 respectively; other *départements* lost between approximately 8 per cent and almost half of their population, through war casualties, flight ahead of invasion, and evacuation during the war. In most places, the population dropped by a quarter or a third: exact total figures for the population in the north-east as a whole are difficult to establish, and depend on the specific category under consideration - an estimate of the whole of the ten *départements* affected by the war, including areas behind the Allied lines along the Western Front and in Alsace-Lorraine which was not under French sovereignty in 1914, gives a total of six and a half million people in 1911 and just over three and a half million by November 1918, 56 per cent of the pre-war figure. Early in 1915, the C.R.B. organisation, which depended on accurate records of the numbers to be fed, gave the figure of 2,200,000 for the civilian population in the occupied area of northern France; this represented many refugees from Belgium, but these migrants were added to a French population reduced by the departure of men to the French army, and families who had escaped ahead of the German invasion.

The excess of deaths over births was around 220,000—in a nation which was already suffering before the war from a low birth-rate, in decline since the mid-nineteenth century—and everywhere in the north marriage and birth rates declined catastrophically, with serious implications for the future. French military deaths were the highest (1,383,000, or 34 per thousand) of all the major combatant nations, and it was the young men, the future leaders, teachers, farmers, manufacturers—and fathers—who were lost. After the immediate post-war surge in births to 1910 levels, the rate sank into a steady decline once more during the 1920s.

The task of clearing the ground and reestablishing normal life—domestic, industrial or agricultural—was almost beyond contemplation, and outside help was needed in the battlefield areas. Chinese and Indochinese labour gangs were used—the former paid only on their return home, to reduce the number of brawls over gambling. Fighting amongst the gangs was not infrequent, and on at least one occasion the apparent culprit was shot out of hand by the supervising British officer.

Meanwhile, displaced families returned and sought their possessions amidst the battlefield litter, and bereaved French families collected bodies from battlefield burial grounds to take them home to their local cemeteries. In extreme old age one man still recalled vividly the long walk home when, as a very small boy, he ended the journey riding on the coffin of his father he had never known. Many of his immediate seniors, too young to have taken part in the war, spent their military service immediately after the war in clearing the battlefields of their dead brothers' and comrades' bodies. Nor did these matters affect only French families; in the mid-Twenties, the English writer Henry Williamson returned to explore the terrain that he had fought over throughout the war, and described what he found to the north of Arras:

> The grass covers the old trenches and the small concrete shelters. Willows, those trees of the wilderness, wave on the ancient parapets, thrice the height of the howitzers which their parent-withies may have helped to camouflage. Reeds spring out of the old shell-holes stagnating with a brown scum, whence arises the ghastly croak of many frogs.
>
> I passed heaps of rusty iron shards piled by the cart-track, with barbed wire, pressed like bales of satanic hay...[5]

These glimpses of the battlefield areas help to illustrate the implications for the post-war construction period; four years after the end of the war, an English visitor was very conscious of the damaged earth:

> The advances and recessions of a battle line more than two hundred miles long, the thrusts and counter-thrusts of invaders and defenders, the struggles for the control of rivers, railways, and highways, the fierce fighting over strategic positions and the stubborn defense of every city or village where a stand could be made, were of themselves enough, without the added weight of a deliberate destruction, to turn large parts of the country into a desert and to leave of civilization only a memory and a name. If the war made familiar to the world the names of Armentières, Lens, Arras, Péronne, St. Quentin, Soissons, Reims, and St. Ménéhould, it is also true that because these communities, like hundreds of others of lesser fame, were long in the thickest of the fighting they were all but completely ruined. Not all of the destruction, of

course, was the work of the enemy, save as responsibility attaches to the enemy as the aggressor; for what one army did not overrun had often to suffer from the operations of the other, and it was as disastrous to a town or a farmhouse to dislodge an invader as it was to resist an attack.[6]

The scale of the work required is almost impossible to evaluate; among many typical examples is the factory in Douai which contained 2,320 cubic metres of concrete, for 25 blockhouses, to be removed; and in the *département* of Meurthe et Moselle alone, 650,000 cubic metres of earth were needed to fill in trenches. Thousands of miles of roads, canals and railways need to be cleared and rebuilt, including hundreds of railway bridges, canal locks and other installations. Of the 6,242,000 hectares of land directly affected by the war, nearly half were severely disturbed or completely devastated, including three-quarters of land under cultivation. The numbers of cattle, horses, sheep and pigs in the area was tiny compared to the pre-war levels (see Appendix).

Repairs would take years, and before they could be started it was essential to remove explosives and ruins, and to assess the damage and the scale of work required in every commune. Many commune survey plans were missing, making the preliminary assessment uncertain and even more complicated. Battlefields and their surroundings, cities, towns, hamlets, roads and railways, buildings of all kinds—there was a colossal task to be undertaken in removing the debris of war, dangerous and cumbersome, to clear away ruins and fill in trenches.

The number of houses destroyed or seriously damaged seems to have been at least 850,000. Temporary housing was established, 20,000 dwellings at first but soon rising to over 24,000 and eventually to a total of more than 800,000 houses and farm buildings (by January 1931).[7] In addition there were more than 5,000 barrack or Nissen-type huts for accommodation, stores, shops, schools, churches, post offices, etc., and nearly 5,000 general agricultural storage units. The reconstruction in northern France was at its peak in the early 1920s but proceeded at varying speeds in different communes. It continued for many years after that, completed in a few cases barely weeks before the outbreak of the Second World War. A number of modest buildings can still be seen in the towns and villages that were rebuilt along the old front line, used as garages or store-rooms, with some notable examples in excellent condition, well-painted and cared for and still lived in. Amidst the sweeping acres of prosperous modern farmland, they are a striking reminder of the years of destruction and renewal.

It was an immensely complicated operation, and lies outside the scope of this work. The many public bodies involved included the Committee for Relief in Belgium, the churches of several nations, social, medical and educational contributions from the British army and other organisations (British military teams made a valuable contribution in testing wells and reinstating water supplies). A number of international 'adoptions' were officially established, arrangements by which towns in Great Britain, Australia, the U.S.A. and other countries took on responsibility for raising funds and collecting clothing, etc., for devastated French communities along both sides of the Western Front. There was usually a direct connection, in the form of the adopting community's battle losses at or near the site chosen for help. Some of the many American organisations which had contributed to the war effort were also involved in this intense period of reconstruction—including, notably, the Quakers, or Society of Friends—helping to restore a sound basis of health and daily life which would put the northern region back on its feet again. The impressive pattern of adoptions and the substantial contributions made to the recovery is generally forgotten now except for some unexpected street names in the reconstructed French towns and villages, although modern twinning arrangements in some cases perpetuate the scheme. Agricultural supplies donated to the area included seeds, young trees and breeding stock for farms that had lost their livestock.

Adoption of French Communes by British Communities

Bexhill	Bayencourt
Birmingham	Albert
Blackburn	Péronne, Maricourt
Brighouse	Courcelettes
Burnley	Colincamps, Courcelles
Canterbury	Lesboeufs
Derby	Barleux
Eastbourne	Bray-sur-Somme
Exeter	Montdidier

Folkestone	Morlancourt
Gloucester	Ovillers-la-Boisselle
Hornsey	Guillemont
Ipswich	Fricourt
Leamington Spa	Biaches
Llandudno	Mametz
Maidstone	Montauban
Portsmouth	Combles
Stourbridge	Grandcourt
Swansea	Carnoy
Tonbridge	Thiepval
Warwick	Longavesnes
Winchester	Engelbelmer, Auchonvillers, Beaumont Hamel

German prisoners of war were brought into the liberated zone in 1919 as labourers, while the original inhabitants were discouraged from returning to the most severely damaged areas too quickly. Basic commodities such as housing, clothing and food supplies must be established before real reconstruction could begin, and in many places it was impossible to define sites exactly; whole villages had ceased to exist, communications were non-existent, and the outline of roads and buildings could often not be identified.

In other areas, away from the wartime front line, repairs and reconstruction work were easier to assess, but the cost of such work was a severe challenge and the system for preparing plans and payment was slow and complicated. The most significant losses were the livestock, farm and factory equipment, and the lack of household and personal possessions after the years of neglect and requisitioning. Taking the whole of the occupied area, many industries had been virtually eliminated. An official German report describes 'devastated' sugar refineries, for example, which would lack primary supplies—sugar-beet—for several seasons. An observer remarked of the Somme area that 'the former prosperity had been destroyed for the next ten years'. The valuable textile industry centred round Lille had no stocks, no raw materials, no looms or equipment, only empty or ruined buildings, and the vital mines were in a similar condition. Large numbers of cooperatives were formed, to receive goods and payments in compensation, to plan the use of construction

'*The devastation of war: Péronne*'

'*The devastation of war: Le Cateau*' (above and below)

equipment and to manage the substantial agricultural supplies needed.

In addition to these industrial losses, the power station in Lille was unusable and the gas works, water mains and railways blown up and destroyed. Roubaix and Tourcoing suffered equally, and indeed the whole of that vital industrial area had virtually ceased to exist as a contributor to national production or local employment.

It was not only the substance for material life that was missing, for many churches (excellent targets, or observation posts) had been destroyed—the Soissons diocese alone required 165 million francs for its reconstruction programme. Farming communities seized the opportunity to incorporate land reform into the clearance and reconstruction work, and ancient strips or patches of land were exchanged to form larger holdings, more practical for modern agriculture.

The population of the invaded and occupied *départements*, which in 1918 stood at 55 per cent of its 1911 figure, rose to 89 per cent by 1921, and by the spring of 1926 was back at 97 per cent of its earlier total. Throughout the occupied region, agricultural land took time to recover its fertility after four years of misuse or neglect, even where it had not been churned up by fighting, shelling and trenches. And although generous quantities of farm animals were donated, full productivity took several years to reestablish.

In some regions, feelings at the end of the war were particularly complicated: Alsace and Lorraine had been part of Germany since 1870 and in the most Germanic region, in the farthest north-east of modern France, there were mixed feelings about the change of nationality: some of this area was firmly German-speaking and felt German, and the forty-seven years since the French defeat in the Franco-Prussian war meant that the prevailing culture for many was more German than French. There had been little overt resistance here during the war—in addition to the heavy German military presence, the area was partially populated by families of German descent. In the Second World War—which was in so many ways a continuation of the first—the measures of control first considered here in 1917-18 (confiscation of businesses, agricultural management, expulsion of intransigent French residents) were put into effect very quickly in 1940.

Some battlefield areas posed specific problems. It was suggested that the battlefields of the Somme front line area could never be restored to productivity—they should be planted over with trees. This proposal was not adopted for the Somme area, but around Verdun it was seen as the best solution; much of the fairly thin layer of top-soil had been literally blown away by the bombardments. Several villages here were not restored, and the sites can still be seen as clearings in a vast forest; a few streets or house sites are indicated, a chapel or shrine may have been rebuilt, but otherwise there is nothing but an information panel and a footpath to follow through the trees and the shell-holes still clearly visible. Parts of the Chemin des Dames battlefield area, in the Aisne, was treated in the same way. As modern visitors will know, the work on the battlefields continues: many tons of shells come to the surface every year, to await the special disposal squads, and fragments of shrapnel, wire and metal items of uniform or equipment can be found on any battlefield site. Away from the battle zone, traces of metal items and concrete structures are still sometimes visible, and repetitive architecture from the 1920s often indicates rebuilding after the destruction or neglect of the war years.

It would take many years for mines and heavy industry to recover. The mining centre of Lens was completely obliterated, Liévin was not much better. The Director General of the Lens coal mines estimated that as the houses of more than one-third of the workforce had been destroyed in neighbouring villages, rather more than 12,000 new dwellings would be needed.

In Lille, the Chamber of Commerce drew up a valuation of the damage to buildings, covering linen and cotton spinning mills, filtrations plant, metal-working factories, tanneries, chemical works, breweries and clothing manufacturers. Evaluation commissions had begun work as early as February 1915, establishing a system for small allocations to be made promptly. Eventually more than three million claims for compensation were recorded, and dealt with much less rapidly than the long-suffering *sinistrés* considered reasonable. Bureaucratic delays accumulated, and those who had suffered the depredations of the war had to undergo demoralising obstacles before being able to resume normal life and work.

It is of course extremely difficult to establish accurate figures for the damage caused by the occupation, and in most cases such attempts reveal dilatory or inefficient official bodies and the impossibility of arriving at a satisfactory over all total figure. One substantial 1925 account of the occupation includes a somewhat grudging comment on the caution and impartiality of British observers. He notes that all lists of losses were drawn up along very rigorous lines:

> In particular, the French figures were examined by English experts and it is well known that, since the peace, they have never tried to increase the reparation figures due to France. The Commission for Reparations, in publishing its figures, is thus correct in stating that the figure given for damage is substantially below the true sum of French losses and can only be considered as a bare minimum in every respect.[8]

Not surprisingly, it is almost impossible to put figures to the reconstruction costs, which extended over many years and every aspect of life in a large and varied area. The Lille Chamber of Commerce detailed the damage in textile and metal-working factories, breweries and chemical works, and arrived at a total of 200 million francs. Another example is the 1918-1920 total money advanced to *sinistrés* by the Office de Reconstitution Agricole for the whole of the ten war-ravaged *départements* (i.e. including areas on the western, Allied, side of the Western Front)—897.7 billion francs. At the other end of the scale, a village householder lists all his household possessions, with their value in 1914 and the greatly increased cost of replacement or full repair in 1920. The dozens of items range from his working shirts, boots and cap, through household furniture and linen (tables, chairs, cooker, bed, mattress, sheets, tablecloths ...), farm and garden tools, and all kitchen equipment. A few items had doubled in cost, such as two large wicker baskets, up from five francs to ten, or a dozen white handkerchiefs at thirty francs instead of 15, but in most cases the cost in 1920 was fully three times the 1914 figure. His new work shoes cost 45 francs rather than the 12 franc price of their pre-war equivalents.

Many other claims survive in the archives, written on all kinds of paper from smart business letter-heads or sophisticated personal paper to squared schoolroom-type sheets. They include a plea for help in restoring extensive glasshouses, the property of a market-gardener who saw his peacetime livelihood disappearing into the chill winter air. Another correspondent listed material left behind in his factory by the Germans, and asked what he should do with it: a weighing machine, dynamo, press, sewing machines, a large quantity of tombs, rags, powdered potassium, cardboard ... the factory owner was anxious to clear his premises and get back to work.

In some cases the end of the war came just in time. In Anzin and Denain the mines had been kept working through the occupation, with the underground workings and equipment being designated for destruction when the Germans retreated, but the rapid Allied advance overtook these plans and, although needing vast renovation and reequipping, they survived and the shafts escaped the blasting and demolition inflicted elsewhere.

For others, however—human victims—the armistice came too late, even though they survived to see peace once more. Many of the young men sent to forced labour gangs came through the demoralising and physically devastating conditions in a mental and emotional state which was equally degrading, for the ill-treatment they had survived had eliminated all sense of moral values or responsibility and many could not adjust to a normal domestic, family and work-place routine. Girls too had suffered in equally disruptive ways: many from a sheltered background had been despatched to rough field work or into brothels, away from family, friends, school or work.

In May 1919, a special tour of some of the devastated battlefield region was arranged for the combined committees for refugees from the occupied area. It was based on Lille, as being the only city near the battlefields which was able to provide accommodation. For some of the delegates (representing all the *départements* which had been occupied, wholly or in part, except Meurthe-et-Moselle), it was perhaps the first sight of the land which had been actively fought over during most of the war. A paragraph headed Hallue—Pont-Noyelles describes the scene:

> On the frontier of the living lands, barely pulling out of the depths, this is the dead land—for mile upon mile, and far out of sight, the ground is full of holes, churned up by the projectiles which fell here beyond numbering. The very few trees which still stand are reduced to skeletons ... in the fields, piles of metal, corrugated iron, or clumps of barbed wire ... piles of shells ... above all, crosses ... grouped on the top of a mound ... or in the ditches along the roadside.

> Train loads of visitors arrive twice weekly, bringing pilgrims ...

there should be more—school children should come from all over
France, so as to remember what war was like for their fellow-
Frenchmen, and to realise the scale of work necessary to start life
again in these dead towns and lands ... to understand too the
colossal scale of the task to be undertaken, to restore life to these
dead towns and these dead landscapes, and the sacred debt that the
entire nation owes to these occupied areas.[9]

The report goes on to list some of the towns that have been virtually
eliminated - Bapaume, Vimy, Albert, Lens:

Number 13 of the Lens mines—the *fosse Saint-Elie*—was brought
into operation shortly before the war; the Germans blew up the
whole installation; the extraction machinery was broken up and
destroyed, the boilers shattered ... a titanic pile of twisted iron and
tangled beams ... this is premeditated deliberate ruin.

A desolate landscape, flooded, inhabited by dead trees, ruined
houses, villages destroyed, towns wiped out. Clearing up alone will
take years ... thousands of hectares are riddled with trenches, and
there are thousands more to sift through; thousands of kilometres
of barbed wire, and there are still thousands of kilometres more;
the fields are being cleared of munitions ... temporary shelters
have been sent, but there are few to be seen, among the chaos of
stones and bricks. Some fields are under cultivation, but how many
remain barren![10]

The visiting delegates tried to find hope in the dismal scenery, but were
overwhelmed by the misery:

Yet there are some people living in these whited sepulchres of
villages and towns. They find shelter in cellars, making rough
rooms, and stove-pipes can be seen sticking out of the ground; no
water, no light, no drainage ... the wretchedness of our refugees
continues, like that of our liberated peoples, the folk who have
been repatriated.[11]

Another trainload of visitors crossed northern France, and Belgium, in the spring of 1919, bringing German diplomats and civil servants from Berlin to Versailles. As it crossed the bleak landscape, it slowed down— either because of poor track or in order to let the destruction be seen more clearly—and the former invaders could see what the war had done: the land and houses in ruins, factories and bridges unusable. The train was greeted by waving German prisoners of war, who now formed part of forced labour gangs, but French units working on the clearance stood and watched the train in silence.

By the summer of 1919, thousands of visitors were travelling out from Paris for the day by train, curious to see the ravaged war zone. The dangers of discarded ammunition were emphasised to tourists, but visitors died as well as many returning farmers, labourers clearing the land and builders engaged on reconstruction.

These reports relate to the long strip of land which was fought over constantly throughout the war, a great expanse in the eyes of the observer on the ground but narrow in relation to the overall area of France. In that sense they do not apply to the rest of the occupied area, which was run-down, deprived, wasted and poverty-stricken, but still functioning after a fashion and recognisable to the returning soldiers and refugee families: yet the atmosphere of undeserved misery, the deprivation of information and the comforts and rewards of everyday living, were applicable to the whole of the occupied lands. Pride in surviving, in winning the war, was balanced by the weight of the four years of defeat.

What Do We Do Now?

The Armistice of November 1918 must have been one of history's greatest moments of triumph, hope and regret combined. Slowly, men returned home from their units, or from hospital, to see how life at home had continued without them and conscious of the need to restore industry and rural activity to its former productivity. Perhaps some people truly believed that they could return to pre-war conditions, that life could pick up again where it left off in the summer of 1914; but for everyone in this region it was a matter of intense and frustrating hard work, learning to live in a new and diminished world surrounded by reminders of the men who were killed, untraced, or permanently hand-icapped by the effects of war.

The now silent battlefields and trenches, and the ruins of shelled-out towns and mines, were a speciality of northern and north-eastern

France. Between that line of war, easily identified on maps as the snaking curve of the Western Front, and the re-established northern and eastern frontiers, residents, farmers and newly-returned soldiers and refugees had uniquely depressing conditions to deal with: even where buildings remained, furnishings, household linen, fittings and domestic and farmyard equipment and livestock were missing. Farming had continued, in deteriorating conditions, through the labour of the women, children and grandparents as the men who had not escaped the occupation had increasingly been taken for forced labour. The housing and industrial premises in which the new post-war life was to be born were often inadequate, ruined, dangerous.

In the struggle of the peace that now began, the French nation of 1918 was not the same as the France which had gone to war. It had changed not only in terms of geography and demography but economically, socially and politically. There was more than one French experience of the war years—and therefore the peace that began in November 1918 was not the same throughout the country. The black enveloping drapes, set up after 1871 to mourn the lost provinces of Alsace and Lorraine, were taken down from the figure of 'Strasbourg' in the Place de la Concorde at the heart of Paris, but this was not enough to put the German-occupied territories on level terms with the rest of the nation.

Everywhere throughout France men were missed and mourned, but here in the north was the added grief of mourning those who had died in prison-camps, in labour gangs or from unnecessary illness and deprivation. Those who had suffered the occupation were not the same as those who had remained free: everyone had suffered loss, but the loss of freedom was different from the loss of individual family members in combat, and this war had taken over their whole lives. No doubt there were families whose day-to-day experience of the occupation was not distressing, who found enough to eat and who did not lose members to forced labour in their own zone or to military action in the free part of France; yet when peace came, 'the war', 'victory' and 'peace' had different meanings for those whose identity as part of France had never been in question than for those who had lived through the enemy occupation.

In the north, the core and focus of private domesticity had been worn down, autonomy and independence eliminated, personal identity as French citizens mocked or disregarded. Some families in the north had suffered the loss of relatives in the French army, yet had remained in ignorance until after the liberation, others had lost no-one but in their enforced isolation had not known of their family's survival until the country was reunited. During their four years without direct news of their own country, they had not known what was happening to their own fellow-citizens, or what their future might be. In such circumstances, the longed-for moment of victory could have nothing simple about it: too much to remember, too many physical and emotional wounds to heal, too much material damage to repair. For over four years, 'Frenchness' was relegated to an official inconvenience, French national identity was a daily handicap. If the war had continued, if they had been 'German' for forty years as Alsace-Lorraine had been after the Franco-Prussian war, perhaps the intensity of French pride and loyalty would have diminished; but the diaries and memoirs quoted, even allowing for the triumphalism of survival and victory, do not show any signs of it, and these qualities of 'Frenchness', of having survived a long and fierce ordeal, were a source of pride and high morale in the long haul back to renewed family life and economic activity.

The social and political philosopher Friedrich Engels prophesied that Germany would inevitably become engaged in a world war, decimating Europe, crowding the Thirty Years' War into three or four years and affecting the whole continent; he foresaw famine and pestilence, and a descent into barbarity and general bankruptcy. He wrote this in 1887. Since the First World War ended, it has often been compared to the Thirty Years War which devastated Europe in the mid-seventeenth-century, in its effects on those who suffered it and its lack of beneficial consequences—a description of that earlier war as 'morally subversive, economically destructive, socially degrading' seems very well fitted to characterize the whole of the 1914-18 war and its aftermath. The north of France was a double victim of the First World War: to the misery and deprivation of the servitude imposed on land and people were added terrible material and psychological scars, greater than those suffered by the rest of their compatriots but frequently disregarded outside their own area.

What about the next decade, the next generation? After the 1919 Treaty of Versailles, martial conflict was officially in the past, a new era was beginning with the new decade; but the language of the new peace was inevitably concerned with consequences of the past—repatriation, returning refugees, reconstruction, reuniting, rebuilding physical, moral and economic health—rather than a fresh start. It is a mark of the significance of the Great War that we cannot now think of the 1920s and 1930s without the background and starting point of the 1914-18 war, and the conflict of 1939-45 is recognised as the continuation of that war; that continuing thread is part of the northern regions, which were forced to live through the invasion and occupation without any solid certainty of final victory except personal determination.

The French nation went to war, and suffered appalling losses before achieving victory and winning back its own territory. The armistice of November 1918 marked the beginning of a new struggle, to rebuild the nation and win the peace, but in addition to their great material losses the people of the north had to rebuild their communities and their morale, recover their inhabitants, and reestablish their identity. For most of France, the men who did not return were the dead heroes of the war, the names on the proliferating memorials still visible at the heart of virtually every commune in the country; the communes of the occupation also remembered men who were missing—fewer deaths in battle but many who died in labour camps, of malnourishment or disease, or who remained where they had settled as refugees or evacuees.

The French army was a single identifiable and representative body, the losses in battle and reverses of strategy were suffered by the French nation as a whole. For those who lived it, the occupation was experienced within small units, families or villages; towns could feel a sense of communal identity, there could be sympathy between neighbours, a recognition of the impotent frustration and depression which was everybody's burden. For many people, the system imposed on the conquered and occupied portion of France made it difficult, when peace came, to respond as part of the larger community whose pride of survival was based on different ingredients.

This fragmentation of identity, over more than four years, added greatly to the fragility of peace and recovery, exacerbated by the confusion and delays of the clearing and rebuilding period. In an echo of the French *poilus*' view of the war in which the officers and the war itself were often felt as the real enemy, the 'enemy' of the post-war years for many French citizens became the official reconstruction bodies.

221

The years of defeat in the north left a memory that was qualitatively different: the pride of victory was not the same for the communities of the north, for there were the bitter months of occupation to remember, and the pride of resistance and survival to add to the universal national triumph at winning the war. Throughout the northern area—on both sides of the long-term battle-front and on across the whole area of occupation—the problems of clearance and reconstruction were distressing, glaring and urgent. The realities and the needs, unprecedented in both the extent and the degree of damage suffered, were almost beyond the imagination of anyone who had not witnessed them.

This includes later generations, who therefore need to bring generous imagination and understanding to this population and terrain in the throes of survival and recovery: we have become too accustomed (particularly through television) to the experience and the consequences of advanced technological warfare and ruthless exploitation to appreciate fully the outrage and impotence felt by the communities and the individuals described in this book. The particular horrors of the 1930s and 1940s could not be foreseen, nor how far they have fundamentally extended our view of 'man's inhumanity to man': our modern view of human psychology and ordinary expectations of life, shaped by the events of later decades, form an almost impenetrable barrier between 1914-18 and the end of the twentieth century.

The legacy of these years in the north to those who faced the Second World War was too great, too rich in experience, bitterness and justifiable pride, to be wholly overcome in the intervening decades. During the winter of 1939-40 the realities of war hung in the air of the whole of France, but when the collapse came in May 1940 it was the communities in the north with their memories of the First World War occupation that were all too well prepared for what was to come.

Notes

1. The period of post-war clearance and reconstruction is fully covered in: Clout, Hugh, *After the Ruins: Restoring the Countryside of Northern France after the Great War*, Exeter, University of Exeter Press, 1996
2. Gromaire, Georges, *L'Occupation allemande en France (1914-1918), Collections de Mémoires. Études et Documents pour servir à l'histoire de la*

Guerre Mondiale, Paris, Fayot, 1929
3. Archives Municipales, Lille
4. Archives Municipales, Lille
5. Williamson, Henry, *The Wet Flanders Plain*, Gliddon Books, Norwich, 1987
6. MacDonald, William, *Reconstruction in France*, London, Macmillan, 1922
7. Direct replacement figures cannot be established, since in many cases one building would replace two or more, or vice versa.
8. Gromaire, *L'Occupation allemande*
9. Wallon, E. & Gobert, L., *Visite faite dans la région du Nord (Somme, Pas-de-Calais et Nord) par une délégation de l'Union des Comités Centraux des Réfugiés des Départements Envahis*, Paris, 1919
10. Wallon & Gobert, *Visite*
11. Wallon & Gobert, *Visite*

Appendix*

* Figures on the extent of devastation, loss and reconstruction required are difficult to establish, and these tables are necessarily approximate. They are based on figures taken from several sources, including Gromaire's *L'Occupation allemande* and the publications of the Ministère des Régions Libérées quoted in Clout's *After the Ruins* (see Bibliography)

1. Industrial and Agricultural Production Lost through German Occupation

Area of France invaded and devastated by War: 10%
Population affected: 12¹/₂% of French total

Lost Industrial Production

	% of French total
Steel	80.00
Coal	55.00
Iron Ore	90.00
Pig Iron	80.00
Electricity	45.00
Machine Tools	20.00
Woollen Goods	94.00
Cotton Goods	60.00
Linen Thread	90.00
Machining Capacity	16.30
Trade Exports	20.00

2. Agricultural Losses

Area of land in liberated region .... 16 million acres
area to be cleared before cultivation ... 8 million acres

Livestock Numbers

	pre-war	1918
Cattle and draught oxen	892,000	58,000
Horses and mules	407,000	32,000
Sheep and goats	949,000	149,000
Pigs	356,000	25,000

Agricultural Production lost throughout the war
Wheat .... 50 %
Oats .... 30 %
Sugar Beet .... 60 %
Potatoes .... 18 %

3. Some Reparation Figures
(approximate)

Demands for indemnity to May 1921.... 2.8 million francs
Total estimated loss .... 34,000 million francs
Indemnities claimed .... 106,000 million francs

Typical Costs of War Damage Clearance
Armentières .... 2 million francs
Lille .... 51,000-63,000 francs/commune
Somme *département* (59 communes) ... 6.9 million francs

Total cost of reparation: 143 billion francs (1925 figures)

4. The Legacy of War

Communes occupied/evacuated 4,329
Communes completely destroyed 1,039
Communes partly destroyed 3,290
Houses destroyed 293,039
Houses seriously damaged 435,961
Public buildings destroyed 6,147
Public buildings damaged 10,731
Industrial and commercial
    establishments destroyed 20,000
Trenches and shell holes to
    be filled .... 436 million cu. yards
Barbed wire to be removed .... 448 million sq. yards
Munitions to be destroyed .... 21 million tons
Wells to be restored 121,108

Railways
network completely destroyed .... 1,500 miles
network needing repair .... 5,250 miles
stations, bridges, tunnels, damaged or destroyed 3,000

Navigable Waterways
to be repaired, dredged and cleared .... 1,200 miles
locks, staithes and basins to be repaired 1,200
sunken barges, etc., to be salvaged 700

Roads
to be remade .... 33,000 miles
bridges, culverts, etc., to be rebuilt 3,200

Bibliography

Les Allemands à Lille et dans le Nord de la France, Paris, Ministère des Affaires Etrangères 1916

Becker, Annette, *Oubliés de la grande guerre: humanitaire et culture de guerre 1914-1918, populations occupées, déportés civils, prisonniers de guerre*, Paris, Noêsis, 1998

Blancpain, Marc, *Quand Guillaume II gouvernait 'de la Somme aux Vosges'*, Paris, Fayard, 1980

Blancpain, Marc, *La Vie quotidienne dans la France du nord sous les occupations (1814-1944)*, Paris, Hachette, 1983

Bocquet, Carlos, *Lille pendant la guerre 14-18*, Lille, Libro-Science SPRL, [c1984]

Bocquet, Léon, *Villes Meurtries de France: Villes du Nord*, Brussels & Paris, G. Van Oest, 1918

Boulin, Pierre, *L'Organisation du travail dans la région envahie de la France pendant l'occupation*, Paris, Presses Universitaires de France, 1927

Burner, David, *Herbert Hoover: A Public Life*, New York, Alfred A. Knopf, 1984

Canini, Gérard, *La Lorraine dans la Guerre de 14-18*, Nancy, 1984

Catalan de la Sarra, Comte de, *La Guerre dans le canton de Ribemont*, Saint Quentin, Société académique de Saint-Quentin, 1931

Celarié, Henriette, *En Esclavage*, 1917

Clout, Hugh, *After the Ruins: Restoring the Countryside of Northern France after the Great War*, Exeter, University of Exeter Press, 1996

Cobb, Richard, *French and Germans, Germans and French*, Hanover, University of New England Press, 1983

Collinet, P. & Stahl, P., *Le Ravitaillement de la France occupée*, Paris, Presses Universitaires de France, 1928

Corday, Michel, *The Paris Front*

Croÿ, la Princesse Marie de, *Souvenirs 1914-1918*, Paris, Plon, 1933

Delahaye-Théry, Mme Eugène, *Les Cahiers Noirs*, Rennes, Editions de la Province, 1934

Delva, Jules, *Au Pays d'Ors avant, pendant et après la grande guerre*, Ors, 1997

Deruyk, René, *Lille: 1914-1918 Dans les Serres Allemandes*, Lille, La Voix du Nord, 1988

Deruyk, René, *La Mort Pour la Liberté, l'Histoire du Comité Jacquet*, Lille, La Voix du Nord, 1993

Deruyk, René, *Lille: 1914-1918 Dans les Serres Allemandes*, Lille, La Voix du Nord, 1992

Bibliography

Douai pendant la guerre 1914-18, Douai, Archives Municipales, 1964

Douchet, Henri, ('FASOL'), *Péronne sous l'occupation*, Péronne, 1929

Ducasse, André, Meyer, Jacques & Perreux, Gabriel, *Vie et Mort des Français*, Paris, Hachette, 1959

Embrey, Robert & Lavalard, René, *La Vie à Péronne et dans sa région*, Péronne, Société archéologique de la région de Péronne, 1988

Fleury, Elie, *Sous la Botte, Histoire de la Ville de Saint-Quentin pendant l'Occupation Allemande, Août 1914-Février 1917*, Saint Quentin, Fleury, 1925-6; Noyon, Éditions de la Tour Gile, 1997

Gay, G. I. & Fisher, H. H., *Public Relations of The Commissions for Relief in Belgium: Documents*, Stanford, Stanford University Press, 1929

Gromaire, Georges, *L'Occupation Allemande en France (1914-1918)*, Paris, Payot, 1925

Hélot, J., *Cinquante Mois sous le Joug Allemand*

Herwig, Holger H., *The First World War, Germany and Austria-Hungary 1914-1918*, London, Arnold, 1997

Les Heures de Détresse: Belgique 1914-1915, Brussels, L'Oeuvre du Comité National de Secours et d'Alimentation et de la Commission for Relief in Belgium, 1915

Huber, M., *La Population de la France pendant la Guerre*, Paris, Presses Universitaires de France, 1931

Jaminet, F., *Sous le Fil Electrisé*, Paris, Nouvelles Editions Latines, 1931

Lançon, J. & Minon, R., *Les Archives Historiques et Patriotiques du Nord de l'Aisne pendant la guerre et l'après-guerre 1914-1921*, Paris, Bibliothèque des Oeuvres documentaires, 1921

Lavalard, René & Embry, Robert *1914-1918 La Reconstruction dans la Somme et les régions dévastées*, Péronne, Société Archéologique de la région de Péronne, 1996

Lille Before and During the War, Paris, Michelin, 1919

Lorédan, J., *Lille et l'Invasion Allemande 14-18*, Paris, Perrin 1920

MacDonald, William, *Reconstruction in France*, London, Macmillan, 1922

Maillard, Béatrice, *Une Famille en pays envahie*, 1925

Martin-Mamy, *Quatre Ans avec les Barbares, Lille pendant l'Occupation allemande*, Paris, La Renaissance du Livre, 1919

Mauclère, Jean, *L'Orage sur la ville*, Paris, Éditions Berger-Levrault, 1933

Mauclère, Jean & de Forge, Henri, *Feuilles françaises dans la tourmente*, Paris, Éditions Berger-Levrault, 1932

Meyer, Jacques, *La Vie quotidienne des Soldats pendant la Grande Guerre*, Paris,

Hachette, 1966

Michaux, Laurette, *La Moselle pendant la guerre (1914-1918)*, Metz, Archives Départementales de la Moselle, 1988

Mortane, Jacques, *Les Civiles Héroïques*

Nash, George, *The Life of Herbert Hoover: The Humanitarian, 1914-1917*, New York, W.W.Norton, 1988

Pauly, L., *Occupation allemande et guerre total*, 1930

Perreux, Gabriel, *La Vie Quotidienne des Civils en France Pendant La Grande Guerre*, Paris, Hachette, 1966

Picard, Maurice, *Les Rapatriés Civils*, la Société des Amis de l'Université de Lyon, Lyon, 1917

La Picardie dans la Grande Guerre 1914-1918, Amiens, Association des Professeurs d'Histoire et Géographie de l'Académie d'Amiens, 1986

Prache, Gaston, *Dans mon pays envahi*, 1924

Premier Journal Clandestin Sous l'Occupation Allemande, Lille-Roubaix-Tourcoing, 1914-5

La Reconstitution de la France devastée, Paris, Archives Nationales, 1932

Redier, Antoine, *Les Allemands dans nos maisons*, Lyon, Cartier, 1937

Redier, Antoine, *La Guerre des femmes*, Paris, Éditions de la Vraie France, 1924

Thébaud, Françoise, *La Femme au temps de la Guerre de 14*, Paris, Stock, 1986

Tierce, Antoinette, *Between Two Fires, a True Story of the German Occupation of Lille*, (tr. J. Lewis May), London, The Bodley Head, 1931

Thuliez, Louise, *Condamnée à Mort*, Paris, Flammarion 1933

Van der Meersch, Maxence, *Invasion '14*, Paris, Albin Michel, 1935

Wallon & Gobert, *Rapport sur la visite faite dans la région du Nord*, Union des Comités Centraux des Refugiés des Départements Envahis, Lille, 1919

Whitaker, J, P. *Under the Heel of the Hun*, 1917

Whitlock, Brand, *Belgium under the German Occupation*, London, Heinemann, 1919

Wibaux, René, *Volontaire dans la Tourmente*, Lille, S.I.L.I.C., 1934

Williamson, Henry, *The Wet Flanders Plain*, Norwich, Gliddon Books, 1987

Yerta, Marguerite, *Six Women and the Invasion*, Paris, Plon, 1917

Index